Building a Knowledge in Reading

SECOND EDITION

Jane Braunger

Strategic Literacy Initiative/WestEd
Oakland, California, USA

Jan Patricia Lewis

Pacific Lutheran University
Tacoma, Washington, USA

INTERNATIONAL
Reading Association
800 BARKSDALE ROAD, PO BOX 8139
NEWARK, DE 19714-8139, USA
www.reading.org

NCTE | The National Council of
Teachers of English
1111 W. Kenyon Road
Urbana, IL 61801-1096, USA
www.ncte.org

Director of Publications   Dan Mangan
Editorial Director, Books and Special Projects   Teresa Curto
Managing Editor, Books   Shannon T. Fortner
Acquisitions and Developmental Editor   Corinne M. Mooney
Associate Editor   Charlene M. Nichols
Associate Editor   Elizabeth C. Hunt
Production Editor   Amy Messick
Books and Inventory Assistant   Rebecca A. Zell
Permissions Editor   Janet S. Parrack
Assistant Permissions Editor   Tyanna L. Collins
Production Department Manager   Iona Muscella
Supervisor, Electronic Publishing   Anette Schütz
Senior Electronic Publishing Specialist   R. Lynn Harrison
Electronic Publishing Specialist   Lisa M. Kochel
Proofreader   Stacey Lynn Sharp

Project Editor   Shannon Fortner

Cover   Design: Linda Steere; Photos (from left): © Dynamic Graphics Inc., © Banana Stock Ltd., © Banana Stock Ltd., © 2001 Image 100 Ltd.

IRA Stock Number: 575

NCTE Stock Number: 03901

Web addresses in this book were correct as of the publication date but may have become inactive or otherwise modified since that time. If you notice a deactivated or changed Web address, please e-mail books@reading.org with the words "Website Update" in the subject line. In your message, specify the Web link, the book title, and the page number on which the link appears.

Library of Congress Cataloging-in-Publication Data
Braunger, Jane.
  Building a knowledge base in reading / Jane Braunger, Jan Patricia Lewis.-- 2nd ed.
    p. cm.
  Includes bibliographical references and index.
  ISBN 0-87207-575-3
  1. Reading. 2. Language acquisition. 3. Language arts. 4. Literacy. 5. Reading (Elementary) I. Lewis, Jan Patricia. II. Title.
  LB1050.B72 2005
  428.4'071--dc22
Third Printing, October 2006   2005020170

Contents

CHAPTER 3

Factors That Influence Literacy Learning   37

CHAPTER 4

Core Understandings About Reading   58

Preface

THE FIRST EDITION of *Building a Knowledge Base in Reading* (*BKBR*), published in 1997, set forth a purpose of providing "a research baseline for teachers, policymakers, decision makers and other interested persons to consider in helping all children meet today's higher literacy standards" (p. 1). Our goal was to compile a broad array of research in the service of a robust view of reading and learning to read. The need for literacy instruction informed by solid research continues, and the stakes today, in light of the target achievement goals set by state standards and by the No Child Left Behind (NCLB) Act of 2001 (2002), are even higher than at the time of the first edition's publication.

In this second edition (*BKBR2*), we reaffirm our original purpose and emphasize that to accomplish it, we must not only bring back to the public discourse on reading the research findings documented in *BKBR* but also describe the instructional implications of key studies published since then. We share a concern with many contemporary researchers and literacy experts that important research was left behind in the crafting of the NCLB legislation and the federal Reading First initiative it launched.

The research that underpins the Reading First initiative is the report of the National Reading Panel (NRP), *Teaching Children to Read* (National Institute of Child Health and Human Development [NICHD], 2000), which lays out findings from a meta-analysis of experimental studies conducted in five topics (phonemic awareness, phonics, fluency, vocabulary, and comprehension). Advocates of the NRP's work hail these research studies as "scientifically-based research in education," and the term has in fact become code for randomized experiments as the gold standard of educational research (Maxwell, 2004). Critics, however, decry the paucity of research studies (in type as well as number) that were examined in drafting the NRP report and take issue with the narrow definition of *scientifically based research* that has come to dominate discussions and decisions about literacy education (Berliner, 2002; Edmondson, 2004; Eisenhart & Towne, 2003; Maxwell, 2004; Olson, 2004; Pressley, 2003).

Following the publication of *BKBR*, we heard repeatedly from teachers, teacher educators, and policymakers how useful the book was to them with its collection of research-based instructional recommendations. Over the past few years, however, the research climate has been narrowed by an increasingly simplistic model of what works in the teaching of reading—scientifically based reading instruction, as described above. This focus on establishing a single line of cause and effect has led to a problem with research in reading: The preferred topics for funded research are increasingly the smallest components of reading that can be controlled or studied in experimental settings. Instructional recommendations based on such studies tend to focus on direct instruction of discrete skills, for example, phonemic awareness and phonics.

In contrast to the narrow criterion of *scientifically based instruction*, the International Reading Association (IRA) has proposed *evidence-based instruction* as the hallmark of literacy instruction, recognizing the many types of research that provide insights into teaching and learning. Its position paper on evidence-based reading instruction (IRA, 2002) asserts that reading research makes it clear that "there is no single instructional program or method that is effective in teaching all children to read." Instead, as the position paper notes, a broad research consensus supports the following best practices set forth by Gambrell, Morrow, Neuman, and Pressley (1999):

1. Teach reading for authentic meaning-making literacy experiences: for pleasure, to be informed, and to perform a task.

2. Use high-quality literature.

3. Integrate a comprehensive word study/phonics program into reading/writing instruction.

4. Use multiple texts that link and expand concepts.

5. Balance teacher- and student-led discussions.

6. Build a whole-class community that emphasizes important concepts and builds background knowledge.

7. Work with students in small groups while other students read and write about what they have read.

8. Give students plenty of time to read in class.

9. Give students direct instruction in decoding and comprehension strategies that promote independent reading. Balance direct instruction, guided instruction, and independent learning.

10. Use a variety of assessment techniques to inform instruction. (p. 14)

The core understandings and the related research base included in this book complement and elaborate on these practices. Chapter 1 discusses key topics in the current discussion of reading and reading instruction, including contemporary definitions of reading, achievement standards, and criteria for relevant research linked to instruction. It also introduces the 13 core understandings to be explained in detail in chapter 4. Chapter 2 summarizes key findings from research on oral language acquisition and connections between oral and written language, across all developmental levels and with particular attention to literacy issues for English-language learners. Chapter 3 addresses factors influencing learners' literacy development, including culture, socioeconomic status, and special needs of learners. Chapter 4 presents 13 core understandings of the current knowledge base about the process of learning to read and continuing to grow as a reader. Representative classroom applications are included to illustrate the core understandings in practice. The conclusion summarizes the instructional implications of the research discussed. In short, readers at all stages of development need access to time for reading and learning, a variety of texts, knowledgeable teachers, excellent instruction, demonstrations of literacy, other readers, and their own reading process.

Our goal in producing *BKBR*2 is to recapture the broad and balanced research perspective that was so welcomed by readers and users of *BKBR*, and to update it to reflect the current research landscape. Since the publication of *BKBR*, significant literacy research has been done in areas such as engagement and motivation, classroom learning contexts, and effective instructional approaches. As a result, readers of *BKBR*2 will find several core understandings—for example, numbers 7, 10, and 11—substantially expanded in chapter 4. In cases where a research study has implications across a number of core understandings, we make repeated references to the findings, focusing on the salient details for specific core understandings. References supporting each chapter and core understanding are grouped at the end of the book by chapter and by core understanding, so that readers have the relevant bibliographic citations available in one place.

It is time for critical and well-documented factors to come back into the public and professional discourse about helping students become effective readers. The RAND Reading Study Group (2002) took up the task of articulating a research and development program in reading comprehension and noted the need for a set of theories and models to provide a coherent foundation for such research. Theories about reading comprehension, the report continued, must be informed by "the multiple perspectives (including educational, cognitive, linguistic, sociolinguistic, discourse analytic, and cultural perspectives) that have been brought to bear in the design and conduct of literacy research" (p. 2).

*BKBR*2 responds to that request by including the recommendations set forth in the NRP report (NICHD, 2000). However, it provides a larger research context because it also draws from findings from studies and documents such as the report of the National Research Council, *Preventing Reading Difficulties in Young Children* (Snow, Burns, & Griffin, 1998); the 2000 and 2002 National Assessments of Educational Progress (see Donahue, Finnegan, Lutkus, Allen, & Campbell, 2001; Grigg, Daane, Jin, & Campbell, 2003); the report of the RAND Reading Study Group, *Reading for Understanding: Toward an R&D Program in Reading Comprehension* (2002); research published by the Center for the Improvement of Early Reading Achievement between 1997 and 2002; the National Research Center on English Learning and Achievement's findings on schools beating the odds, published since 1998; and other recent literacy research.

*BKBR*2 has broadened the focus on reading development to include research with instructional implications for older readers, specifically middle and high school students. To reflect this longer developmental continuum, many of the core understandings have been reframed. Readers of *BKBR* noted that the core understandings applied to all stages of reading development. We agree and make that application explicit in *BKBR*2.

Two other changes are intended to make *BKBR*2 more accessible and useful to readers. One is the addition of a summary at the end of each of the first three chapters, to pull together the key ideas. The second is the inclusion of teacher resources at the end of each chapter or core understanding, to help teachers translate the core understandings into classroom practice.

This updated synthesis of research on reading is needed by a number of groups directly engaged or otherwise involved in literacy instruction. First and foremost are teachers, at various stages of their professional lives. Teachers need reliable resources to support local decision making about instructional programs and materials, and teachers in training need a compilation of research findings from various traditions with instructional implications for reading along the developmental continuum.

Without a solid knowledge base about the nature of reading and how it develops, teachers may function more as program deliverers than as thoughtful providers of instruction based on their knowledge of literacy and learning and informed daily by professional assessment of the young readers in their charge. With a national goal of a qualified teacher in every classroom, it is important to provide all teachers with current and complete research-based knowledge about reading. *BKBR2* is offered to support teachers as professionals. Their understandings of literacy and learning underpin their decisions—from overall curriculum design to in-the-moment instruction and materials choices. Teachers, not programs, are the critical factor in developing independent readers who are engaged and thoughtful. It is our hope that *BKBR2* serves teachers in this important work.

Acknowledgments

We are grateful to the many teachers and teacher educators who found the first edition of *Building a Knowledge Base in Reading* useful and asked us to write a second edition. They provided the impetus to revisit and update the original. For very helpful response to early drafts of key chapters, we wish to thank Ruth Schoenbach. Finally, we appreciate the suggestions for teacher resources linked to core understandings provided by Kathy Egawa, Yetta Goodman, and Margaret Phinney.

CHAPTER 1

Literacy for the 21st Century

AS IN THE first edition of *Building a Knowledge Base in Reading* (*BKBR*), throughout this second edition (*BKBR2*) the terms *literacy* and *reading* are used interchangeably. The close connections among reading, writing, speaking, and listening are well understood, and current U.S. state standards incorporate all aspects of literate behavior. Research in the field may focus on one mode of literacy development—for example, reading—but an important lesson of recent research in reading has been that all forms of language and literacy develop supportively and interactively. Children build on oral language knowledge and practices as they learn to read and write; they develop key understandings about reading—especially phonics—through writing, and they extend their writing range through reading. This dynamic, supportive interaction of language and literacy continues throughout readers' development.

Beyond the National Reading Panel Report

This broader, more interconnected view of literacy compels us to enlarge the picture of reading and how it develops beyond the recommendations set forth by the National Reading Panel (NRP). As we noted in the preface, the NRP summary report *Teaching Children to Read* (National Institute of Child Health and Human Development [NICHD], 2000) based its instructional recommendations on a meta-analysis of experimental research done on five topics: phonemic awareness, phonics, fluency, vocabulary, and comprehension. (The limitations of this approach, both in methodology and in the research content available for study, are discussed later in this chapter.) The report was the basis of the Reading First initiative and has been extremely influential in shaping U.S. federal, state, and local literacy policy and practice. Given this impact, it is reasonable to ask whether the NRP adequately studied the field in the course of its work. Many would say it did not (Allington, 2002b, 2005; Coles 2003; Garan, 2002; Krashen, 2005). In fact, a significant criticism of the NRP report is that the panel looked neither at interactions among aspects of reading such as phonemic awareness, fluency, and comprehension; nor at interactions between forms of literacy (Olson, 2004; Yatvin, Weaver, & Garan, 2003); nor at interactions between instruction and various personal and social contextual factors (Berliner, 2002; Maxwell, 2004). The consequence of this fragmented research perspective has been, not surprisingly, a narrowing of recommended instructional practice and learning experiences in literacy.

Literacy as a Complex, Developmental Process

Literacy development has always been a central concern of schooling. So important is learning to read, Boyer (1995) contends, that the success of an elementary school is judged by its students' proficiency in reading. He suggests, "Speaking and listening come first. But learning to read is without question the top priority in elementary education" (p. 69). In fact, early reading achievement is a reliable predictor of later school success. Language is essential to learning, and reading, as a specialized form of language, is not only a basic skill, it is an indispensable tool for critical and creative thinking. Literacy allows us to make connections between our own and others' experiences; to inquire systematically into important matters; and to access, analyze, and evaluate information and arguments. In short, literacy is key to success in school and beyond for effective participation in the workforce, the community, and the body politic.

Becoming a competent, effective reader is a developmental process. And though most students have attained basic reading skills, there is growing concern regarding the low attainment of more complex literacy, especially among older students (Kamil, 2003; RAND Reading Study Group, 2002; Snow & Biancarosa, 2003).

Evolving Definitions of Literacy

In the United States, the definition of literacy has steadily evolved to suit the increasing demands of our personal, social, economic, and civic lives. Myers (1996) traces this process through specific literacy periods in the United States, each with a different operational definition of literacy. "Signature literacy," the ability to read and write one's name, was the mark of a literate person at the time of the American Revolution. By the mid-19th century, "recitation literacy" was the standard, demonstrated by oral recitation of memorized texts, such as Bible verses. Then in the early 20th century, the bar was raised: The measure of literacy was the ability to read previously unseen text. As the United States brought more people, including a number of immigrants, into productive employment and citizenship, the need for this "decoding/analytic" literacy was clear. It placed a high priority on decoding individual words and comprehending literal text. As a definition of literacy, it persisted well into the 1980s, and by all accounts our schools have succeeded in teaching this type of literacy, roughly equivalent to the basic reading achievement level of the National Assessment of Educational Progress (NAEP).

Our definition of reading leads inevitably to the way we teach reading at all phases of a student's school experience. The following statements incorporate current definitions of reading as a complex, interactive process, using basic skills and advanced strategies to make meaning:

- "Reading is an interactive and constructive process involving the reader, the text, and the context of the reading experience. Reading involves the development of an understanding of text, thinking about text in different ways, and using a variety of text types for different purposes." (from the framework for the NAEP reading assessments, Grigg, Daane, Jin, & Campbell, 2003, p. 3)

- "Reading is a complex developmental challenge that we know to be intertwined with many other developmental accomplishments: attention, memory, language, and motivation, for example. Reading is not only a cognitive psycholinguistic activity but also a social activity." (Snow, Burns, & Griffin, 1998, p. 15)

- "Reading comprehension is an interactive process involving the reader, the text, and the activity or purpose for reading. These elements interact in and are affected by the larger sociocultural context. Learning to read well is a long-term developmental process. At the end point, the proficient adult reader can read a variety of materials with ease and interest, can read for varying purposes, and can read with comprehension even when the material is neither easy to understand nor intrinsically interesting." (RAND Reading Study Group, 2002, p. xiii)

- "Reading is a complex and purposeful sociocultural, cognitive, and linguistic process in which readers simultaneously use their knowledge of spoken and written language, their knowledge of the topic of the text, and their knowledge of their culture to construct meaning with text." (National Council of Teachers of English [NCTE], 2004, n.p.)

- Reading should be conceptualized as an engagement. Engaged readers not only have acquired reading skills but also use them for their own purposes in many contexts. They possess beliefs, desires, and interests that energize the hard work of becoming literate (Guthrie & Anderson, 1999). Recent research shows engagement as essential to achievement in reading (Campbell, Voelkl, & Donahue, 1997; Guthrie & Wigfield, 2000; Kamil, 2003) and engaged reading as conceptual, strategic, and social (Guthrie & Anderson, 1999).

- "Being literate in contemporary society means being active, critical, and creative users not only of print and spoken language but also of the visual language of film and television, commercial and political advertising, photography, and more." (International Reading Association [IRA] & NCTE, 1996, p. 5)

Tensions Between Literacy Demands and Student Performance

Given the literacy demands contained in the foregoing definitions, it is reasonable to ask how well our students are measuring up. The 2002 NAEP data (Grigg et al., 2003) provide some insight, continuing the trends noted in *BKBR*. Most students achieved at or above the basic level on the NAEP: 64% of 4th graders, 75% of 8th graders, and 74% of 12th graders. But while 4th- and 8th-grade average scores were higher than in the two most recent administrations of the NAEP, average 12th-grade scores in 2002 were lower. In fact, the percentages of 12th-grade students who performed at or above basic and proficient levels decreased between 1998 and 2002, and thus fell below the levels seen in 1992. Only about one third of students in all grades scored at or above the proficient level, and the percentage who achieved the advanced level remained disturbingly low: from 7% at 4th grade to 3% at 8th and 5% at 12th.

These numbers should concern us because the literacy demands on students now and in the future are for *proficient* and *advanced*—not merely *basic*—reading ability. To achieve NAEP's proficient level, readers should be able

> to demonstrate an overall understanding of the text, providing inferential as well as literal information...to extend ideas in the text by making inferences, drawing conclusions, and making connections to their own experiences and to other readings...to summarize and apply information. (Grigg et al., 2003, pp. 11–13)

At the advanced level, readers should be able to generalize about topics in the reading; apply critical standards to texts; analyze both meaning and form; develop a perspective on a text and explain the reasons for it; and analyze, synthesize, and evaluate points of view.

These literacy behaviors are typical of what Myers (1996) calls "critical/translation" literacy; it is the standard that will be required of 21st-century "knowledge workers" now learning to read in our schools (Green & Dixon, 1996). And yet the current NAEP data (Grigg et al., 2003) support the conclusion Allington and Cunningham (1996) drew that only about 15% of our students are achieving higher levels of literacy.

Although basic skills are essential components of literacy, reasoning and critical thinking are increasingly important. The NAEP data (Grigg et al., 2003) provide additional support for teaching reading in ways that support these higher literacy skills. In both fourth and eighth grades, higher NAEP scores are associated with teaching for meaning, including instruction in metacognitive skills, reading "real" books instead of passages from basal readers, and writing in response to literature; yet, ironically, funding for professional development under the Reading First initiative favors basic skills approaches (Wenglinsky, 2004).

The need for a high degree of literacy, including the ability to comprehend and apply complex texts, makes the relatively poor comprehension outcomes among adolescents a grave concern (Kamil, 2003; RAND Reading Study Group, 2002). Such sophisticated literacy ability is also required for the ongoing learning essential to an ever-increasing knowledge base in all fields.

A Continuing Need: Bringing More Students to Higher Literacy Levels

Clearly, the standards for literacy are higher than they have ever been. Productive functioning in our society will require higher levels of literacy than in previous eras, and these higher levels will be required of a larger percentage of the population. At the same time, increasing numbers of children who are likely to experience difficulty learning to read are entering school (Graves, van den Broek, & Taylor, 1996). Overwhelmingly, it is poor and minority children who fail to succeed as readers, and their numbers are growing in our schools. The recent NAEP data (Grigg et al., 2003) show that achievement gaps between white students and black and Hispanic students, while narrowing, still persist, showing no significant difference since 1992. And with growing diversity in the school-age population, these gaps are actually likely to widen (RAND Reading Study Group, 2002). Another concern for educators is the gap in NAEP scores between higher performing large town and suburban populations and lower performing urban and rural populations.

Poverty as a Factor in Literacy Development
Children who are poor or who are members of ethnic and cultural minorities do not by definition experience difficulty in learning to read. However, these are the

groups with whom public schools have had the least success overall in achieving high levels of literacy. We mention the growth in these populations mainly to emphasize the urgency of ensuring successful literacy learning for all children. Without question, literacy is the goal of the No Child Left Behind (NCLB) Act of 2001 (2002). What is questionable in the legislation, though, are the means to the end: high-stakes accountability based on single measures of reading performance and Draconian consequences for students and schools that do not measure up to the mark. The schools most often at risk for these consequences are those that serve significant populations of students living in poverty—an equity issue that needs to be addressed. As the remaining sections of this book will argue, more attention to quality of instruction, learning contexts, and literacy resources would serve underperforming and disadvantaged students better than a singular focus on accountability.

To ensure that indeed no child is left behind, it is important to examine the fit between reading instruction and current high standards for literacy. Instruction in pronouncing words, understanding texts at a literal level, locating and remembering details, and answering factual questions is appropriate to teach basic reading or the decoding/analytic literacy Myers (1996) describes. However, such an approach is inadequate to ensure that all children develop more advanced, critical/translation literacy. Unfortunately for many poor and minority students, especially those in urban schools failing to make adequate yearly progress as stipulated by NCLB, the instructional emphasis is on basic skills.

> "To ensure that indeed no child is left behind, it is important to examine the fit between reading instruction and current high standards for literacy."

Long before they come to school, children are building on their experiences and their oral language to become strategic thinkers and readers in a process known as emergent literacy. We already know that children raised in safe, nurturing, and stimulating environments are better learners than those raised in less stimulating settings, and that the cognitive and affective effects can be long lasting (Carnegie Task Force, 1994). For children in the former, supportive settings, home influences and school experiences combine to support them as they make steady progress in the more formal and complex tasks involved in conventional reading and writing (Snow et al., 1998). Research also points to the importance of language exposure and experience to children's vocabulary growth and cognitive development and to the differential impact of poverty on these critical aspects of children's development: Well before the age of 3, children are on a trajectory of language development in which "the amount and diversity of their past experience influences which new opportunities for experience they notice and choose" (Hart & Risley, 1995, p. 194).

As Hart and Risley (1995) note, poor children are at a distinct disadvantage regarding the amount and richness of language interactions that stimulate cognitive development. The consequences for their success in school, specifically learning to read confidently and critically, are alarming. Too many children move into the intermediate grades without control of reading skills and strategies necessary for effective, satisfying uses of literacy. Yet, as tenacious as the reading problem is, we know more now than we ever did about the reading process and about how to teach reading. Steady gains in the basic reading abilities of students in the lowest performing groups have been documented over the 30 years of the NAEP reading assessment (Grigg et al., 2003). As previously noted, the performance gap between privileged middle class students and poor minority students is closing, but it is still too wide. Pearson's (1996) observation still holds true that "as a profession we seem most able to provide help to those students who need it least and, conversely, least able to provide help to those who need it most" (p. 304).

No easy solutions exist to the dilemma of bringing all students to high levels of literacy, so it is all the more important that teachers have a great deal of knowledge to apply to the design of instruction. As Allington (2002a) notes, perhaps the best research-based strategy available to schools to accomplish high literacy for students is investing in good teaching, whether through sound hiring practices or effective professional development. It is widely understood that teachers must continually enhance their own knowledge to ensure students' success, but a growing reliance on programs, rather than teachers, to teach literacy threatens positive outcomes for students and diverts critical funding from teacher professional development in literacy (Allington, 2002a; Darling-Hammond, 2000; Land & Moustafa, 2005; Moustafa & Land, 2002). Poor students with limited out-of-school opportunities for literacy extensions and applications need knowledgeable teachers who know how to design productive and engaging literacy experiences.

Social, Cultural, and Linguistic Factors in Literacy Development

Part of the knowledge required of teachers is how sociocultural and linguistic variables affect learning to read. Teachers need to understand the uses and values of literacy in the many cultures from which children in any classroom may come. Extensive home- and community-based research by Heath (1983); Moll, Amanti, Neff, and Gonzalez (1992); Purcell-Gates (1995); and others offers teachers a wider lens through which to see rich traditions of literacy and funds of knowledge to tap in developing school-based literacy practices (Paratore, 2002). These home and school connections are explored more fully in chapter 3.

For children whose first language is not English, teachers must address many variables. Such factors as literacy in the first language, health issues for immigrants, the decision of whether to teach literacy in the first or in the second language (English), worldview and background experiences and knowledge, and schooling experiences in the home country are critical to effective acquisition of literacy. The diversity of students in public schools today does not support a "one size fits all" program of reading instruction; rather, teachers must be able to provide instruction appropriate to the wide range of students' experiences and needs.

Furthermore, teachers must recognize and work to eliminate the ways in which students' ethnicity, culture, language, and social class are used by schools, consciously or unconsciously, as an explanation for students' success or failure (Haycock, 2001; Obidah, 1998; Orange & Horowitz, 1999). For students learning to speak and to read in English, issues of intergroup hostility, subordinate status of a minority group, cultural stereotyping, and patterns of acculturation versus assimilation have a profound effect on their acquisition of English and their success in school (Collier, 1995). Teachers working to help new English speakers develop academic literacy must understand and scaffold for them the social and cognitive processes involved (Walqui, 2002).

Core Understandings About Reading: Striving for Consensus

The challenge to public schools to bring all students to high levels of literacy is unprecedented and complex. The task is made even more daunting by a lack of public consensus on (a) literacy goals and (b) the relevant knowledge base to inform initial and continuing reading instruction.

*BKBR*2 aims to contribute to an important professional dialogue and help build a consensus on literacy and its knowledge base by detailing what is known about how children learn to read and grow as readers and the environments that support the process. To that end, we return, with added research support, to the 13 core understandings identified and explained in *BKBR*. The core understandings listed here will be explained in detail in chapter 4:

1. Reading is a construction of meaning from text. It is an active, cognitive, and affective process.

2. Background knowledge and prior experience are critical to the reading process.

3. Social interaction is essential at all stages of reading development.

4. Reading and writing are reciprocal processes; development of one enhances the other.

5. Reading involves complex thinking.

6. Environments rich in literacy experiences, resources, and models facilitate reading development.

7. Engagement in the reading task is key in successfully learning to read and developing as a reader.

8. Children's understandings of print are not the same as adults' understandings.

9. Children develop phonemic awareness and knowledge of phonics through a variety of literacy opportunities, models, and demonstrations.

10. Readers learn productive strategies in the context of real reading.

11. Students learn best when teachers employ a variety of strategies to model and demonstrate reading knowledge, strategy, and skills.

12. Students need many opportunities to read, read, read.

13. Monitoring the development of reading processes is vital to student success.

Current Dilemmas in Designing Literacy Instruction

The Need for Agreement on a Model of Reading

The evidence for a complex and high-performance view of literacy today is abundant. And yet a debate about the teaching of reading continues, partly because public agreement is lacking on what we mean by reading and how it is learned. For example, some would argue that reading is a bottom-up or part-to-whole process and should be taught as incremental skill building. In this view, the reader moves from sounding out and identifying the meanings of individual words to understanding sentences, then paragraphs. In a similar way, word recognition and comprehension strategies are skills for getting at the meaning in the text, skills that are acquired through sequenced instruction in their subskills. Others would argue for a different model of reading, one in which reading can be described as a top-down or whole-to-part process. Readers bring their knowledge of the world to the text and actually develop facility in decoding print in the process of reading for meaning. In this view, students learn to read and improve as readers primarily through the meaning they bring to text. Still others propose a third model, one that can be described as interactive. In this approach, reading is the process of constructing meaning as the reader interacts with the various cue systems—graphophonics, meaning, language structure, and purpose—available in the text. In this view, both the reader and the text contribute to the process of comprehension (Wilhelm, Baker, & Dube, 2001).

Continuing concerns about low achievement among some students have intensified the debate about how best to teach reading. These concerns have been heightened in the current climate of high-stakes accountability linked to state tests, a key component of the NCLB legislation. And the NRP report (NICHD, 2000), though it claims to provide research-based guidelines for instruction that will bring all children to desirable levels of literacy, may have muddied the waters instead of charting a clear course for teachers. As Yatvin (2002) points out, the NRP never articulated a definition of reading to use in guiding their selection of research and conclusions about instruction. However, their selection of topics to study—phonemic awareness, phonics, vocabulary, fluency, and comprehension—and their investigation of them as individual factors reflect an implicit shared view among most of the panel members of the reading process as a hierarchy of skills that begins with decoding and builds to comprehension—the bottom-up or part-to-whole model previously described.

U.S. schools, districts, and states are feeling some consequences of these procedural decisions by the NRP as they apply for federal funds under the Reading First initiative. *Put Reading First* (Center for the Improvement of Early Reading Achievement [CIERA], 2001), a guide for teachers on grade K–3 implementation of the NRP's findings, is organized around the five areas of reading instruction studied by the panel. Not surprisingly, proposals typically set forth instructional plans in each of the five categories of the NRP study, as if these aspects of reading constitute the universe of reading and even operate independently of one another. Also predictably, the plans are often heavy on the first four topics, and almost relegate comprehension to the last aspect of reading to address, in sequence, if not in importance. In contrast, the RAND Reading Study Group (2002) has set forth a research agenda with comprehension at the center of the reading process and specifically points to the need for a definition of reading comprehension and for understanding reading as a developmental process. As noted earlier in this section, the NRP's decision to look only at five topics, and not at the integrated nature of the reading process and at related literacy topics, limited the recommendations the panel ultimately set forth. The limitations of the scope of research examined will be discussed in the final section of this chapter.

A further problem with the lack of a clearly articulated definition of reading in the NRP report is the lack of fit between assessments used in the studies examined by the panel and measures of actual reading performance. For example, a number of the studies included in the meta-analysis of research on phonics and phonemic analysis used reading of words in isolation or pronunciation of nonsense words as measures of reading achievement (Yatvin et al., 2003). Without comprehension involved, how is this reading?

The NRP's assertion that reading instruction should be based on scientifically reliable and replicable research has been translated at the institutional level to a requirement that reading should be taught scientifically. No agreement exists on what this means. However, the proliferation of basic skills programs with a sequenced program of instruction that is often highly scripted suggests that reading as decoding is the model driving instruction.

The Need for Instruction Grounded in a Research-Based Model of Reading

Prior to the report of the NRP (NICHD, 2000), the field of literacy education was not without well-researched, theoretically sound, and clearly articulated recommendations for instruction in reading. In its seminal report, *Preventing Reading Difficulties in Young Children* (Snow et al., 1998), the National Research Council (NRC) set forth a description of the ways in which teachers work with young children to address the complex factors involved in learning to read:

> Briefly put, we can say that children need simultaneous access to some knowledge of letter-sound relationships, some sight vocabulary...and some comprehension strategies. In each case, "some" indicates that exhaustive knowledge of these aspects is not needed to get the child reading conventionally; rather, each child seems to need varying amounts of knowledge to get started, but then he or she needs to build up the kind of inclusive and automatic knowledge that will let the fact that reading is being done fade into the background while the reasons for reading are fulfilled. (pp. 79, 84)

Snow and colleagues (1998) echo Clay's (1991) description of how readers develop a self-extending system of strategies. Her model of reading, developed after extensive research into good readers' behaviors, speaks to the purposeful, meaning-driven nature of reading:

> Once a reader is using a set of strategies which enable him to monitor his own reading and check one source with other sources in a sequential problem-solving process, then engaging in these activities serves to extend the potential of the reader to engage in more difficult activities and he assumes the major responsibility for learning to read by reading. (p. 317)

In both of these descriptions, the model of reading is not simply immersion and inductive learning, as some have characterized it, but rather the orchestrated use of various skills, strategies, and knowledge that converge to make meaning with text. And the process of becoming a reader continues, with new lessons to be learned at various stages. In *Supporting Young Adolescents' Literacy Learning*, a joint position statement of IRA and the National Middle School Association (2001), we are reminded,

> The ability to comprehend a variety of texts, to use sophisticated comprehension and study strategies, to read critically, and to develop a lifelong desire to read are not acquired entirely during the early years. A good start is critical, but not sufficient. Middle school students deserve continued and systematic instruction in reading. (n.p.)

The position statement on evidence-based reading instruction mentioned in the Preface (IRA, 2002) noted the shaky ground earlier researchers had found in attempting to identify one best way to teach reading. In *The Cooperative Research Program in First-Grade Reading Instruction*, Bond and Dykstra (1967/1997), far from declaring one instructional approach "the winner," conclude,

> Children learn to read by a variety of materials and methods.... No one approach is so distinctly better in all situations and respects than the others that it should be considered the one best method and the one to be used exclusively. (p. 416)

Debate about models of reading and resulting instruction affects not only the school and classroom levels, but also the larger, more influential level of education policy. And such policy may privilege a single point of view or be a result of negotiation among conflicting viewpoints. In literacy policy, Edmondson (2004) traces this process from the 1965 Elementary and Secondary Education Act (liberal viewpoint) to its reauthorization in 2001 as the No Child Left Behind Act and its Reading First initiative (conservative viewpoint). Edmondson argues that liberal literacy policy generally reflects a view of reading in which individuals and communities benefit from improved literacy and research informs teachers' professional decisions. In contrast, she describes conservative literacy policy as sharing the overall goal of improved literacy but being more concerned with identifying and mandating the best way to teach to ensure literacy goals are accomplished.

A case in point is the NRC report *Preventing Reading Difficulties in Young Children* (Snow et al., 1998), which cited voluminous research in recommending ways to support children's development as readers, such as a focus on construction of meaning with print, frequent opportunities to read, and learning about the alphabetic principle. Readers of the document could see it as a negotiated statement, reflecting the hard work and earnest dialogue among the prestigious members of the committee that produced it. *Preventing Reading Difficulties* was in fact viewed as "a sensible, comprehensive look at a variety of strategies and approaches to reading" (McDaniel & Miskel, 2002, p. 15). However, within a year of the report's publication, the NRP report was commissioned by the U.S. Congress to go further than *Preventing Reading Difficulties* had, to "assess the status of research-based knowledge, including the effectiveness of various approaches to teaching children to read" (NICHD, 2000, p. 1). The NRP report and subsequent No Child Left Behind Act and its Reading First initiative show an increasing interest at the U.S. federal level with translating research into what works in classroom instruction. Some have argued that linking achievement test results to federal funds in effect narrows instructional options as schools increasingly turn to reading programs that promise results tied to scripted instruction. More broadly, critics see a movement away from setting forth research-based principles for teachers to use in designing instruction and toward convening selected literacy experts to review research and subsequently dictate practice (Edmondson, 2004; McDaniel & Miskel, 2002).

What Counts as Knowledge About Reading Development?

Insights From a Wealth of Research Perspectives

Over the past 50 years, research has focused on language arts, on reading and writing, more than ever before (Purcell-Gates, 1997). We have come to understand that reading, in and out of school, is part of a much larger, more complex array of making sense of the world around us. Further, we have come to appreciate how a variety of disciplines and research traditions informs us about how reading is first learned and continues to develop. Cognitive psychology, educational anthropology, linguistics, and sociology have all contributed to the knowledge base about reading, its acquisition, and its processes (Kamil, Mosenthal, Pearson, & Barr, 2002; Pearson & Stephens, 1994). Research in language acquisition and emergent literacy has provided especially rich insights into our knowledge of reading at the early stages, and research in discipline-based literacy and genre studies offers new understandings of literacy as a developmental process. Critical approaches have come to represent a critique of widely held functionalist views about the role of schooling and society, bringing more focus on the political and economic context of power and knowledge, particularly in language and literacy acquisition and use (Freire & Macedo, 1987; Gee, 1996; Siegel & Fernandez, 2000).

Research on the brain, for example, has shown the enormous effect on later learning of children's early experiences with language and exposure to the world (Carnegie Task Force, 1994; Hart & Risley, 1995; Healy, 1990). Research on miscue analysis and retrospective miscue analysis has helped us understand readers' errors in the context of their attempt to construct meaning with text (Goodman, 1965; Goodman, 1976; Goodman & Marek, 1996). Research on engagement has offered insights into motivation, self-monitoring, independence, and achievement in reading (Guthrie & Wigfield, 2000; Morrow, 1996). And research on emergent and intergenerational literacy has shown us the importance of home and community literacy practices in learning to read and growing as a reader in school (Purcell-Gates, 1997).

In addition, recent studies of middle and high school readers have supported insights from research on adult literacy. Adolescents and adults need real-world applications of literacy that build on current knowledge (Moje, Young, Readence, & Moore, 2000; Sticht, Caylor, Kern, & Fox, 1972), and they need to use literacy to accomplish their own purposes (Freire, 1970; Moore, Bean, Birdyshaw, & Rycik, 1999). These findings are relevant to children as well and have been incorporated into many classrooms' literacy designs.

Evidence of Literacy Learning Depends on the Model in Use

If one believes that decoding is the major task in learning to read (the bottom-up or part-to-whole model), it follows that children are successful to the extent that they learn to decode print accurately. Likewise, what counts as professional knowledge is evidence of how and to what degree children learn to pronounce words on the page. Knowledge about reading development in this view comes from empirical studies with control and experimental groups; testing in these studies is typically standardized tests of letter–sound knowledge, word knowledge in isolation, and accuracy of oral reading. These are the types of studies that the NRP relied on for its meta-analysis and subsequent recommendations (NICHD, 2000).

Such studies and their test data provide valuable information about reading, but they do not give the complete picture. Left out of these studies are contextual factors in the reading process, the relationship between reading and writing, the role of engagement, and the impact of holistic, integrated teaching approaches, to name a few critical variables (McCracken, 2004). The current focus on how and when children learn—or can be taught—phonemic awareness (Adams, 1990; CIERA, 2001) may stem from a misperception of reading as solely decoding. Perhaps a more serious factor is the more recent misrepresentation or misinterpretation of the findings on phonemic awareness published by the NRP (Allington, 2002b; Coles, 2003; Yatvin et al., 2003). Allington (2005) decries the fact that the NRP's summary recommends instructional practices, such as an emphasis on systematic phonics, that are not supported by evidence in the full report.

If one sees reading as a process of constructing meaning as described in the interactive model, then evidence of reading growth will include many indicators from numerous sources, including, but not limited to, achievement data. Additional evidence of literacy development comes from naturalistic studies of students actually reading, for example, teachers' observations and analyses of literacy experiences; classroom research on the impact of social interaction, strategic modeling, and materials on literacy learning; readers' use of all cue systems in reading (letter–sound, meaning, syntax, and pragmatics); connections between learners' reading and writing; and a host of other variables involved in the reading process. In this view, the test of readers' achievement is based on observation and analysis of their reading of complete texts and on data collection with tools such as miscue analysis, retellings, and records of discussion.

Concerns About a Narrow Model of Research

As noted earlier, the NRP's reliance on control, or experimental, studies for the meta-analysis on which it based its recommendations has led to a dominant view at the federal level of education that experimental research is the gold standard for educational research. But educational researchers from a variety of perspectives have weighed in to caution against a reliance on this limited form of research to inform instruction (Berliner, 2002; Eisenhart & Towne, 2003; Maxwell, 2004; Olson, 2004; Pressley, 2003). Glass, the principal architect of meta-analysis as a research methodology, offers a wry critique of this elevation of randomized experiments as the only way to know something:

> If the federal government wishes to be consistent (a dubious assumption), then they will have to back off their policies on smoking, coal dust, speeding on interstate highways, and a host of other things that have never been verified by randomized experiments. (as cited in Robinson, 2004, p. 26)

Pressley (2003), like Glass no stranger to experimental research, sees a problem basing instructional decisions on data drawn from meta-analysis of such research:

> Determining that instruction is effective only if its effects are replicated across a number of studies (i.e., there are enough replications to do a meta-analysis) is a decision to ignore the many instructional effects that have been studied in only one or a few investigations. Such a decision can also lead to the misconception that there are only a few forms of instruction that enjoy scientific validation through the rigorous application of experimentation. (p. 65)

Pressley and others (Bullock, 2004; IRA, 2002) support evidence-based reading instruction but voice concern that it is being too narrowly understood in policy circles as reading instruction based exclusively on findings from experimental research. For example, the NRP's decision to use meta-analysis for their examination of research on reading instruction limited the number of studies they looked at, and totally left out correlational and observational studies, two branches of scientific study long accepted by the educational research community as valid and productive (NRC, 2002). This decision further constrained the panel's study, already limited by the decision to focus on five aspects of reading as noted earlier in this chapter.

But the most powerful critiques of overreliance on experimental research as a basis for instructional decisions get at the heart of the educational enterprise. Unlike medicine or agriculture, where a treatment may actually be isolated as a variable, and clear causal relations can be uncovered in controlled experiments, education is by nature a collection of many, variously interacting variables (Berliner, 2002; Bullock, 2004; Maxwell, 2004; Olson, 2004). In education, there is not a simple causal line between teaching and learning. This is why Berliner (2002) describes educational research as, in fact, the "hardest science of all," meaning that it is the most difficult to research. He cites three factors that bedevil researchers: (1) the dynamic and complex contexts in which teaching and learning operate; (2) the ubiquity of interactions in a classroom among a host of variables in the student, the teacher, and the materials (to name just three sites of variations); and (3) the shifts in the social and knowledge environment that can invalidate earlier research findings (e.g., behaviorist models of learning were replaced with constructivist models when new information about learning became available).

> *Research should acknowledge the multiple and varied contexts in which teachers work and provide support by informing their professional decision making.*

Put another way, when experimental studies control out factors, the findings do not map well onto the messy, real-world classrooms of teachers who might want to apply the lessons of research to improve students' learning. Given the importance of local knowledge and of context and interactions in classroom learning, Berliner (2002) supports educational research that includes ethnographic models, case studies, survey research, time series, design experiments, and action research. He asserts that we need these types of research to collect "reliable evidence for engaging in unfettered argument about education issues" (p. 20). Eisenhart and Towne (2003) also raise the importance of a constructive debate and dialogue about educational research (as we have had in the past). They note, as do many others quoted here, that the current narrow definition of educational research and its use as the standard for federal support works against long-held and productively exercised values of scholarship and discourse among the educational research community. In *Scientific Research in Education* (2002), the NRC reaffirms the goal of genuine inquiry in educational research and stresses that researchers must be able to choose "methods based on their research questions and to draw conclusions that are valid for the questions and methods used" (p. 34). Olson (2004) adds that rather than using research to search for what works—and then mandate it—research should acknowledge the multiple and varied contexts in which teachers work and provide support by informing their professional decision making.

Large-scale generalizations for policy and insights for classroom teaching may emerge from either quantitative or qualitative research. The discussion of what counts as knowledge about how beginning and developing readers learn goes beyond the relative merits of quantitative and qualitative research. In fact, most literacy researchers see the value in both for different lines of inquiry and application to literacy learning. And educational researchers are increasingly concerned that the current narrow definition of scientifically based research misrepresents anything other than randomized control studies—and especially qualitative research—as not scientifically based (American Educational Research Association, 2003). The association notes that qualitative research is far superior to experimental research in getting at critical educational knowledge such as the influence of contextual factors in learning, learning processes in specific situations, and the role of participants' beliefs and values in shaping outcomes (Berliner, 2002; Maxwell, 2004).

With regard to reading, the attention to the context of the teaching–learning situation in qualitative research is a big plus. Often the researcher functions as a participant observer. The presumed loss of objectivity (highly valued in quantitative research) can actually benefit the research and its potential application in the classroom. As Glesne and Peshkin (1992) point out, "The more you function as a member of the everyday world of the researched, the more you risk losing the eye of the uninvolved outsider; yet the more you participate, *the greater your opportunity to learn*" (p. 40, italics added). For teachers researching their own classrooms, Lytle and Cochran-Smith (1992) note that "systematic subjectivity" is essential.

The Importance of Practitioner Knowledge

In this book, we cast a broad, cross-disciplinary net to capture knowledge about how children learn to read and young people continue to develop as readers. One important knowledge source is teachers themselves. It is important to understand how teachers develop and deepen their knowledge about the process of reading. They do this through their own formal education, their reading and reflecting on the work of published researchers, their close observation of and reflection on students reading in their classrooms, and their sharing of classroom-based insights with one another.

Teachers' classroom studies provide invaluable knowledge about reading. Through their classroom research, teachers develop their personal theories, practical knowledge, and theoretical expertise. They recognize themselves and are recognized by others as professionals in the classroom, school, and communities (Taylor, 1993). In addition, teachers design curricula, either alone or with others, based on their research, and they adjust their practice based on their conclusions from the study (Patterson & Shannon, 1993). Research by teachers into students' learning in their own classrooms is "a distinctive and important way of knowing about teaching" (Taylor, 1993, p. 129). Knowledge about learning to read and growing as a reader must include teachers' knowledge obtained by such close observation, reflection, and analysis.

Shanahan and Neuman (1997) highlight the impact of teacher research on what we know and how we teach literacy. Among the 13 research studies they selected as most affecting literacy instruction since 1965 were Graves's study of children's writing (1982) and Atwell's (1987) study of middle school students' writing and reading. In both these studies, the teachers told their stories of immersing learners in authentic reading and writing tasks, and through their reflections on daily classroom life, drew a map for other "teacher-travelers" to follow in making their classrooms places where young people become readers and writers.

These teacher-researchers took the learner's perspective to discover what makes children want to read and write, how children develop increasing control over literacy processes, and the types of teacher interventions and classroom interactions that support those processes. Taking the learner's perspective turns out to be good advice for researchers as well as for teachers.

Summary: Toward a Knowledge Base in Reading

How do children learn to read? How do young people expand their capacity as readers to meet increasingly complex literacy demands? We are asking these questions at a time when the knowledge base is informed by research from a wide array of perspectives and methodologies as well as by more traditional treatment-effect studies. Sadly, however, we are also asking these questions at a time when control, or experimental, studies have assumed a larger influence on classroom instruction than other, more contextualized and potentially useful studies. As we have pointed out in this chapter, critiques of this narrow definition of research used by the NRP's report abound. In fact, rich studies of literacy development before, during, and outside of school add to our growing knowledge of the process and allow us to identify classroom practices that help or hinder young people in the process of becoming literate.

As we inquire into the best ways to teach beginning reading and to support students' ongoing development as readers, it is important to be clear about what we mean by reading. Again, we wish that the NRP had begun its work by agreeing on a model of reading before looking at individual research studies and making instructional recommendations based on them. In the absence of a clear definition of reading, the panel's report has been translated into instructional recommendations on five discrete areas of reading.

In this book, we adhere to a model of reading that is developmental, purposeful, interactive, and socially constructed. Our model of reading naturally leads to decisions about effective instruction as well as about relevant evidence of reading achievement. For example, rather than seeing reading as a technical skill acquired through systematic instruction in discrete skills by the time a child reaches third grade, we see reading as a developmental process in which skills and strategies are best learned in the context of authentic engagements with texts. In this model, skills and strategies continue to develop as learners encounter new texts and tasks across the spectrum of schooling and beyond. What counts as evidence of reading achievement in this model is, above all, comprehension attended by the reader's ability to acquire and use various strategies appropriately and flexibly.

A clear understanding of the nature of reading and what to look for in assessing students' growth as readers presumes a deep knowledge base about language and literacy among teachers. This is especially critical today as we address the need to close achievement gaps between groups of students and to bring all students to proficient and advanced levels of reading, as set forth by the NAEP. It is critical that all students have well-prepared, knowledgeable teachers who can make professional judgments about instruction based on their familiarity with research and also on their understandings of the unique strengths and needs of their students.

In sharing relevant research on reading in this book, we act out of a commitment to teachers as decision makers. "What works" is a relative term, and we trust knowledgeable teachers to draw from the research summarized here appropriate implications given their teaching context. We also see research as prompting dialogue—among researchers as well as teachers—about classroom implications and applications. We reject a model of research that dictates practice based on narrow definitions of both reading and research. In this book, criteria for research contributing to knowledge about reading include (a) evidence of seminal studies, (b) recency, (c) validation of current perspectives or evidence of new perspectives on learning, and (d) application to a broad range of learners.

In the next chapter we provide a discussion of current knowledge of learning theory and development based on such research and essential to the important teacher understandings described above.

TEACHER RESOURCES

National Council of Teachers of English (NCTE). (2004). *A call to action: What we know about adolescent literacy and ways to support teachers in meeting students' needs* (NCTE guideline by the Commission on Reading). Urbana, IL: Author. Retrieved May 21, 2005, from http://www.ncte.org/about/over/positions/category/read/118622.htm

National Council of Teachers of English (NCTE). (2004). *On reading, learning to read, and effective reading instruction: An overview of what we know and how we know it* (NCTE guideline by the Commission on Reading). Urbana, IL: Author. Retrieved March 18, 2005, from http://www.ncte.org/about/over/positions/category/read/118620.htm

Reading research. (2005, February). [Special section]. *Phi Delta Kappan, 86*(6).

Short, K.G., Schroeder, J., Kauffman, G., & Kaser, S. (Eds). (2003, September). Literacy: What matters? [Special issue]. *Language Arts, 81*(1).

Yatvin, J., Weaver, C., & Garan, E. (2003). Reading First: Cautions and recommendations. *Language Arts, 81*(1), 28–33.

CHAPTER 2

Acquiring and Developing Literacy: Basic Understandings

How Do We Learn?

The complexity of the human brain has long been the focus of scholarly research. Since its rise at the beginning of the 20th century, the discipline of psychology continues to document our quest for understanding the mysteries of the mind, striving to describe how the mind does its work and develops its resources.

Historically, a variety of theories through which to understand cognition and thinking have emerged as understandings; they continue to become increasingly more complex. The discipline has moved through a straightforward behaviorist model (Skinner, 1974; Thorndike, 1971), to a more complex cognitivist, information-processing model (Anderson, 1977), and on to a still-evolving constructivist model (cf. Alexander & Fox, 2004; Schallert & Martin, 2003). Although the field itself hosts a wide range of perspectives and interpretations, several aspects seem important as underlying, foundational understandings about cognition.

General Notions

Cognition is active, rather than passive; we act on, rework, and transform input rather than simply receive environmental stimuli to trigger responses; and prior knowledge plays a major role. Theories have begun to distinguish between simple information acquisition versus the construction of meaning: The construction of meaning is a much more complex and personal interaction than the processing of information (cf. Schallert & Martin, 2003). Our current understandings of cognition include several important foundational concepts:

- *Schema theory* provides a description of knowledge use that puts interpretation at the heart of cognition (Schallert & Martin, 2003). In essence, schema theory describes the organization of individual and social knowledge, experience, background, and connection as a means for interpreting and understanding the world (Anderson, 1977; Rumelhart & Ortony, 1977; Schank & Abelson, 1997).

- *Prior knowledge* is thus critical to making meaning of social situations, experiences, and texts (Anderson & Pearson, 1984; Rumelhart, 1980). The extent of an individual's world and experiential experiences helps to bring meaning to new experiences, connections, and understandings.

- *Patterning*—the ability to assign knowledge, both acquired and innate, into maps and categories that are meaningful and connected—is emphasized as a critical learning strategy. Caine and Caine (1991) found that the brain simultaneously perceives and creates parts and wholes; that is, the brain reduces information into parts and perceives holistically at the same time. Learning involves both focused attention and peripheral perception; it always involves conscious and unconscious processes. In sum, learning is a complex process, embedded within our social interactions.

- *Metacognition*, the ability to think about one's own thinking, combines the interacting processes of self-appraisal and self-management and has been found to be critical in effective cognition and learning (Paris & Winograd, 1990). Current conceptions of metacognition focus on learners becoming strategic (Paris, 1988; Paris, Lipson, & Wixon, 1983).

- *Social and cultural contexts* must be considered in understanding cognitive processes. No longer can we focus solely on the individual to consider the impact of the cultural, social, and historical milieu in which every person is born and lives (Bakhtin, 1981, 1990; Bruner, 1990; Gee, 1996, 2000; Wells, 1999; Wertsch, 1991).

- *Emotions* affect cognition. Different affective states influence cognitive processing by encouraging the adoption of different strategies for dealing with information from the environment (Schallert & Martin, 2003). Csikszentmihalyi (1990) describes the state in which an individual is so caught up in the event that attention is rapt as "flow."

- *Motivation* has critical impact on cognitive processing (Guthrie & Wigfield, 2000). An individual's desire to participate in various activities and his or her clarity of purpose and connection to real life are critical aspects of motivation.

The Place of Prominent Theorists

How young people learn, be it language or any other knowledge, has long been at the heart of research in psychology, the sciences, and education. Currently, most models of how students acquire knowledge, particularly language knowledge, have a foundation based in Piagetian constructs (Piaget & Inhelder, 1969); that is, students learn via interactions and experiences within their environment. The work of Russian psychologist Vygotsky (1934/1978) adds another critical dimension to children's learning with an emphasis on the importance of *social* interaction. Vygotsky's theories put a focus on the construction of meaning as central: Both personal and social meanings are socially constructed. In contrast to Piaget's theories, language is central to this process rather than reflecting but not determining thought (Pace, 1993).

In the case of language and literacy development, the theories of Piaget and Vygotsky are compatible, yet conflicting (Teale, 1987). Researchers and teachers alike tend to make ubiquitous references to either, or both, but without serious consideration to the theoretical work that remains to be done. Yaden, Rowe, and MacGillivray (2000) suggest that researchers, particularly those focusing on emergent literacy processes, pay closer attention to examining the deeper connections between sociocognitive studies and sociocultural perspectives.

Nevertheless, Vygotsky's (1934/1978) work is prominent in current and emerging thinking around cognition, language, and learning. The main tenets of his sociocultural theory include the following:

- Knowledge is constructed by individual learners (Bodrova & Leong, 1996).

- Language is the main vehicle of thought (Walqui, 2003) and plays a central role in mental development (Bodrova & Leong, 1996).

- Learning precedes development (Walqui, 2003); in fact, it can lead development (Bodrova & Leong, 1996).

- Development cannot be separated from its social context (Bodrova & Leong, 1996). Social interaction is the basis of learning and development. Learning is a process of apprenticeship and internalization in which skills and knowledge are transformed from the social into the cognitive plane (Walqui, 2003).

Vygotsky's (1934/1978) notion of a Zone of Proximal Development (ZPD) in learning is central to understanding the development of cognitive processes. This is the range of social interaction between a novice and more knowledgeable other in which the child can perform with degrees of assistance from an adult that which the child cannot yet perform independently. The ZPD ends at the level at which the learner can operate independently.

These social interactions involve scaffolding—the support needed by the learner—to progress in understanding and ability. Cognitive development is promoted when thought and language processes that begin interpersonally later become intrapersonal (Pace, 1993). Wood (1988) describes scaffolding as tutorial behavior that is contingent, collaborative, and interactive. (See Core Understanding 11 for discussion of instructional implications of scaffolding.)

Considering the Developmental Nature of Cognitive Processing

Early Learning. Current research on the early development of the brain assigns more and more emphasis to the experiences and interactions that occur. Interaction is the key: How those around the child—parents, siblings, caregivers—talk and engage in experiences with the child seems to hold critical importance. Ability is not fixed within each individual but rather is a process where experience and environment are key factors in development of potential. Such research has powerful implications for work with beginning readers.

A Carnegie Task Force (1994) study synthesizing research on brain development within the first three years points to five key findings:

1. Brain development that takes place before age 1 is more rapid and extensive than we previously realized.

2. Brain development is much more vulnerable to environmental influence than we ever expected (Hart & Risley, 1995).

3. The influence of early environment on brain development is long lasting.

4. The environment affects not only the number of brain cells and number of connections among them, but also the way these connections are "wired."

5. We have new scientific evidence for the negative impact of early stress on brain function. (pp. 7–9)

Work in the cognitive sciences and the neurosciences, as well as advances in other fields, builds on these notions. It shows that effective learning occurs when these factors are in place: direct engagement of the learner, social process, the learner's purposes and intentions driving the learning, hypothesis testing, and a search for meaning (Caine & Caine, 1991, 1997).

Critical to this evolving view of early learning, particularly for language learning, is the increasing number of researchers focusing on the child's perspective on learning, rather than focusing on an adult's perspective of what learning ought to be (Dahl & Freppon, 1995; Ferreiro & Teberosky, 1982; Teale, 1982; Yaden et al., 2000). Research methodologies have emerged that allow a closer view of what students do as they think and learn, particularly as they learn to speak, listen, write, and read; of their developing understandings of reading; and of how they learn to make sense of the meaning they create. Dahl and Freppon (1995) believe these developments to be particularly important in the context of current debates about differing instructional approaches, particularly for low-income students who are most at risk for failure. It is important to better understand how students view reading and writing behaviors from different perspectives in order to provide instruction and experience that best meet their needs.

Childhood. Strickland and Feeley (2003) describe elementary school-age students as able to operate on a basis of rules. In Piagetian terms, they are within the period of concrete operations, grasping the mental tasks of reversibility and conservation. They are able to classify, understand hierarchical relationships, and arrange objects in an orderly series. At this stage, learners are beginning to think more critically, posing questions as they are working through tasks (Gillet & Temple, 1996). They become more metacognitive, able to make their thinking more and more transparent. Interactions between teachers and students highlight this growing awareness.

Adolescence. Adolescents' behaviors are also often interpreted through a Piagetian frame (Pikulski, 1991). Simmons and Carroll (2003) describe young adolescents as arriving in middle school or junior high still in the concrete operational stage as found in elementary school students. However, they soon begin the transition into formal operational thought, able to think in terms of hypotheses as well as to use trial-and-error problem solving.

By middle school, students are on the threshold of a cognitive explosion (Carr, Saifer, & Novick, 2002), building capacity for more complex thinking that will continue to develop through young adulthood (Jackson & Davis, 2000). But cognitive development is only one aspect of the dynamic of adolescence. Physical and social development, as well as intellectual growth, are more rapid than at any other developmental stage except infancy (Jackson & Davis, 2000). Adolescents are intensely concerned with their own opinions and understandings, even as they are aware that others may have different opinions or ideas (Woolfolk, 2001). This self-awareness makes early adolescence an ideal time to support development of metacognition—the ability to reflect on and monitor one's thinking and learning processes (Garner, 1994; Schoenbach, Greenleaf, Cziko, & Hurwitz, 1999). Adolescents are very interested in interacting with their peers; at the same time, they are increasingly interested in larger social, political, economic, and cultural issues in the world around them. Key learning principles of construction of meaning, active engagement, and meaningful content have been shown to support learners of all ages (Carr et al., 2002). Within these principles, some aspects have special relevance to adolescent learners:

- Learning occurs through social interaction, and knowledge is socially constructed. Scaffolded support in a learning experience allows the individual to move beyond his or her current capabilities (Palincsar & Brown, 1984; Pearson & Stephens, 1994; Vygotsky, 1934/1978). Learning occurs at the edge of possibility, literally in the ZPD, so learning experiences should offer support and challenge, moving the learner toward new competence.

- Learning occurs when the individual is motivated and actively engaged in the experience; both intrinsic and extrinsic motivation can lead to engagement, but the goal is to develop strong intrinsic motivation to drive ongoing learning (Guthrie & Wigfield, 2000).

- The goal of learning is conceptual understanding beyond acquisition of facts of details (Guthrie & Davis, 2003; Langer, 2001). Inquiry-driven learning generates new questions and understandings, ideally with relevance beyond the classroom (Wiggins & McTighe, 1998).

Teachers of adolescents must see the strongest learning potential in Vygotskian terms as "on the edge of possibility," not focusing on facts but encouraging young people to think more complexly about the intersections of academic and world knowledge (cf. Ivey, 1999).

Language Learning: Acquisition and Development

Holdaway (1979) observes, "Anything that can be said of human language and language learning has some vital bearing on the processes of literacy" (p. 13). Consequently, investigation into how children and adolescents acquire language has grown immensely during the past 40 years. Chomsky's (1959, 1965) notion that all humans actively construct meaning led to questions beyond the long-held behaviorist view of response theory. Chomsky's new perspective and alternative questions have led to a series of investigations that have given increasing insight into how students learn oral language, which in turn invites consideration of how students then acquire written language. Because of the relative newness of this area of investigation, consensus remains elusive on many points. Roller (2001) confirms this in her review of the development of comprehensive reading instruction: She finds that though curricula for learning to read and write presume a cognitive, developmental sequence, empirically grounded descriptions of those developmental sequences are definitely lacking.

Disciplines and subdisciplines interested in such investigations (e.g., cognitive and developmental psychology, psycholinguistics, sociolinguistics, linguistics, anthropology, education) consider questions from such a wide variety of perspectives that difference is found more often than is similarity. These investigations have, however, helped us to gain insight into the processes of acquisition and development of children's language. In general, this research helps us to understand that oral language development is all of the following:

- *Reconstructive*: It is a process of reconstructing the child's home language through interactions with more sophisticated language users. Language learning is much more than simple imitation; rather, it is a complex process of trial and error through approximations. Learning language is an intellectual, cognitive process (Brown, 1973; Halliday, 1975; Piaget & Inhelder, 1969).

- *Meaning based*: Language has a purpose: to communicate needs, wants, and feelings. Halliday (1975) suggests learning language is "learning how to mean" in one's culture. Children will take on a language form because of its function—initially understanding the function, and through use, becoming clear about the form itself. For example, young children, as they are learning to talk, approximate the forms of language (e.g., "ba" for *bottle*) while clearly understanding the function of language (e.g., communicating "I want my bottle now!"). In this way, form follows function.

- *Social*: Language is for communication among people, and it is acquired and expanded through purposeful and meaningful interactions (Bruner, 1975; Gee, 1996; Harste, Woodward, & Burke, 1984; Neuman & Roskos, 1992; Vygotsky, 1934/1978; Wells, 1986).

- *Interactive*: Children learn language via scaffolds provided by sophisticated language users; that is, they offer opportunities for children to try out approximations and through constructive and positive feedback, assist children toward gaining conventions of the language (Applebee & Langer, 1983; Bruner, 1975; Cambourne, 1988; Vygotsky, 1934/1978; Wells, 1986).

- *Developmental*: Children's language acquisition occurs in stages that are documentable. Often, children's processes of hypothesis generation (i.e., figure out how language works) are demonstrated through their language "errors" (Brown, 1973; Wells, 1986).

- *Interrelated*: Oral language development is in a dynamic relationship with listening, reading, and writing: Each influences the other in the course of development. Brown and Cambourne (1990), elaborating on a visual metaphor designed by Harste, Burke, and Woodward (1982), describe this relationship in terms of a "linguistic data pool" (p. 24); this means that all language learners have an ever-increasing pool of knowledge about language and are continually adding to it whether reading, writing, listening, or speaking.

Language as Function

It is important to consider Halliday's (1975) notion that language is functional. According to his theory of language development, what a child can do during interactions with others has meaning, and meaning can be turned into speech: What can be said reflects what can be done. In his work, he describes the following functions of language:

- *Instrumental*: language to satisfy a personal need and to get things done.

- *Regulatory*: language to control the behavior of others.

- *Interactional*: language to get along with others.

- *Personal*: language to tell about oneself.

- *Imaginative*: language to pretend, to make believe.

- *Heuristic*: language to find out about things, to learn things.

- *Informative*: language to communicate something for the information of others.
(cf. Pinnell, 1985, p. 60)

Children's acquisition of oral language does seem to follow a pattern: Children seem to be more interested in the functions of literacy first, then the form, and later the conventions (Halliday, 1973, 1975; cf. Morrow, 1996). As children become more sophisticated in their knowledge and use of language, the expected conventions (e.g., "I would like to have a glass of milk, please.") become the norm.

A Model of Acquisition

Based on a synthesis of Halliday's (and others') work and his own investigations, Cambourne (1988) provides a useful model of conditions that support successful oral language learning:

- *Immersion*: From birth, we are immersed in the language of our culture. Learners need to be immersed in all kinds of language.

- *Demonstration*: Learners need to receive many demonstrations of how language is constructed and used.

- *Engagement*: Deep engagement with demonstrations is maximized when learners are convinced that (a) they are potential doers of whatever is being demonstrated; (b) engaging with what is being demonstrated will further the purposes of the potential learners' lives; (c) engagement with whatever is being demonstrated will not lead to pain, humiliation, denigration—it is safe to have a go at it. In addition, learners are more likely to engage with demonstrations provided by those who are significant to them.

- *Expectation*: Expectations of those to whom learners are bonded send clear messages to children as to what they are expected to learn *and* what they are capable of learning. Learners respond positively and confidently to supportive expectations.

- *Responsibility*: Learners need to participate in making decisions about when, how, and what bits to learn in any learning task.

- *Approximation*: Learners must be free to approximate the desired model—mistakes are essential for learning to occur.

- *Use*: Learners need time and opportunity to use, employ, and practice their developing control in functional, realistic, nonartificial ways.

- *Response*: Learners must receive feedback from exchanges with more knowledgeable others. Response must be relevant, appropriate, timely, readily available, nonthreatening, with no strings attached. (pp. 28–75)

For adolescent learners, Applebee, Langer, Nystrand, and Gamoran (2003) translate these conditions into three approaches to classroom discussion: (1) emphases on dialogic interaction (Nystrand, 1997), (2) support for envisionment building (i.e., those cognitive and linguistic processes that readers and writers draw from as they begin to envision an evolving text world [Langer, 1985]), and (3) extended curricular conversations (Applebee, 1996). Langer identified four classroom practices for adolescents that parallel Cambourne's conditions for younger learners:

1. Teachers treat all students as capable envisionment builders with important understandings and potential contributions to classroom discussion;

2. Teachers use instructional activities such as discussion to develop understandings rather than to test what students already know;

3. Teachers assume that questions are a natural part of the process of coming to understand new material, rather than an indication of failure to learn, and that questions provide productive starting points for discussion; and

4. Teachers help students learn to examine multiple perspectives (from students, texts, and other voices) to enrich understanding rather than focusing on consensus interpretations. (as cited in Applebee et al., 2003, p. 691)

Connections Between Oral Language and the Language of Print
Cambourne (1988) believes these conditions also support the learning of written language. Similarly, Applebee and colleagues (2003) agree the role of oral language (specifically conversational discourse) supports the learning of adolescents. Although parallels between the learning of oral language and the learning of print (reading and writing) have engendered much debate, it is important to note both the similarities and the differences and how these apply to acquisition and development.

Similarities. Reading, writing, speaking, and listening, at the deep levels of production and comprehension, are parallel manifestations of the same vital human function—the mind's effort to create meaning (Cambourne, 1988). Cognitively, the same processes seem to be in effect with all language processes. Children go through developmental stages in ways similar to oral language development. Trumbull and Farr (2005) note that all areas of language proficiency contribute to proficiency in reading and writing, including verbal memory, phonological skills, semantic (vocabulary) skills, grammatical skills, pragmatic skills, and discourse skills.

Differences. The two modes of language are different in many complex and interesting ways. These differences are due to such pragmatic factors as psychological and physical distance from audience, function, amount of time people have to produce language, and degree of permanence (Chafe & Danielwicz, 1987; Olson, 1977; Rubin, 1978; Tannen, 1982). The most salient difference is that the two require different kinds of knowledge that learners must acquire in order to operate with and on them. And certain uses of the written mode require specific knowledge that cannot be carried over from the oral mode, and vice versa (e.g., in written language, using capitalization, indentations, commas, periods, and question marks; in oral language, using pauses and fillers).

Trumbull and Farr (2005) note an important cognitive difference between oral and written language—the fact that written language is doubly symbolic; readers and writers must become at least somewhat conscious of their knowledge of oral language, which isn't necessary in speaking most of the time (Flood & Menyuk, 1981).

Cambourne (1988) discusses these differences in detail. Written language is not merely oral language that has been written down because it is used for different purposes, in different contexts, under different conditions. The same access for learning the written mode is not as readily available as that for the oral. That is, while oral language is constantly surrounding us in a variety of means (personal, recorded, and so on), print language must be created and made accessible. Someone must construct a text—a newspaper, a letter, a list, a sign, a billboard—and make it available for others to read. Classrooms must provide a wide variety of opportunities to access print—through books, charts, lists, labels—so that children have opportunities to interact with print in real and meaningful ways parallel to oral language.

Moustafa (1997) suggests that children need to learn the language of print; that is, based on their knowledge of oral language, they need to learn how the language of print works. Just as with oral language, children are figuring out how print works concurrently with learning to read (reminiscent of Halliday's learning through language and about language while learning language). Clay (1985) similarly speaks of children's learning about language in their lives. These understandings must be developed through scaffolded experiences specifically with print. Wells (1986) points out that reading to children also helps them acquire the language of print. The work of Mason (1992), Sulzby (1985), and Purcell-Gates (1988) also supports the importance of reading aloud to children. These experiences give children a sense of the language of print, putting them in an even better position to figure out print on their own (Moustafa, 1997).

Cambourne's (1988) work suggests this learning must be supported by the same conditions as oral language. In fact, Cambourne goes further, saying that his model of language learning reflects how humans go about learning in general. His conditions for learning language reflect basic principles that can guide effective teaching and learning of language. Thus, experience in and out of schools must be provided by teachers and parents to assist children in their development.

Language Development Over Time

Emergent Literacy

Traditionally, adults viewed a discrete set of skills deemed necessary for children to begin to read as *readiness*. Typically, this state included knowledge of colors, shapes, and the alphabet. The notion of *emergent literacy*—coined by Clay (1966)—turned the focus from this adult idea of readiness to what children acquire from their surrounding environments that provides a foundation for beginning literacy. Research across cultures has provided substance to the idea of emergent literacy. These researchers have focused explicitly on how children go about their learning, rather than on a set of tasks configured by adults to represent the learning. In a very general sense, *emergent literacy* describes those behaviors shown by very young children as they begin to respond to and approximate reading and writing acts. By the time children enter first grade, they are often ready to move into more sophisticated behaviors. However, development varies. Ferreiro and Teberosky (1982), Harste and colleagues (1984), Heath (1983), Morrow (1978, 1997), Sulzby (1985), Taylor (1983), Teale (1982, 1986), and Wells (1986) provide insight into how young children use the same type of learning strategies seen in oral language to begin to make sense of the print they find in their world, highlighting children's active construction of increasingly more sophisticated conventional literacy strategies (Yaden et al., 2000). Generally, the following behaviors describe children's emergent literacy:

> " *In a very general sense, emergent literacy describes those behaviors shown by very young children as they begin to respond to and approximate reading and writing acts.* "

- *They have gained oral language structures*. In particular, young children are becoming aware of syntax (structure) and meaning. In oral language, they have begun to experiment with the sounds language makes. This understanding and knowledge is an important foundation transferred to learning the language of print. They begin to understand the different registers of print from being read to (Bus, van IJzendoorn, & Pelligrini, 1995; Pappas, 1991; Purcell-Gates, 1988; Purcell-Gates, McIntyre, & Freppon, 1995; Sulzby, 1985).

- *They find meaning in symbols around them*. Early on, signs and symbols (e.g., McDonald's golden arches, labels from familiar products) take on important meaning: The environmental print in children's lives has a real function. These signs and symbols reflect what is available and meaningful within the lives of those around the child, from letters to symbols found in everyday life (Goodman, 1984; Harste et al., 1984; Mason, 1980; Smith, 1971).

- *They begin to gain metalinguistic awareness*. They begin to become aware of different individual sounds and words, often by word play and rhyming games (Sulzby, 1985).

- *They begin to write, using symbols, signs, and letters in their attempts to reconstruct the symbolic language around them* (Bissex, 1980; Harste et al., 1984; Sulzby, 1985). Children begin to represent the variety of visual symbols they see as part of their everyday lives, often creating lists and visual representations.

- *They begin to approximate print behaviors modeled to them.* This includes storybook reading, use of storybook language and behaviors, and the approximation of writing tasks modeled (lists, stories, and so on). Often, these approximations occur within the child's play (Heath, 1983; Sulzby, 1985; Wells, 1986). These activities also support growth in metalinguistic awareness.

- *They follow a developmental pattern in reading and writing* (Morrow, 1997). These patterns reinforce the use and emergence of language cues for the knowledge systems of sound–symbol relationships, meaning, structure, and purpose. The patterns suggest process, and as these processes are repeated, they are refined. Language acquisition is not additive; rather, children are repeating the whole process, refining, and getting clearer and clearer with time and experience.

- *They begin to categorize speech sounds to print patterns* (Read, 1975). They create their own spelling patterns, based on their perception of how language works and how they can fit it together.

- *They begin to include dramatic play as a strategy for understanding literacy processes* (Christie, 1991; Pellegrini & Galda, 1991, 1993). In this type of play, children use make-believe transformations of objects and their own identities to act out scripts they invent (cf. Yaden et al., 2000). Through such play, children are provided with opportunities to build important cognitive and linguistic skills needed for emerging reading and writing abilities.

Childhood Literacy Development

Oral language remains as the foundation of reading and writing development for children throughout the elementary school years. Again, development will vary from child to child and grade to grade; however, certain particular language development stages can be recognized by teachers as they plan for effective classroom experiences. Generally, the following behaviors describe elementary school-age children's literacy development:

- *They continue in language development.* Chomsky (1959, 1965) studied the development of certain sentence structures with school-age children. By ages 9 and 10, most children had mastered structures they had misinterpreted or misunderstood at ages 5 and 6. Teachers need to provide opportunities where they can understand children's understandings as different from adults', probing and exploring language meaning and function in the process. Children at this stage tend to be literal in their language usage.

- *They continue to need many opportunities to talk.* Loban (1963) found that children who had many opportunities for classroom interactions with both teachers and peers had increased the complexity of their sentence structure and increased their vocabulary knowledge.

- *They continue to develop metalinguistic abilities and strategies.* At this stage, this ability to reflect on and manipulate the structural features of language (Tunmer, Herriman, & Nesdale, 1988) is important to vocabulary development (Anderson & Nagy, 1992; Graves, 1986) as children continue to develop "word awareness" or "word consciousness" (cf. Nagy & Scott, 2000, pp. 273–279).

- *They continue to enjoy read-aloud experiences.* These experiences model what good readers do, support vocabulary and language growth, and develop response and questioning strategies. Nagy and Anderson (1984) found that children gain vocabulary through both listening to and individually reading a rich variety of literature.

- *They continue to develop a sense of story.* Children are able to predict, to add details, and to discern the differences between text genres. Although they begin their elementary years at a literal level, they are increasingly able to make inferences, compare and contrast, and synthesize and evaluate their interpretations of a variety of text genres (cf. Strickland & Feeley, 2003).

- *They continue to need many opportunities to write.* Much research of the last two decades has focused on the impact of process writing opportunities on literacy development (reading, speaking, and listening) (Bissex, 1980; Calkins, 1983, 1986, 1994; Clay, 1975; Dahl & Farnan, 1998; Graves, 1983, 1994; Hansen, 1987). Children need daily writing opportunities where they are able to choose topics and compose their own pieces over time. Ongoing, successful writing experiences support successful growth in reading ability and skill (Hansen, 1987).

- *They continue to develop strategies for reading.* Readers in the elementary years are increasingly able to be metacognitively aware; that is, they can know the strategies they are successfully, or not so successfully, using (Myers & Paris, 1978).

Adolescent Literacy Development

Reading is not a set of technical skills acquired in elementary school and then applied throughout life. Rather, the literacy demands of each stage of a learner's development require new knowledge and skills from the reader (National Council of Teachers of English [NCTE], 2004). As middle and high school students deepen their study of subject areas such as mathematics, science, and social studies, they encounter text structures, concept-related vocabulary, and discourse features that necessitate discipline-based ways of reading—ways of reading best learned in practice and modeled by subject area teachers (Kucer, 2005; Moje & Sutherland, 2003; Schoenbach et al., 1999). As students read expository as well as narrative texts, they must make sense of more abstract, complex topics removed from their personal experiences (Moore, Bean, Birdyshaw, & Rycik, 1999). At the same time, adolescent readers are expected to engage more critically with texts. This means not only drawing inferences, reasoning, and problem solving for comprehension but also recognizing and critiquing the perceived message of the text on such topics as race, ethnicity, social class, and gender (Moje, Young, Readence, & Moore, 2000). Langer's (2001, 2002) studies depict adolescent literacy as a dynamic interaction of the social and cognitive realms. In this process, textual understandings continue to grow from students' knowledge of their worlds to knowledge of the external world with increasing sophistication.

Differences among students as readers, shaped by development and experience, magnify as the grade level increases. Complicating the challenge of meeting the needs of students across this range is the growing number of middle and high school students who are English-language learners (ELLs), some already literate in their first language, others without that tradition. Academic progress will vary, given these factors (Moore et al., 1999).

What do we know about proficient literacy practice in adolescence? How well are teens measuring up? Effective reading among adolescents adds sophistication to the development process begun in early childhood. Some key features of growing sophistication in teens' literacy development include the following (cf. Shanklin, 2000):

- Flexible and purposeful use of an array of strategies for determining meanings of new vocabulary and for comprehending text.

- Ability to use a range of reading and thinking strategies to comprehend, remember, analyze, and synthesize what they read.

- Knowledge of text structures and how to use them to make meaning with text.

- Ability to set authentic purposes for reading.

- Motivation and engagement in reading.

- Metacognitive awareness of their own reading process (i.e., how and what they are understanding, and when and how to take action to correct a breakdown in comprehension).

- Ability to read and understand a wide range of genres.

- Ability to link reading to other sign systems.

- Ability to activate relevant schema and build on or revise them as necessary to fit new content area topics.

If adolescents are to develop the literacy skills necessary to meet the personal, economic, social, and civic demands of the 21st century, we must help more of them move beyond current competence levels to reach these advanced literacy levels.

What do adolescents bring to the task of developing advanced literacies? Middle and high school students already engage in "multiple literacies" (Moje et al., 2000), using texts across various formats (the Internet, film, music, as well as print) to suit various personal, social, and cultural purposes. They use literacy both to make meaning and to act on their world (NCTE, 2004). Adolescents' purposeful and critical use of the multiple literacies in which they currently engage provides excellent motivation for them to expand their repertoire of forms and their understanding of literacy. In the process they gain access to more academic discourse communities (Moje & Sutherland, 2003).

What kinds of instruction and experiences do adolescents need to develop as readers? Recommendations from a variety of literacy professional organizations and researchers converge on critical components of an effective literacy curriculum for adolescents (Kamil, 2003; Langer, 2000; Moore et al., 1999; NCTE, 2004; Schoenbach et al., 1999). Adolescents need the following:

- Wide reading across a range of texts and genres linked to curriculum.
- Opportunities to build fluency and stamina through extensive reading in books of their own choice.
- Instruction that develops both motivation and ability to read increasingly complex texts.
- Teacher modeling of these advanced ways of reading.
- Strategy instruction embedded in reading to learn with curricular texts.
- Instruction that helps them connect knowledge and skills across the curriculum and between school and life.
- Authentic conversations about texts with student-to-student talk as the mode and diverse interpretation of text as the norm.
- Classrooms that foster cognitive collaboration.
- Practice in being reflective about their own reading process and opportunities to recognize and appropriate others' productive strategies.
- Practice in reading texts critically so they can learn how texts are organized in particular disciplines, investigate content and purposes within texts, make personal connections to text and connections between texts, and explore multiple meanings of texts.
- Assessment that identifies strengths as well as areas of need.

Family Literacy: From Theory to Practice

The role of families is important in emergent literacy processes. Literacy is deeply embedded in the social processes of family life (Taylor, 1983). Families influence literacy development in three ways (Leichter, 1984): through interpersonal interaction (literacy experiences shared by family members), the physical environment (literacy materials found in the home), and the emotional and motivational climate (the relationships and their attitudes toward literacy). In general, parent involvement in education is directly related to significant increases in overall student achievement (Bloom, 1985; Clark, 1983).

Home and school connections are critical to learning to read. Children who have had a wide variety of language experiences—in both oral and written modes—fare better as they begin to learn to read within the school setting (Purcell-Gates, 1996). These experiences include the following:

- *Many opportunities to talk*. Descriptions and conversations with positive interactions and feedback from those around the child support growth and development of increasingly sophisticated language patterns (Bruner, 1975; Cazden, 1988; Hart & Risley, 1995; Ninio & Bruner, 1978).

- *Experiences with stories, both oral (storytelling) and written (storybook reading)* (Holdaway, 1979; Sulzby, 1985; Teale, 1978, 1982; Wells, 1986). Storybook reading experiences are considered by many to be the most important aspect of emergent literacy experiences (Purcell-Gates et al., 1995), giving children the structure and syntax of written language as well as demonstrating purpose and function of reading (Heath, 1982; Morrow, O'Connor, & Smith, 1990; Sulzby, 1985; Taylor & Strickland, 1986). If children do not have this background framework on which to hang the more explicit literacy experiences received in schools, they may have difficulty acquiring and developing literacy.

- *Appropriate verbal interaction between adult and child during story readings* (Cochran-Smith, 1984; Ninio, 1980). Edwards (1989, 1991) found that nonmainstream parents can successfully be taught how to interact with books in ways that support successful literacy development.

- *Opportunities to draw and write* (Clay, 1975). Drawing and writing support children's interest in and growing awareness of print in their environment. Experiences at home and with other family members highlight their importance as everyday means of communication.

Purcell-Gates (1995) concludes that print in the world is "phenomena"; that is, it must be experienced in authentic contexts in order to be recognized as communicating meaning. This conclusion strengthens the concept that the home is an essential locus of learning about print (Purcell-Gates, 2000).

Recent research has focused on the connection between home and school literacies. A position statement of the International Reading Association (IRA; 2002) refers to several studies as indicative of the positive impact of home–school connections on literacy development. Among the studies are those of Morrow and Young (1997), who created a program to connect home and school literacy contexts; results showed those children who participated in home–school related activities did significantly better in academic tasks in school than those who did not participate. Another study by Bevans, Furnish, Ramsey, and Talsma (2001) found that parent-involvement intervention led to increased at-home reading, improvement in home–school communication, and an increase in parents' knowledge about reading. Paratore, Melzi, and Krol-Sinclair (1999) found similar results in a study of Latino families' involvement in a home–school literacy project.

It is important to note that home–school partnerships should be developed across K–12 schools; however, such programs must respond to the different needs of students at elementary, middle, and high school levels (IRA, 2002).

Gadsen (2000) suggests that a wide circle of caregivers are likely to make significant contributions to children's cognitive and social development, complementing those of the immediate family (Auerbach, 1989; Paratore, 1993; Taylor, Chatters, Tucker, & Lewis, 1990). The literature on intergenerational literacy has helped researchers and educators to think more broadly about the families of children in classrooms and the possibilities of supporting all children as effective learners. Gadsen suggests this work helps us to understand that there is not one appropriate, prototypical model of family structure; rather, there is a vast range of family constellations. She also notes that for all families, irrespective of ethnic background, their past and contemporary experiences have dictated or defined the family structures in which they function, with varying degrees of socially valued success. Each family brings a repertoire of beliefs, knowledge, skills, and experiences that are as likely to strengthen as to debilitate its members.

> " *Language and literacy are developmental across the span of childhood, from emergent and early stages to increased sophistication in adolescence. Oral language development is foundational.* "

Summary: Research Findings on Literacy Acquisition and Development

This chapter has focused on the cognitive, social, and developmental aspects of language and literacy learning. Brain research has affected current notions about cognition and learning; theories have begun to distinguish between simple information acquisition versus the construction of meaning. Foundational concepts include schema theory, prior knowledge, patterning, metacognition, social and cultural contexts, emotions, and motivation.

Prominent theorists whose work has informed our understandings of language and literacy development include Piaget and Vygotsky. In particular, Vygotsky's work has highlighted the importance of both social and cultural contexts and social interaction within those contexts. His theory of ZPD and the use of scaffolding within this zone illustrate ways in which children reconstruct language.

Language and literacy are developmental across the span of childhood, from emergent and early stages to increased sophistication in adolescence. Oral language development is foundational. It is a process of reconstructing the child's home language through interactions with more sophisticated language users. It is reflective of the cognitive processes described above, including that it is a social process, it is meaning based, it is interactive, it is developmental, and it is in a dynamic relationship with listening, reading, and writing.

While oral language and written language seem to share many of the same processes, there are different kinds of knowledge that learners must recognize and acquire in order to operate with and on them. These parallel processes are, again, developmental across time, increasing in complexity and sophistication.

Families are critical in support of language and literacy acquisition and development. The very foundation of language and literacy acquisition is focused on the interaction of more sophisticated users within a child's familiar social and cultural contexts.

In the next chapter, we provide a synthesis of factors that influence literacy acquisition and development important to teacher understandings.

TEACHER RESOURCES

Bransford, J.D., Brown, A.C., & Cocking, R.R. (Eds.). (1999). *How people learn: Brain, mind, and school*. Washington, DC: National Academy Press.

Trumbull, E., & Farr, B. (2005). *Language and learning: What teachers need to know*. Norwood, MA: Christopher-Gordon.

CHAPTER 3

Factors That Influence Literacy Learning

MANY FACTORS INFLUENCE literacy acquisition and learning. Research efforts over the past three decades have continued to explore these factors and the extent to which they affect students and their literacy knowledge.

Currently, the notion of the achievement gap between ethnic groups in K–12 schooling has been the focus of both discussion and research, perhaps more than ever before. An Educational Testing Service report, *Parsing the Achievement Gap: Baselines for Tracking Progress* (Barton, 2003), describes factors influencing successful learning in the following categories:

Before and Beyond School

- *The Development Environment*: The early experiences and conditions of life and living, including weight at birth, exposure to environmental hazards such as lead, environmental stimulation necessary for cognitive development, and hunger and nutrition.

- *The Home–Learning Connection*: Generally, the support for learning in the home, including parental expectations for academic achievement, reading to young children, access to quiet study space, attention to physical and health needs, amount of TV watching, and parent availability.

- *The Community*: The extent to which the community and its essential institutions support or hinder the efforts of families and schools. Student mobility (that is, how frequently students change schools) is related to socioeconomic status and can result in a myriad of problems in school.

- *The Home–School Connection*: The two-way street of parents trying to be supportive of school efforts and schools reaching out to inform, encourage, and show receptivity to parent participation. It includes getting students to attend school regularly and encouraging them to do their homework.

School

- *Teaching and Learning*: The instructional infrastructure, including the quality of leadership, pedagogy, professional development, rigor of the curriculum, teacher preparation, teacher experience and attendance, class size, and availability of appropriate technology-assisted instruction.

- *The Learning Environment*: The general conditions and ambiance of the school, such as expectations, commitment of teachers and staff, and school safety. (p. 6)

Although the summary of these findings is not surprising, the focus of interpretation puts much more emphasis on the ability of teachers, administrators, and schools to work effectively across a wide range of cognitive, social, emotional, and cultural needs found within the current school population. Increased emphasis on curricula that are equally rigorous for all students (of all backgrounds and need) is found: "Not surprisingly, research evidence shows that students' academic achievement is closely related to the rigor of the curriculum" (Barton, 2003, p. 8; cf. Bryk, Lee, & Holland, 1993; Chubb & Moe, 1990). Singham (2003) agrees, stating that strong curriculum reform, coupled with intentional, sustained professional development of teachers, has the most impact on the gap in teaching quality and, thus, of the achievement gap itself.

Labov (2003) describes factors that influence learning in much the same fashion. Although these factors are critical and cannot be neglected, he insists the field must apply the knowledge of the reading process to the actual teaching of reading. He states,

> Current summaries of the state of reading interventions propose no solution (NICHD [National Institute of Child Health and Human Development], 2000; Snow, Burns, & Griffin, 1998). The field of reading has not presently an answer to the question of what to do about healthy children who do not learn to read.

To understand the problem of struggling readers, we have to know more than what their dialects sound like—we need to know the structure of the linguistic knowledge that children bring to school and how words are represented in that system. (p. 129; cf. Labov, 2001; Labov, Baker, Bullock, Ross, & Brown, 1998)

Gee (1996, 1999) looks closely at the linguistic and cultural backgrounds of individuals and groups and the ways of using language that relate to identity, social relationships, and contexts. These can be represented by *d/Discourses* in at least two ways. He describes *d* discourses as "connected stretches of language that make sense, like conversations, stories, reports, arguments, essays, and so forth" (1996, p. 127; cf. Van Sluys, 2004). *D* Discourses are "ways of being in the world" that bring together "acts, values, beliefs, attitudes, social identities, gestures, body positions, clothes" (1996, p. 127; cf. Van Sluys, 2004). Social systems work to position people in various ways via these d/Discourses as individuals manipulate resources within given contexts in efforts to construct a recognized, cohesive self. Individuals acquire the primary discourse within the immediate context of home and community. Acquisition usually occurs in the primary discourse, and learning occurs in the secondary Discourse. Thus, as described by Labov (2003), students whose home, or primary discourse, is closely aligned with the school, or secondary Discourse, will have an easier transition between these two spheres. What is not commonly attended to in the process of learning secondary Discourse (in this case, that of schooling) is that students are also immersed in and acquire the values, beliefs, and structures connected to that Discourse (cf. Rogers, 2002). Heath's (1983) work exemplifies this notion, highlighting the fact that different models of literacy processes and thus Discourses were reflected in the values and expectations of individual communities.

Culture and Literacy: What Difference Does Difference Make?

As noted in the opening section of this chapter, a match between cultural expectations for literacy and school expectations for literacy is critical to the successful acquisition of reading. These expectations are not always the same, and students' experiences with literacy will vary accordingly. For example, in some cultures storytelling is as highly valued as the use of print materials (Morrow, 1996). Families help students to appreciate and understand the social significance of literacy—however it may be defined for individuals (Clay, 1979; Taylor, 1983). However, studies have found the types and forms of literacy practiced in some homes—often of low-income, ethnic and cultural minority, and immigrant families—to be largely incongruent with the literacy encountered in school (Heath, 1983; Taylor & Dorsey-Gaines, 1988). This research identifies families as literate in ways defined by their cultures and communities—for example, cultures rich in oral traditions—rather than in ways defined by school literacy. These studies challenge assumptions about uniform definitions of literacy as well as about the concern of parents for their children's education (cf. Chavkin, 1989; Comer, 1986; Paratore, 2002; Snow, Barnes, Chandler, Goodman, & Hemphill, 1991).

Oral language provides the foundation and framework for written language acquisition; therefore, a mismatch between family literacy and school literacy can cause difficulty for children learning to read within a school situation. With increasing diversity among the population, students come to school with a wide variety of oral language patterns and expectations, as well as a wide variety of experiences with print language (Hall, 1987). As schools find themselves in this richness of diversity, they need to be attentive to what students bring as a framework, building on their experiences, values, and background knowledge to introduce them to more public forms of literacy (cf. Gee, 1996, 1999; Labov, 2001, 2003; Labov et al., 1998).

Dyson (1997), with the San Francisco East Bay Teacher Study Group, sees the issue to be one of identifying differences as problems or as possibilities. She describes this potential (to go either way) as an intersection of the many *horizontal differences*—that is, those differences of language, cultural style, familial circumstance, or other sociocultural and linguistic differences—with *vertical* differences—those where students fall on the very narrow band of abilities and skills that mark even young children as "smart" or "not," "ready" or "not," or "at risk" or "not" via a kind of standardized achievement test (p. 11). She notes that the teachers she worked with in this study of inner-city students "worked hard to make visible children's competence and to acknowledge the breadth of language, symbolic and problem-posing and -solving skills needed in our world—without abandoning the need to straightforwardly help children learn traditional school knowledge and skills" (p. 12). Schools need to move away from equating horizontal differences with risk for students who are different from the dominant cultural group. Schools must create bridges to literacy for students of all backgrounds.

Key studies have provided findings about fostering positive relationships among culture, language, and schooling.

Au and Mason's (1981, 1983) work with the Kamehameha Elementary Education Program (KEEP) to construct a curriculum that was attentive to the native language structures of Hawaiian students shows the importance of a match between native language and dominant language as key to moving students into successful literacy experiences (cf. Gallimore, Boggs, & Jordan, 1974; Jordan, 1984, 1992).

Delpit's (1986, 1988) work argues that many linguistic and ethnic minority students must be made aware of and taught the "language of power" (e.g., the conventions of written language and the academic register) to be successful in school.

Goldenberg's (1987) ongoing work with Hispanic students in metropolitan Los Angeles, as well as other diverse locations in California, focuses on a view of cultural discontinuity rather than of cultural deprivation as a way to consider students' success in school. For example, many Hispanic families place emphasis on moral development in preschool experiences, whereas the school may expect the families to place a higher value on academic achievement. This difference in emphasis points out a discontinuity between cultures rather than confirming that some children lack particular experiences.

Heath's (1983) study of three groups within an Appalachian town found that the differences in language patterns and expectations affected school success. The school was not attentive to what some students did know (e.g., creative uses of oral language for storytelling).

The KEEP work in collaboration with the Rough Rock Demonstration School (Jordan, 1995) showed that a "culturally responsive school"—that is, a school that acknowledged the cultural heritage of students—provided a successful milieu for native students. Teaching and learning in these schools acknowledged the differences in the amount, initiation patterns, and volume of talk, as well as the use of questions, between native cultures and the mainstream culture.

Michaels's (1981) study of show-and-tell showed how everyday language and the language of school often clashed. Children were not able to make the transitions to school language without help from teachers aware of the discontinuity, and thus were at a disadvantage to progress according to school standards of language, especially the school value for linear, topic-centered oral presentations.

Moje and colleagues (2004) studied a group of 30 Latina/o adolescents over five years, focusing on how they bridged home and school funds of knowledge and Discourse in science. Their findings show that though these students were capable of skilled and strategic uses of multiple funds of knowledge and Discourse outside of school, they did not actively volunteer to engage and use these at school within science classes. Moje and colleagues suggest that teachers must explicitly plan for the inclusion of such funds and Discourse, as well as make clear to students that many different kinds of knowledge are welcomed in classrooms, particularly content classes at the secondary level.

> **These data highlight the important role of perceptions and expectations within a classroom and their appropriate focus and interpretation in the continuing achievement gap between minority students and those in the dominant cultural group.**

Orange and Horowitz (1999) surveyed and interviewed a group of 10 English teachers and a total of 83 male adolescents of diverse ethnic backgrounds (63 African American and 20 Mexican American) about their perceptions of a wide variety of literacy tasks found in high school English classrooms. The researchers termed their findings an "academic standoff": Perceptions by teachers were often the exact opposite of the students'. An important finding of their study is that students felt they needed the challenge of more difficult texts, whereas teachers felt the students were not interested in such texts. In addition, students felt teachers should read and provide feedback on writing and reading activities, whereas teachers felt students did not care to read feedback and respond to their suggestions. These data highlight the important role of perceptions and expectations within a classroom and their appropriate focus and interpretation in the continuing achievement gap between minority students and those in the dominant cultural group.

Philips's (1983) study of Native American students (Warm Springs Reservation in Oregon) found that differences between Native American students and a white teacher in language styles and expectations prevented learning from taking place. School experiences that focused on single performance, provided no opportunity for practice, and lacked support for learning in small groups did not match the cultural expectations for learning for Native American students.

Street's (1995) research on literacy practices and attitudes in middle class homes revealed what he called a "relentless commitment to instruction" (p. 127). Students were engaged in literate activities expressly to teach them reading and writing. In many school settings, this explicit instruction in literacy is continued; but where teachers base the timing and amount of literacy instruction on the learner's needs, there can be a discontinuity between the home values for adult-determined literacy lessons and the school's use of learner-centered, learner-responsive literacy instruction to build on what the child already knows. The obverse can be equally true: Students from homes where literacy instruction was not provided come to school and are judged to be lacking, not ready to read.

Taylor and Dorsey-Gaines's (1988) study of six inner-city families showed a great number and variety of early literacy experiences displayed within their everyday lives, but it also showed a mismatch between school expectations and the cultural expectations and interpretations. Although many reading and writing experiences were available to the students in their homes, school provided mainly workbook and drill-oriented experiences. This study points out the danger in global generalizations about the literacy needs of low-socioeconomic status (SES) cultural and ethnic minority students.

Valdes (1996) studied 10 immigrant Mexican American families and their children. Although many educators have interpreted these families as "disinterested" in their children's education, Valdes points out that their goals, values, and experiences are often incongruent with the expectations of school and makes the case that educators must come to respect and understand the strong family values and goals to create culturally sensitive and responsive classrooms.

Wells's (1986) longitudinal study of preschool children in London found a critical relationship between reading aloud to children and their success as readers at school. The amount of storybook reading children had experienced prior to beginning school was the single strongest factor in determining their later school success.

Wilhelm and Smith (2002) studied the discrepancy between the literate lives of 49 adolescent boys outside of and within school. They suggest that classroom activities can be more engaging if students respect and respond to these rich outside-of-school activities as a valued and important basis for school literacy tasks.

Clearly, a variety of indicators point to a gap between the literacy achievement of minority students and those in the dominant cultural group. Educational anthropologists Ogbu and Erickson offer two perspectives from which to consider the issues surrounding this disparity. Ogbu's (1981, 1990, 1993) work focuses on a theory of "cultural inversion": a phenomenon where minority students choose to fail to do well in school as a way to maintain their own culture rather than to become subsumed by the dominant culture. This suggests teachers must work to gain students' trust, so that students become willing to acquire the strategies and attitudes necessary for academic success. It is important to support positive connections between the home culture and school. For example, Erickson's (1993; Erickson & Mohatt, 1982) research describes the importance of culturally responsive instruction as a way of providing for success for minority students. He suggests teachers use communication patterns responsive to or compatible with the norms, beliefs, and values of students' home cultures. Moll, Amanti, Neff, and Gonzalez (1992) similarly describe the need for students to be able to use their "funds of knowledge"; that is, they need to be able to use their own cultural background knowledge and experiences as beginning points to make real-world connections.

In addition, parents of students who are not in the dominant cultural group must be supported to become partners with the school in their student's literacy development. It is not lack of interest in school success that keeps these parents at a distance from the school. Rather it may be that the school lacks the appropriate strategies and mechanisms to involve them (Edwards, 1991). Beyond giving parents generic advice to read to their children, schools can share resources, demonstrate strategies, and otherwise invite parents into the literacy process.

Gay (1988) states that the variety of interests, aptitudes, motivations, experiences, and cultural conditioning determines how, not whether, students can or cannot learn. For school, then, the learning context is very important, not simply how students achieve on a standardized test. How do we, as educators, begin to recognize when mismatches occur? How do we know a child is not successful at reading because, for example, the texts do not match his or her experiences? Many horizontal differences exist among students, but these differences are in themselves not positive or negative with regard to students' learning. It is when institutions (e.g., the school) equate or correlate these risk factors to academic deficiencies that they become problems rather than possibilities. The danger is a narrow focus on literacy skills, emphasizing or even distorting vertical differences. The issue is for the school to provide what the child needs now, not to explain away failure as the home's fault.

The underpinnings of oral language—the ways in which students have come to *mean* in their home culture—are critical to the development of written language modes of reading and writing. Reading is language. Although the tasks of written language differ in many ways, the *processes* through which they are learned are, in principle, the same. However, the home language of students provides the foundation for the emergence of reading and writing behaviors. If there is a mismatch between the structures, values, and expectations of the home language and school language, students may be at a disadvantage for success in early reading tasks and thus spend their entire school careers attempting to catch up.

Students at Risk of Failing to Succeed

According to McDermott (1987),

> By making believe that failure is something kids do, as different from how it is something done to them, and then by explaining their failure in terms of other things they do, we likely contribute to the maintenance of school failure. (p. 363)

Many characteristics are associated with students who experience difficulty in learning to read. Individual differences are important, but should they lead to students' failure to succeed in school? Although cultural factors are critical in consideration of these students, the complexity of our society and the structure of our schools encompass a much wider range of factors. Consideration of socioeconomic status, language-minority status (English as a second language [ESL], English-language learner [ELL], and bilingual), and other special needs are important. Invariably, these factors are often intertwined. For example, some remedial reading programs (most specifically Title I programs and Reading First grants) are based on the needs of students of poverty; often, this includes language-minority students. The question remains, however, How can our schools best meet the needs of these students to support them in successful ways?

Snow and colleagues (1998) present a list of risk factors in learning to read, particularly for young children. These include group risk factors and individual risk factors, as listed in the following sections.

Group Risk Factors

Some groups of children are at risk for reading difficulties because they are affected by any or all of the following conditions:

- They are expected to attend schools in which achievement is chronically low;
- They reside in low-income families and live in poor neighborhoods;
- They have limited proficiency in spoken English; and,
- They speak a dialect of English that differs substantially from the one used in school. (Snow et al., 1998, p. 131)

Individual Risk Factors

Individual children, whether or not faced with the adverse conditions describing group risk factors, may be at greater risk for reading difficulties for any or all of the following reasons:

- They are children of parents with histories of reading difficulties;
- They have acquired less knowledge and skill pertaining to literacy during the preschool years, either through limited home literacy experiences that support a match between home and school expectations, and/or as a result of some inherent cognitive limitations;
- They lack age-appropriate skills in literacy-related cognitive linguistic processing, especially phonological awareness, confrontational naming, sentence-story recall, and general language ability;
- They have been diagnosed with having specific early language impairment;
- They have a hearing impairment; and,
- They have a primary medical diagnoses with which reading problems tend to occur as a secondary symptom. (Snow et al., 1998, p. 132)

Although these lists of factors for "at-riskness" are important to note and consider, understanding perceptions and definitions of at-riskness is also important. Edwards, Danridge, and Pleasants (2000) considered teachers' and administrators' perceptions and definitions of at-riskness and found that Head Start teachers and administrators, in general, saw families as generally interested in their students' education, albeit in different ways, and tended to focus on the family unit. In contrast, elementary school teachers and administrators tended to view a lack of parental involvement as disinterest and to place the responsibility for at-riskness within the family.

Allington (1977, 1980, 1983), Allington and McGill-Franzen (1989), Durkin (1978), and Hiebert (1983) describe the stark differences in teaching low-achieving students as compared to their more adept peers. Stanovich (1986) describes a "Matthew effect" in reading achievement. Simply put, the rich get richer, and the poor get poorer: Capable readers get to read more books and engage in reinforcing activities such as talking and writing about what they have read, while struggling readers get a steady diet of skill instruction and few opportunities to actually read real books. The evidence suggests that it is the amount of reading that differentiates low-achieving students from high-achieving students.

Allington and Walmsley (1995) assert that throughout studies of effective instructional intervention with special student populations, no truly specialized materials or teaching strategies demonstrated advantages over the best teaching available in regular education classrooms (Larrivee, 1985; Lyons, 1989). What we see instead is that a particular instructional strategy used with at-risk students is not as important as simply attending to their needs (Allington & Walmsley, 1995). This finding points to the need to provide equal access to school resources for all students to increase the chances of success for all students in literacy learning (Kozol, 1991).

Snow and colleagues (1998) report in *Preventing Reading Difficulties in Young Children* that it is generally accepted that most children who struggle to read do not require instruction that is substantially different from their more successful peers; rather, they require a greater intensity of high-quality instruction. They also state that it is critical to detect problems early and implement effective preventions and early interventions during the developmental span of birth through grade 3.

As learners advance through their years of schooling, their lives and responses to school become more complex. Although many educators now propose that learning problems can be solved with early attention and intervention, many others propose that developmental, social, economic, and cultural contexts continue to create diverse learning needs in today's classrooms (Moore, Bean, Birdyshaw, & Rycik, 1999).

Poverty

As the number of students living in poverty increases, the impact of living without critical resources is increasingly apparent in the lack of school success of many students (Allington & Cunningham, 1996). Although many of these families living in poverty engage in rich literacy practices related to their community and culture, they often do not have access to books and other print materials, either to borrow or to own; to varied childhood experiences such as trips to the zoo; to see everyday uses of literacy on which school literacy activities are based (e.g., newspapers, shopping, entertainment); or to a wide variety of rich oral language interactions. Although many of these students are of cultural and ethnic minority, many, too, are of European American descent. Regardless of poor students' culture or ethnicity, researchers have found a pattern of schools having low academic expectations for them (Allington & Cunningham, 1996). Teaching methods and instructional materials reflect this belief. Often, schools assume these students are capable only of low-level drill in basic skills. In addition, schools may provide such students with less-qualified teachers, little opportunity to read real texts, and little access to interaction with more skilled readers. Moll (1991) states,

> When "disadvantaged" students are shown to succeed under modified instructional arrangements, it becomes clear that the problems these students face in school must be viewed, in great part, as a consequence of institutional arrangements that constrain students and teachers by not capitalizing fully on their talents, resources, and skills. (p. 62; cf. Diaz, Moll, & Mehan, 1986; Moll & Diaz, 1987)

When a commitment to modify instructional arrangements based on current best practice is made, students of poverty gain opportunities to succeed (Allington, 1991). Other research has supported this finding.

Purcell-Gates, McIntyre, and Freppon (1995) found that students from low-SES backgrounds with little previous experience with print gained linguistic competence in story structure, vocabulary, and concepts about print when involved in experiences designed to promote this type of knowledge.

Adams (1990) concludes that while it is true that some students can figure out the letter–sound system without much instruction, students with little exposure to reading and writing often need some explicit phonics instruction. Many rich experiences with reading and writing must support such instruction.

Allington (1994a, 1994b; Cunningham & Allington, 2003) asserts that specifically because of the lack of experience and exposure, students considered at risk need more time to read—really read real texts—in contrast to drills on particular skills.

Snow and colleagues (1991) found a complex set of interactions of both home and school factors that influenced the successful literacy development of low-income students. The enormous impact of consistent, high-quality classroom instruction was clear; in situations where students did not have high levels of literacy support at home, anything less than high-quality instruction at school had dramatically negative impacts on school achievement (Allington & Cunningham, 1996; Allington & Johnston, 2002; Barton, 2003; Langer, 2002; Pressley, Allington, Wharton-McDonald, Block, & Morrow, 2001).

Edwards (1989, 1991) and others found that parent-directed book-reading interactions allow at-risk students to acquire literacy skills that will help them become better readers at school. Some parents may need support in how to provide these experiences at home (Gallimore & Goldenberg, 1989; McCormick & Mason, 1986; Teale, 1981, 1987).

Neuman and Celano (2001) argue that as a sociocultural phenomenon, literacy develops in settings that provide resources and opportunities for students to become involved with its cultural tools. Differences in these settings (particularly the lack of access for high-poverty students) are likely to contribute to the considerable variations in patterns of early literacy development (cf. Allington & McGill-Franzen, 2003).

Allington and McGill-Franzen (2003) argue that summer reading setback is a critical factor in the achievement gap between poor and rich students and that reform must focus not only on making curricular and instructional change, but also on making structural changes that provide year-round access to high-quality materials that provide engaging, successful reading experiences throughout the calendar year (cf. Entwisle, Alexander, & Olson, 1997; Hayes & Grether, 1983).

Snow and colleagues (1998) provide the following synopsis of research on SES and reading achievement:

> We are not saying here that SES is not an important risk marker. What we are saying is that its effects are strongest when it is used to indicate the status of a school or a community or a district, not the status of individuals. A low-status child in a generally moderate or upper status school or community is far less at risk than that same child in a whole school or community of low-status students. (p. 127)

English-Language Learning

As immigration into the United States continues, many students enter school with a language other than English. Statistics predict that by the year 2050, the percentage of students in the United States who arrive at school speaking a language other than English will reach 40% (Lindholm-Leary, 2000). These students have become fluent in this language via oral language processes parallel to those described earlier (Ellis, 1985; Hakuta, 1986). Snow (1992) suggests that a sociocultural perspective is most appropriate for defining literacy in the context of language variety: *Literacy* can be defined in terms of what is appropriate to get along in one's culture for everyday life rather than solely on an indefinable standard language. Thus, literacy is much more than simply being able to read and write; it is, rather, a set of complex tasks and behaviors that may, for some individuals, encompass the use of several languages and literacies. Ada (n.d.) reminds us "no one learns to read twice" (p. 1): Learning to read in a first language, the language that encompasses those things familiar and meaningful, is critical to success in learning to read in a second language.

A recent study indicates that ELLs receive lower grades, are judged by their teachers to have lower academic abilities, and score below their classmates on standardized tests of reading and math (Moss & Puma, 1995). Statistics show that language-minority students are 1.5 times more likely to drop out of school than native speakers (Cardenas, Robledo, & Waggoner, 1988); more recently, as this trend continues, one in five speakers from non–English-speaking homes drops out of high school (Waggoner, 1999). It is important to note that some (Carnegie Task Force, 1996) believe a constructive way in which to address the issue of second-language learning is to promote learning two or more languages for all students.

Debate continues, however, on the best way to assist students as they learn English as their second language. Collier (1995) asserts it is a misassumption to believe that the first thing students must do is learn English, thus isolating the language from a broad complex of other issues. Much of the debate rests on the question, Should students know English before they are allowed to join their peers in classrooms?

Cognitive and academic development in the first language has been found to have critically important and positive effects on second-language learning (Bialystock, 1991; Collier, 1989, 1992; Garcia, 1994; Genesee, 1987, 1994; Thomas & Collier, 1997). Academic skills, literacy development, concept formation, subject knowledge, and strategy development learned in the first language will transfer to the second language. However, because literacy is socially situated, it is equally critical to provide a socioculturally supportive school environment that allows the first language and academic and cognitive development to flourish. Self-esteem and self-confidence are also critical components for success.

It is clear, however, in recent research syntheses within the field (August & Hakuta, 1997; Cuevas, 1997; Thomas & Collier, 1997, 2002) that native language use is advantageous in English-language acquisition. This use is defined within a range from a firm commitment to a bilingual program to programs where, although most instruction took place in English, native language was used to clarify and extend. The second-language learner makes sense of the second language by using many of the same strategies that worked so well in acquiring the first language (cf. Hudelson, Poynor, & Wolfe, 2003). What is different, however, is that the second-language learner already has an understanding of the meanings, uses, and purposes of language; he or she now must go on to learn how the second language—orally and in print—expresses those purposes, uses, and meanings (Lindfors, 1987). Oral language learning is a lifelong process (Berko Gleason, 1993; Collier, 1992); school-age learners are still acquiring subtle knowledge in oral language expertise.

Krashen's (1981, 1982; Krashen & Terrell, 1983) work has had an important impact on second-language learning and teaching. His theories are based in current beliefs about first-language oral acquisition. Basic principles include the following: Understanding precedes speaking; production is allowed to emerge in stages; the goals of instruction are communicative in nature; and activities must "lower the affective filter of students," that is, provide interesting and relevant topics and tasks and encourage the expression of ideas, opinions, and feelings (Krashen & Terrell, 1983).

It is important to understand the consequences of various program designs for students learning English:

- In U.S. schools where all instruction is given through the second language (i.e., English), nonnative speakers with no schooling in their first language take 7 to 10 years to reach age- and grade-level norms (Cummins, 1984; Thomas & Collier, 1997).

- Immigrant students who have had two to three years of schooling in a first language in their home countries take at least five to seven years to reach age- and grade-level norms (Cummins, 1984; Thomas & Collier, 1997).

- Nonnative speakers schooled in a second language for part or all of the day typically do reasonably well in early years; however, from fourth grade on, when academic and cognitive demands of the curriculum increase rapidly, students with little or no academic and cognitive development in their first language fail to maintain positive gains (Collier, 1995; Thomas & Collier, 1997).

- Students who have spent four to seven years in a quality bilingual program sustain academic achievement and outperform monolingually schooled students in the upper grades (Thomas & Collier, 1997).

Clearly, research with second-language learners has found that learning to read in the first language supports success with reading in the second language (cf. August & Hakuta, 1997; Cuevas, 1997; Roberts, 1994):

- Oral and written language are reciprocal; that is, many experiences in oral language—conversations, reading aloud, and so on—in both languages are critical. The Center for Research on Education, Diversity, and Excellence (CREDE; 2000) suggests that engaging students through dialogue, especially the instructional conversation, is important.

- Environments filled with print examples in both languages are important to successful acquisition (Hudelson, 1987). For example, children's and young adult literature in both languages should be in classroom and school libraries for students to access at both school and home; newspapers and other examples of community literacy should be available in both languages at home and at school; signage in classrooms should be in both languages as appropriate.

- A variety of authentic opportunities to read and write in both languages should be available in the classrooms (Janopoulos, 1986; Moll, 1992).

- Literacy skills related to decoding tasks of reading do indeed transfer between languages (Bialystock, 1997; Goodman, Goodman, & Flores, 1979; Hudelson, 1987; Mace-Matluck, 1982). However, instruction must contextualize these skills within meaningful, authentic tasks and texts for full transfer to occur.

- English vocabulary is a primary determinant of reading comprehension for second-language readers. Those whose first language has many cognates with English do have an advantage in English vocabulary recognition but often require explicit instruction to optimize transfer for comprehension (Garcia & Keresztes-Nagy, 1993; cf. August & Hakuta, 1997).

- Instruction that allows students to learn to read in their first language and then to transfer this knowledge to reading in a second language supports the growth of students' self-confidence. Ada (n.d.) asserts that students taught in this way will "have better opportunities for discovering the meaning and joy of reading" (p. 2).

- Joint productive activity among teachers and students facilitates literacy learning (CREDE, 2000; International Reading Association [IRA], 2001). Collaborative learning supports learners, particularly in new expectations.

- Teachers should help students develop competence in the language and literacy of instruction throughout all instructional activities (CREDE, 2000; IRA, 2001). Teachers must be familiar with a wide range of instructional strategies to support learning across developmental stages.

- It is important for teachers to contextualize teaching and curriculum in the experiences and skills of the home and the community (CREDE, 2000; IRA, 2001). This context helps to create authentic and meaningful experiences for classroom members.

- Instruction should challenge students toward cognitive complexity (CREDE, 2000; IRA, 2001). It is important that teachers support students in increasingly sophisticated language tasks and experiences to which they can apply their growing skill and strategy.

Many studies support the notion of a balanced literacy program as appropriate for students whose first language is not English, that is, programs that provide a balance of explicit instruction and student-directed activities and that incorporate aspects of both traditional and meaning-based curricula (Goldenberg & Gallimore, 1991; Goldenberg & Sullivan, 1994; Moll, 1988). However, no single right way to educate ELLs has been determined; different approaches are necessary because of the great diversity of conditions faced by schools and the varying experiences of ELLs with literacy and schooling in their first language (August & Hakuta, 1997). Current debate around bilingual programs has found (a) increasing political pressure to solely implement English-only programs and (b) academic criticism of a wide variance in research quality surrounding second-language acquisition (Hudelson et al., 2003). However, many research studies continue to point to the overall effectiveness of bilingual programs in providing opportunities for students to gain grade-level achievement in the native language and achieve in English as well as native speakers (Thomas & Collier, 1997). Moll (1988) observes that effective teachers share a belief in the power of their teaching but create their own instructional programs that are attuned to the needs of their students. Clearly, educators must rethink their assumptions about the literacy skills of ELLs in their first language as well as in English. They may find a potential for reciprocity between the two languages.

ESL learners in secondary schools have specific needs. Generally, these students have likely had sporadic or limited schooling in their native countries (Garcia, 1999). In addition, many secondary schools, particularly those who have not traditionally served ESL students, are not prepared to work with very different students who often have had little access to quality education in their own countries (Valdes, 1999; cf. Hudelson et al., 2003). Unfortunately, these students are often adversely affected by the tracking system in U.S. high schools, which often isolates and restricts access to more rigorous and academic curriculum (Fu, 1995; Harklau, 1999).

Several studies have highlighted the elements of effective secondary classrooms and schools for ELLs. These elements include the following:

- Offering a wide variety of courses and programs of instruction (Lucas, Henze, & Donato, 1990).
- Training teachers in secondary bilingual and ESL-related methodology (Huerta-Macias & Gonzalez, 1997; Lucas et al., 1990).
- Providing ample and appropriate opportunities to develop both their native language and English proficiency (Lucas et al., 1990).
- Embracing a schoolwide commitment to valuing and encouraging the success of ELLs (Huerta-Macias & Gonzalez, 1997; Lucas et al., 1990).
- Inviting local minority communities to participate in school decision making (Corson, 1992).

In "A Framework for Teaching English Learners," Walqui suggests that teachers use the following strategies to create classrooms that are particularly supportive for adolescent ELLs:

- Reintroduce key information and ideas at increasingly higher levels of complexity and interrelatedness.
- Help students understand and reflect upon their own learning, particularly the feelings of vagueness and frustration that are a natural part of the learning process.
- Observe students in order to know when to gradually hand over more responsibility as students become capable of handling it.
- Amplify and enrich—rather than simplify—the language of the classroom, to give students more opportunities to learn the concepts involved. (WestEd, 2004, pp. 1, 8)

Special Needs

The programs for students with special needs encompass varied definitions in regard to individual students. For some students, an individual education program (IEP) might result in participation in a Title I program, which is determined by a gap between achievement and grade level. For others, needs may dictate a special education program, which is warranted when handicapping conditions—the most common being learning disabled (LD) or reading disabled (RD)—are involved. Spear-Swerling and Sternberg (1996) contend that "there is currently little educational basis for differentiating school-labeled students with Reading Disability (RD) from other kinds of poor readers" (p. 4; cf. Allington, 2002; Allington & McGill-Franzen, 1989; McGill-Franzen, 1987). And yet public perceptions, often fed by the media, are describing a large portion of the school population as LD because they are struggling readers.

Educational definitions of reading disability contain the three elements that historically have been central to definitions of the concept: (1) the notion that students with RD are achieving well below their true potential for learning; (2) the assumption that RD is due to an intrinsic deficit—sometimes described in psychological terms as a "disorder in processing" but assumed to have a biological cause; and (3) exclusionary criteria, which rule out other disorders (e.g., mental retardation, emotional disturbance, or sensory impairment) and the environment as the primary causes of RD (Spear-Swerling & Sternberg, 1996). Many find research in the RD field to be especially contradictory and confusing. Isolated research findings support almost any position one wishes to take; in fact, consensus is increasing in regard to the lack of a consistent definition for both reading disabilities and learning disabilities (cf. Allington, 2002). Research has shown mildly handicapped special education students received significantly less reading instruction than remedial students (Haynes & Jenkins, 1986; Vanecko, Ames, & Archambault, 1980), and there is evidence that both groups actually received less reading instruction than better readers (Allington & Walmsley, 1995).

> **Spear-Swerling and Sternberg (1996) contend that 'there is currently little educational basis for differentiating school-labeled students with Reading Disability (RD) from other kinds of poor readers' (p. 4).**

Jenkins and O'Connor (2002) contend that schools must find ways to identify RD students earlier than the middle grades, as is the norm. However, they note that despite a strong correlational knowledge base connecting students' phonological language skills to later reading acquisition, predicting exactly which students will develop RD specifically has proved problematic, particularly in regard to how early and how reliably identification can occur.

Spear-Swerling (2004) proposes a roadmap for understanding reading disabilities via cognitive profiles that may be more educationally useful. She proposes assessing specific abilities known to be important in learning to read, as well as interpreting patterns of performance in relation to research evidence on typical reading development and difficulties. The use of these cognitive profiles is relevant to poor readers in general, not only those with RD. She agrees that at present no definitive way exists for educators to diagnose genuine RD in individual students; she goes on to point out that this can make early identification difficult and may, in fact, misidentify as disabled poor readers whose problems are largely experiential or instructional in nature.

Debate centers around the question of whether struggling readers—of any definition, but particularly those determined to have disabilities—need qualitatively different instruction. Some argue that these students need frequent, intensive, explicit, and individual support and direction from teachers, but within authentic and meaningful experiences that are not unlike those offered to other students in the classroom (Allington & Walmsley, 1995; Rhodes & Dudley-Marling, 1996; Snow et al., 1998). Others argue for specific types of instruction that focus on the specific needs of such readers as different from other students in the classroom, usually within the range of phonological skills taught in the context of meaningful texts (Spear-Swerling & Sternberg, 1996). Still others believe that a sole focus on decoding—learning specific phonemic awareness and phonic knowledge tasks—is the appropriate type of instruction, before the addition of reading in meaningful texts (see Core Understanding 11 for further discussion).

Spear-Swerling and Sternberg (1996) observe that current research in reading instruction is only slowly making an impact within special education and remedial programs. Instruction within these programs still often focuses solely on isolated drill. Although many students in such programs do need some type of explicit instruction, just as any child learning to read does, they also require many other types of instruction to succeed. These include instruction in strategy use, practicing in appropriate texts, and employing metacognitive strategies (cf., Spear-Swerling, 2004).

Of particular concern to many educators is the growing overrepresentation of minority students in special education in the United States (cf. Allington, 2002; IRA, 2003). The lack of appropriate reading instruction and early reading interventions among low-performing minority students contributes to these students being placed into the high-incidence disability categories of mental retardation (MR), emotional disturbance (ED), and specific learning disability (SLD) (Artiles & Trent, 1994; Artiles, Trent & Palmer, 2004; Donovan & Cross, 2002; Losen & Orfield, 2002; Parrish, 2002; Zhang & Katsiyannis, 2002). Three issues seem to be at the heart of the matter (IRA, 2003):

1. *Ineffective instruction*. Overrepresentation seems to increase as both poverty and the proportion of minority students present in the population increase (Oswald, Coutinho, Best, & Singh, 1999). This trend suggests that poor instruction is a possible explanation for students' low achievement; data continue to point to the fact that high-poverty schools often lack qualified teachers, appropriate and good-quality materials, and safe environments and buildings that support high-quality instruction. Teachers must work to overcome the deficit model of learning that preordains students of poverty to reading failure. Although strong correlations exist among poverty, minority status, and achievement, an increasingly significant proportion of schools help students to "beat the odds" to become successful in school (Taylor, Pearson, Clark, & Walpole, 1999).

2. *Uncoordinated services*. Another major factor contributing to low reading achievement is the lack of coordination among regular education, Title I, and special education programs and teachers (Allington & Walmsley, 1995).

3. *Starting out behind*. Data indicate that the achievement gap is present when students arrive at school. However, as noted earlier in this chapter, it is critical that teachers become aware of the language and literacy skills all students bring to school as found in their cultures and background, and, more important, use them to bridge and build literacy knowledge, skill, and strategy. What teachers often see as lack of achievement are the different forms of diverse learners' preliteracy experiences (Donovan & Cross, 2002; Neuman & Celano, 2001).

Klenk and Kibby (2000) suggest that the field of "remedial reading," whether dealing with struggling readers in general or RD and LD students specifically, is "rooted in noble social intentions, yet mired in theoretical and practical contentions" (p. 668). They acknowledge limited success in remediating reading difficulties despite a century of investigation. They describe a tension between well-informed reading educators who view reading difficulty as "having no precise etiology" and consider the only instructional response to be a print-based reading instruction program. In contrast, special educators tend to view reading difficulty as a learning disability based on perceptual or neurological deficits that require extraordinary forms of instruction, including development of perceptual abilities. They propose a sociohistorical perspective (Cole, 1990; Tharp & Gallimore, 1988; Vygotsky, 1934/1978) that focuses on *mediation* rather than on *remediation*; that is, learners are actively involved in problem solving with print with guidance and assistance from more knowledgeable others. This view is in stark contrast to traditional and usual portraits of struggling readers.

Supporting Struggling Readers

Context is critical to dealing with the variety of needs for struggling readers. Although no one method can be found, nor is there any one definition of a struggling reader, teachers must be aware of the child's background (social, economic, cultural) and needs (type of variability, learning style).

Allington and Johnston (2002), Langer (2002), and Pressley and colleagues (2001) describe teachers who work with students in ways that support the needs of all learners. Langer (2001) and Taylor and colleagues (1999) describe such effective teachers and schools as being able to beat the odds; that is, they are able to overcome the myriad factors (described in this chapter) presenting obstacles to learning in K–12 classrooms.

Experiences and programs designed for students who struggle with learning to read reflect these factors. For example, Reading Recovery (Clay, 1979; Deford, Lyons, & Pinnell, 1991) is a program that focuses on short-term (usually less than one year), intensive, one-to-one interventions with students who struggle very early on (usually in first grade). The program is given in addition to regular classroom experiences. Roller (1996) suggests a workshop model where students choose from a wide variety of reading materials, participate in literature discussion groups, and carry out personal writing projects in a classroom paired with one-to-one and small-group instruction during other times of the day. Although the organizational structures may be different, these designs continue to focus on rich, meaningful language experiences as the context for a variety of types of instruction. For struggling adolescent readers, focus on explicit comprehension strategy instruction, coupled with a responsive literacy environment and sufficient time engaged with connected text using authentic materials, supports growth in confidence and ability (Primeaux, 2000; cf. Beers, 2003; Greenleaf, Schoenbach, Cziko, & Mueller, 2001).

Taylor and colleagues (1999) found that the intervention programs used in the most effective schools within their study were of regional or local origin, rather than one of the more large-scale reform-based programs available (Herman, 1999). Teachers successful at "beating the odds" with struggling readers are well trained and able to make appropriate instructional decisions based on both their knowledge of best practices and of their students. Studies over the past four decades have continued to show that the teacher is the critical factor in success in learning, particularly in learning to read (cf., Bond & Dykstra, 1967/1997).

Current legislative mandates (i.e., the No Child Left Behind Act of 2001 [2002]) call for increased accountability within what many educators consider to be narrow definitions of learning; many believe this is particularly the case in defining appropriate reading skills and abilities (Allington, 2004a, 2004b; Camilli, Vargas, & Yurecko, 2003; Camilli & Wolfe, 2004; Coles, 2001; Coles, 2003; Cunningham, 2001; Garan, 2002; Krashen, 2004; Yatvin, Weaver, & Garan, 2003). Others believe these scientifically based definitions, based on the findings of the National Reading Panel's report (NICHD, 2000), to be at the foundation of success in learning to read (Lyon, 2004; Lyon & Chhabra, 2004; Lyon, Fletcher, Torgeson, Shaywitz, & Chhabra, 2004; Shaywitz & Shaywitz, 2004). However, some are concerned that this stance of "scientifically based" reading methodologies may negatively affect the ability of teachers to make appropriate instructional decisions based on their knowledge of learners, understanding of best practice, and flexibility in classroom assessment and instruction (Coles, 2001; Coles, 2003; Garan, 2002; Yatvin et al., 2003). Regardless of stance, it is clear that the impact of broad and well-defined teacher knowledge, as well as the ability for teachers to make appropriate instructional decisions based on this knowledge, remains the most critical element in the creation and implementation of instruction that supports all students, particularly those who are at risk or struggling, in learning to read.

Variability (e.g., in literacy experiences, preferences, understandings, abilities, and language) must be acknowledged as a central part of understanding students and their needs (Roller, 1996). Alternative ways of viewing individual differences provide insight into a variety of organizational patterns for instruction that can best meet the needs of all students.

> *Teachers successful at 'beating the odds' with struggling readers are well trained and able to make appropriate instructional decisions based on both their knowledge of best practices and of their students.*

Summary: Understanding Factors That Influence Literacy Development

Factors that influence literacy learning can be categorized across the developmental environment, the home–learning connection, the community, the home–school connection, teaching–learning strategies, and the learning environment. The focus of interpretation of the findings on these factors puts much more emphasis on the ability of teachers, administrators, and schools to work effectively across a wide range of cognitive, social, emotional, and cultural needs found within the current school population.

Schools must find ways to foster positive relationships among culture, language, and schooling; in particular, teachers and administrators must support families' involvement in literacy. Matches between cultural expectations and school expectations must be explicitly made by teachers to support learners from all cultural backgrounds.

Increasing numbers of students are at risk of failing to succeed as readers. The complexity of U.S. society and the structures of U.S. schools call for addressing a wider range of more complex factors than in the past, including SES, language, and learning needs. These factors are invariably intertwined.

The important question remains, How can our schools best meet the needs of these students to support them in successful learning? Allington and Walmsley (1995) suggest that instructional intervention with special student populations using specialized materials or teaching strategies demonstrated no advantages over the best teaching found in regular education classrooms. Snow and colleagues (1998) agree that most children who struggle to read do not require instruction that is substantially different from their more successful peers; rather, they require a greater intensity of higher quality instruction. In general, equal access to school resources for all children appears to be the bottom line.

Debate continues over the best way to assist students as they learn English as their second language. Research clearly shows that cognitive and academic development in the first language has been found to have critically important and positive effects on second-language learning. Native-language use is advantageous in English-language acquisition because the learner makes sense of the second language by using many of the same strategies that worked so well in acquiring the first language.

Jenkins and O'Connor (2002) contend that schools must find ways to identify RD students earlier than in the middles grades, as is now the norm. Debate continues as to the kind of instruction that best meets the needs of children with reading disabilities. In addition, the growing overrepresentation of minority students in special education programs is a matter of concern to educators. IRA (2003) attributes this trend to three factors: ineffective instruction, uncoordinated services, and children who start out behind.

Context is critical to dealing with the variety of needs for struggling readers. Although no one method can be found, nor is there any one definition of a struggling reader, teachers must be aware of the child's background (social, economic, and cultural) and needs (type of variability, learning style).

Chapters 2 and 3 have provided essential contextual underpinnings for learning to read and developing as a reader. In the following chapter, research-based core understandings with specific implications for classroom instruction are described.

TEACHER RESOURCES

Allington, R.L. (2001). *What really matters for struggling readers: Designing research-based programs*. New York: Longman.

Beers, K. (2003). *When kids can't read: What teachers can do: A guide for teachers 6–12*. Portsmouth, NH: Heinemann.

Freeman, Y.S., Freeman, D.E., & Mercuri, S. (2002). *Closing the achievement gap*. Portsmouth, NH: Heinemann.

Tatum, A.W. (2005). *Teaching reading to black adolescent males: Closing the achievement gap*. York, ME: Stenhouse.

Tovani, C. (2000). *I read it but I don't get it*. York, ME: Stenhouse.

When readers struggle. (2001, May). [Special issue]. *Voices From the Middle*, 8(4).

Wilhelm, J.D., & Smith, M.W. (2002). *"Reading don't fix no Chevys": Literacy in the lives of young men*. Portsmouth, NH: Heinemann.

CHAPTER 4

Core Understandings
About Reading

THIS CHAPTER DISCUSSES 13 core understandings about reading that knowledgeable teachers have, understandings informed by various research traditions and demonstrated by the classroom environments such teachers design. As teachers, parents, and policymakers act in their respective roles on these understandings, they support all students to develop the sophisticated literacy skills required for personal, social, civic, and economic fulfillment.

The core understandings reflect the nature of reading as language; as such, it is always about meaning and communication. However, they also illustrate that reading is a learned rather than an acquired language behavior. Reading is dependent on mastering a written code based on the alphabetic principle. Allington and Cunningham (1996) sum up the essential tension, "Reading and writing are meaning constructing activities, but they are dependent on words" (p. 49). The core understandings that follow summarize current research on best practice in literacy instruction that keeps the focus on reading as a construction of meaning while developing the wide range of print-based skills and strategies necessary to the effective use of literacy.

Reading is a construction of meaning from text. It is an active, cognitive, and affective process.

CORE UNDERSTANDING 1

For all modes of language—reading, writing, listening, and speaking—making meaning is the ultimate purpose (Pearson, Roehler, Dole, & Duffy, 1990; Rosenblatt, 1938/1995, 1978). And from the earliest stages, reading is for comprehension. Lest this goal be lost in current debates on how best to teach beginning reading, the RAND Reading Study Group (2002) identified comprehension research as a priority from primary grades through secondary school.

Readers do not take in print and receive words off the page. They actively engage with the text and build their own understanding. Engagement presumes motivation, interest, and purpose, even emotional involvement (both positive and negative). This interaction between the reader and various aspects of text is necessary for comprehension to occur, and it includes the surface features, such as the wording and organization of the text, the ideas involved, and the mental models embedded in the text (RAND Reading Study Group, 2002). With comprehension as the goal, readers purposefully sample print, constructing meaning efficiently and effectively (Duke & Pearson, 2002; Goodman, 1996; Kucer & Tuten, 2003; Smith, 2004).

Reading is a sociocultural process: That is, it occurs within a situation whose participants, time, place, and expectation will affect the reader and the meaning he or she constructs with the text (Gee, 1996; Halliday, 1973, 1975). And from a constructivist perspective, what one learns about reading is linked inextricably to how one learns it. A learner taught to read in ways that emphasize construction of meaning with texts that are semantically and syntactically authentic will develop a useful model of reading (Cambourne, 2002).

To support reading as a purposeful sociocultural, cognitive, and linguistic process, instruction should help readers make sense of written language. This may include construction of essential schema and explicitly taught comprehension strategies for reading various types of texts, as well as many opportunities to read a variety of texts.

TEACHER RESOURCES

Bomer, R. (1995). *Time for meaning: Creating literate lives in middle and high school*. Portsmouth, NH: Heinemann.

Goodman, K.S. (1996). *On reading*. Portsmouth, NH: Heinemann.

Wilson, L. (2002). *Reading to live: How to teach reading for today's world*. Portsmouth, NH: Heinemann.

CORE UNDERSTANDING 2

Background knowledge and prior experience are critical to the reading process.

The work of Anderson and Pearson (1984) and Rumelhart (1980) has demonstrated the importance of prior knowledge in reading. According to this view, called *schema theory*, readers understand what they read only as it relates to what they already know. Because text is not fully explicit, readers must draw from their existing knowledge in order to understand it. Sweet's (1993) summary suggests prior knowledge should be looked at in two ways:

1. *Overall prior knowledge* represents the sum of knowledge individuals have acquired as a result of their cumulative experiences both in and out of school.

2. *Specific prior knowledge* represents the particular information an individual needs in order to understand text that deals with a certain topic. This type of knowledge can be

    - *text-specific knowledge* that calls for understanding about the type of text, or

    - *topic-specific knowledge* that calls for understanding something about the topic.

It is important for teachers to understand and build on the range of background knowledge, both overall and specific, that students bring to school. Opportunities to expand background knowledge are provided in classrooms through a variety of experiences, including teacher read-alouds, discussions during and following reading, independent reading, written response to what has been read, and access to many books and other reading materials. The more students read and write, the more their prior knowledge grows, which in turn strengthens their ability to construct meaning as they read (Allington & Cunningham, 1996; Sweet, 1993).

Reading volume has been found to be a powerful predictor of vocabulary and knowledge differences among individuals (Cunningham & Stanovich, 1998). In turn, vocabulary knowledge is a strong predictor of a reader's ability to understand text, so we can see that vocabulary is an important marker for background knowledge. Numerous studies have confirmed the importance of extensive reading to build vocabulary and background knowledge (Anderson & Nagy, 1992; Stahl, 1998). In addition, a meta-analysis by Swanborn and de Glopper (1999) confirms the superiority of wide reading over vocabulary instruction in building vocabulary and background knowledge. Because words and the concepts and knowledge that they represent are learned incrementally, extensive reading provides the necessary repeated encounters with a new word for a reader to develop a good working knowledge of that word, and by extension, to build new schema, or background knowledge, associated with it (McKeown, Beck, Omanson, & Pople, 1985; Nagy, Anderson, & Herman, 1987). Also, background knowledge figures prominently in successfully learning a new word in context (Trumbull & Farr, 2005).

> " *Numerous studies have confirmed the importance of extensive reading to build vocabulary and background knowledge.... In addition, a meta-analysis...confirms the superiority of wide reading over vocabulary instruction in building vocabulary and background knowledge.* "

Once students understand the functions of print, they can better learn its different forms. Activating only students' topical prior knowledge without helping them to consider the actual structure of the text does not improve their meaning-making abilities (Beck, Omanson, & McKeown, 1982). Moustafa (1997) describes the need to learn the "language of print"; Clay (1985) stresses the importance of learning "the concepts of print." This need to understand the language of print also applies to students learning English as a second language: Using relevant background knowledge of how they use their first language in all its language modes (speaking and listening, reading and writing) offers the scaffold necessary to learn the second language (Roberts, 1994). Students who are learning English at the same time they are leaning academic content require more intense and intentional scaffolding to bridge from their experience to the content of the text, develop appropriate schema, build understandings of context, and internalize academic language. For these students, it is important that teachers not simplify but rather amplify and enrich classroom language to support development of academic concepts (Walqui & DeFazio, 2003).

Culture, as well as language, presents both challenges and opportunities for bridging from home and community to school. Lee's (1995) work with urban African American students shows the value of drawing on and making explicit the tacit knowledge that students have from their own discourse communities that can be applied to academic learning. Trumbull and Farr (2005) note the importance of varying classroom participation structures to accommodate students less comfortable with recitation and more likely to contribute and learn communally. In similar ways, Goldenberg's (1991) instructional conversation and Moll, Amanti, Neff, and Gonzalez's (1992) funds of knowledge offer ways to support nonmainstream students' successful acquisition of school language and concepts. Based on a study of content area literacy learning of urban secondary Latino students, Moje and her colleagues (2004) urge subject area teachers to help students construct a "third space" that merges the "first space" of home, community, and peer networks with the "second space" of the Discourses they encounter in more formalized institutions such as school. These third spaces can build bridges between everyday and academic Discourses to support literacy and content learning. But teachers need to consciously work to construct these spaces and must help students develop new reader identities and behaviors appropriate to engaging in academic Discourses new to them.

For middle and high school students, the need to acquire and apply new schema suited to various academic Discourses is critical. In addition, they need to learn discipline-based ways of reading to access valued concepts and information (Kucer, 2005; Schoenbach, Greenleaf, Cziko, & Hurwitz, 1999). Research with adolescents has shown that even a modicum of background knowledge in a domain related to the content of a subject area text can improve comprehension of that text. Background knowledge even helps readers overcome comprehension problems arising from poorly written or incoherent text (Snow & Biancarosa, 2003).

The knowledge of how print works and of disciplinary-specific ways that texts are constructed and approached is essential and must operate in tandem with a reader's topical knowledge to construct meaning from text. Teachers can effectively improve these abilities when they activate all levels of students' prior knowledge appropriately. It is important for teachers to be aware of the schema students bring to a text as well as the ones they may need to develop. Especially in settings with students from culturally and linguistically diverse backgrounds, teachers need to be alert for mismatches between students' schema and the structure, content, and language of texts that they are expected to read.

CORE
UNDERSTANDING

Social interaction is essential at all stages of reading development.

Learning and literacy are acquired through social interactions. They are cultural and historical activities, representing how a cultural group or discourse community interprets the world and communicates this information from one generation to another (RAND Reading Study Group, 2002). In this socially constructed literacy environment, readers need the opportunity to interact with both peers and adults in a wide variety of settings as they learn and practice language and literacy knowledge, skills, and strategies. It is through social interaction that readers at all stages develop their individual understandings and knowledge (Cambourne, 2002).

It is important to talk about *how* and *why* one reads as well as *what* one reads. Vygotsky (1934/1978) emphasizes the importance of social interactions to actually drive any learning process. Bruner (1975) and Applebee and Langer (1983) elaborate on this notion with their descriptions of *scaffolding*—the interaction between the learner and more sophisticated others that provides guidance, support, and models as new learning takes place. Socially scaffolded instruction at the edge of the individual's independent capability actually supports the learner's internalization of skills and strategies, and eventually his or her independent application of them. And in this process, *metacognition* develops, that is, the ability to be aware of what one does as a reader, as well as to talk about what is read, and to consciously realize problems and reach solutions for them (Pressley, 2002; cf. Sweet, 1993).

Critical knowledge of both the reading processes and what one does as a strategic reader is built through discussion (Eeds & Wells, 1989; Langer, 1993). Goldenberg (1993) suggests an instructional conversation model that combines conversational aspects (the supportive elements of the discussion) and instructional aspects (the lesson focus). The teacher takes the role of a mentor, urging children to think about how they are thinking rather than only what they are thinking. Listening carefully to how children construct their responses provides teachers with an opportunity to discuss their use and knowledge of strategies with them. Teachers phase in to demonstrate and name particular strategies, then phase out to give students a chance to use the new strategies on their own (Walker, 1996). This model provides the support of scaffolding and modeling, then allows children to practice and implement new knowledge about reading on their own. In this way, understanding of the reading process and metacognitive strategy develops through social interaction.

Applebee, Langer, Nystrand, and Gamoran's (2003) study of the role of discussion—among students and between teacher and students—in middle and high school English classes points to its importance for student achievement. Their research confirms and extends findings from earlier studies (cf. Langer, 1999) showing authentic discussion that includes the exploration of ideas in a true dialogue as central to the developing understandings of readers and writers. In fact, several features of *dialogic instruction* were associated with achievement gains for students: These included more use of authentic questions (to explore rather than to test students' understanding); more time for open (student-to-student) discussion; and more "uptake" of student comments by the teacher and other students to create continuity of discourse (Applebee et al., 2003). The increased achievement reported with discussion-based approaches occurred in classrooms with high academic demands, across a range of settings, and among students of varying abilities. In other words, classrooms with high academic demands and greater emphasis on discussion-based approaches show higher end-of-the-year achievement across track levels than other classrooms (2003). Given this finding, the relative lack of discussion-based approaches found in lower track classes raises concerns about access to academic success.

As Vygotsky (1934/1978) first proposed and a wealth of studies have since proved, learners gradually internalize and effectively control ways of thinking, learning, and doing that they originally acquire and practice in supportive social interactions.

TEACHER RESOURCES

Avery, C. (1993). *And with a light touch: Learning about reading, writing, and teaching with first graders*. Portsmouth, NH: Heinemann.

Daniels, H. (2002). *Literature circles: Voice and choice in book clubs and reading groups* (2nd ed.). Portland, ME: Stenhouse.

Peterson, K., & Eeds, M. (1990). *Grand conversations: Literature groups in action*. New York: Scholastic.

Schlick-Noe, K.L., & Johnson, N.J. (1999). *Getting started with literature circles*. Norwood, MA: Christopher-Gordon.

Short, K.G., & Pierce, K.M. (1990). *Talking about books: Creating literate communities*. Portsmouth, NH: Heinemann.

CORE UNDERSTANDING 4

Reading and writing are reciprocal processes; development of one enhances the other.

Both reading and writing are constructive processes (Cambourne, 2002; Pearson & Tierney, 1984; Squire, 1983). A similar, if not the same, level of intellectual activity underlies both reading and writing: Interactions between the reader/writer and text lead to new knowledge and interpretations of text (Clay, 1975; Langer, 1986; cf. Sweet, 1993).

Research shows that writing leads to improved reading achievement, reading leads to better writing performance, and combined instruction leads to improvements in both areas (DeFord, 1981; Smith, 1994; Tierney & Shanahan, 1991). In this interaction, quality as well as quantity matters. Taylor, Peterson, Rodriguez, and Pearson (2002) found that teachers' use of higher level questions after reading led to more growth in student writing than did the use of literal-level questions. And extensive opportunities for students to write in the variety of genres that teachers want them to comprehend as readers actually build capacity in both areas; students learn to read like writers and write like readers (Duke & Pearson, 2002). As students move through the grades, nurturing the integral relationships among speaking, listening, reading, and writing becomes even more fundamental for learning in the content areas (Langer, 2001; Ogle & McMann, 2003). Current research clearly reaffirms that engaging learners in many combined reading-and-writing experiences leads to a higher level of thinking than when either process is taught alone. Because thinking is a critical part of meaning construction, students will become better thinkers if they are taught in classrooms where meaning is actively constructed through reading and writing (cf. Sweet, 1993).

When young children engage in activities that promote verbal and written language, reading and writing develop together (Morris, 1981; Sulzby & Teale, 1991). For beginning readers, writing actually supports the development of phonological and phonemic awareness (Vernon & Ferreiro, 1999). When children have opportunities to write their own stories, to read their own and others' stories, and to write in response to reading, they are able to employ much of their knowledge of reading in meaningful and purposeful ways. Wilde (1992) and others (e.g., Clarke, 1988) have found young children's use of invented spelling as they write provides a window into their evolving understanding of the alphabetic principle of language while they are acquiring important phonics knowledge.

Yet Burgess, Lundren, Lloyd, and Pianta (2001) found that most preschool teachers devote little time to writing activities, despite recommendations of writing as an appropriate literacy activity for preschoolers (International Reading Association & National Association for the Education of Young Children, 1998). In this instance, teachers' beliefs that writing is not important for preschoolers were the stronger influence on their instruction.

Teacher beliefs can indeed drive instructional practice in opposition to recommendations based on research. With regard to the positive interaction of reading and writing, currently another factor is operating in this way—the emphasis on raising student scores on tests of reading achievement. Opportunities for students at all grade levels to write extensively in response to reading are being limited as reading instruction focuses on preparing students to perform well on standardized, short-answer, or multiple-choice tests of reading. As noted, the reciprocal relationship between reading and writing development has been well documented; sacrificing writing opportunities to focus on improving reading scores flies in the face of research and of teachers' professional knowledge. More seriously, such a limitation in practice can hamper students' growth in both of these literacy processes.

TEACHER RESOURCES

Dorn, L., French, C., & Jones, T. (1998). *Apprenticeship in literacy: Transitions across reading and writing*. York, ME: Stenhouse.

Hansen, J. (2001). *When writers read*. Portsmouth, NH: Heinemann.

Reading involves complex thinking.

CORE UNDERSTANDING 5

Research across disciplines, but particularly in cognitive and developmental psychology and education, has shown that reading (like all language modes) is the result of particular cognitive processes (Caine & Caine, 1991, 1997; Scherer, 1997). Readers consciously orchestrate a variety of thinking skills to make meaning of the texts they read. They rely on a wide range of background knowledge, both about the world they live in and the ways in which they can get meaning from a text. They know they must make many types of decisions and choices in order to do this all effectively. Readers think as they read, not only about what they understand about the text but also about the strategies and processes they are using to construct these understandings. (See Core Understandings 1 and 2.)

> *Readers think as they read, not only about what they understand about the text but also about the strategies and processes they are using to construct these understandings.*

Although many theories and models pertain to the workings of written language, most are in agreement that written language relies on four cueing systems, representing types of knowledge readers use as they interact with text: (1) pragmatic (social context), (2) semantic (meaning), (3) syntactic (structural), and (4) graphophonic (the alphabetic, orthographic, sound–symbol aspects). All of these systems must be operating in tandem for optimal meaning. Effective readers are active in the reading process, consciously monitoring their comprehension and, based on this here-and-now metacognition, taking action to repair comprehension problems (Pressley, 2002; cf. Ruddell, Ruddell, & Singer, 1994). The most basic mental operations—decoding, lexical access, and syntactic parsing—become automatic for proficient readers. But more sophisticated operations continue to demand readers' cognitive attention, such as constructing a mental model and generating inferences from text (RAND Reading Study Group, 2002).

For example, as students read a piece of literature they respond to it by using their prior knowledge to construct meaning. This *transaction* with the text results in the construction of their own personal meaning (Rosenblatt, 1938/1995, 1978). Response and discussion help students develop metacognitive skills important to constructing meaning (Palincsar & Brown, 1984). In Langer's (1999) study of schools that beat the odds—produced higher than expected language arts achievement in middle and high school students—this attention to metacognitive procedures and strategies was evident in high-performing classrooms. Engaging students in constantly thinking about what and how they read helps them move from response to analysis (cf. Sweet, 1993).

The power of instructional tools such as anticipation guides, advance organizers, questioning strategies, and reciprocal teaching for comprehension of expository texts demonstrates that reading is a meaning-driven process and that cognitive strategy instruction is essential for achievement of content area learning goals (Guthrie & Davis, 2003). Readers ultimately grapple with information and ideas; print is only the entry point for this interaction (Alfassi, 1998; Duke & Pearson, 2002; Greenleaf, Schoenbach, Cziko, & Mueller, 2001; Guthrie, Wigfield, & VonSecker, 2000).

Reading instruction that probes and expands students' thinking about what they read has proved more effective in fostering students' literacy growth than instruction that relies more on telling and recitation, a classroom model that might be described as traditional or teacher directed (Applebee, Langer, Nystrand, & Gamoran, 2003; Taylor, Peterson, Rodriguez, & Pearson, 2002).

Current educational reform highlights the need for critical thinking and problem solving. Models of the reading process that portray reading as thinking support this perspective (Moje, Young, Readence, & Moore, 2000; RAND Reading Study Group, 2002). The emphasis has come to rest on the need for higher standards and expectations for students within public schools, most recently represented in the No Child Left Behind Act of 2001 (2002) and articulated in the framework of the National Assessment of Educational Progress (Grigg, Daane, Jin, & Campbell, 2003). This model of reading as thinking is the basis of U.S. national standards (International Reading Association & National Council of Teachers of English, 1996) and various state standards developed in successive years.

TEACHER RESOURCES

Keene, E.O., & Zimmermann, S. (1997). *Mosaic of thought: Teaching comprehension in a reader's workshop*. Portsmouth, NH: Heinemann.

Miller, D. (2002). *Reading with meaning: Teaching comprehension in the primary grades*. Portland, ME: Stenhouse.

Schoenbach, R., Greenleaf, C., Cziko, C., & Hurwitz, L. (1999). *Reading for understanding: A guide to improving reading in middle and high school classrooms*. San Francisco: Jossey-Bass.

Environments rich in literacy experiences, resources, and models facilitate reading development.

CORE UNDERSTANDING 6

Learners need many opportunities to interact with print in meaningful ways. Both social and physical factors are important for creating supportive environments for successful literacy acquisition and development. Teale (1982) views the development of early literacy as the result of children's involvement in reading and writing activities mediated by more literate others. Although the physical context is important, it is the social interactions of these activities that give them so much significance in the learner's development. These interactions—with others and within a variety of print settings—teach children the societal functions and conventions of reading and writing and help them link reading with enjoyment and satisfaction, thus increasing their desire to engage in meaningful literacy activities.

As learners become increasingly sophisticated readers and writers, the importance of social interactions remains a critical component of effective learning experiences (Rosenblatt, 1978; Vygotsky, 1934/1978). Opportunities to interact with others using a variety of language processes (reading, writing, listening, and speaking) become a cornerstone for success.

Physical Environment

Historically, educators and theorists have emphasized the importance of physical environment in learning and literacy development. Pestalozzi (cited in Rusk & Scotland, 1979), Piaget (Piaget & Inhelder, 1969), and Froebel (1974) describe real-life environments in which learning flourished among young children; they recognize that the use of appropriate manipulative materials can foster literacy development. Vygotsky (1934/1978) asserts that learning takes place as young people interact with peers and adults in social settings and conducive environments. Learners in purposefully arranged rooms demonstrate more creative productivity, greater use of language-related activities, more engaged and exploratory behavior, and more social interaction and cooperation than do children in randomly or poorly defined settings (Moore, 1986). Studies of classroom interactions have demonstrated the influence of settings on children's purposes for literacy and on their uses of metacognitive strategies, once again indicating the intricate connections between context and cognition (Neuman, 1995; Neuman & Roskos, 1997; cf. Neuman & Celano, 2001).

> *Learners in purposefully arranged rooms demonstrate more creative productivity, greater use of language-related activities, more engaged and exploratory behavior, and more social interaction and cooperation than do children in randomly or poorly defined settings.*

For young learners, several factors are important in creating an effective physical environment. Physical setting has an active and pervasive influence on both the teacher's and the students' activities and attributes (Loughlin & Martin, 1987; Morrow, 1990; Rivlin & Weinstein, 1984). For example, the inclusion of writing centers, library corners complete with a wide variety of materials to read (e.g., different genres and levels of difficulty), areas to read independently and with others, and opportunities to use literacy in play are important for young learners. Rooms partitioned into smaller spaces facilitate peer and verbal interaction and imaginative, associative, and cooperative play more effectively than do rooms with large open spaces (Field, 1980).

For older learners, other factors are important in producing an effective physical environment. When teachers can offer an organized set of choices in which students can work independently, in small groups, or in whole groups, students benefit (RAND Reading Study Group, 2002). When students have a wide variety of print materials, including classroom, school library, and community collections (e.g., public libraries), their access to literacy experiences increases (Allington & Cunningham, 1996; Atwell, 1987; Cunningham & Allington, 2003; Kaufman, 2001; Krashen, 1996). An organized system and routine for accessing important classroom materials independently facilitates students' literacy acquisition (Kaufman, 2001). And easy access to a wide range and variety of texts for middle and high school students to participate in extensive reading of their choice supports their reading development (Schoenbach, Greenleaf, Cziko, & Hurwitz, 1999).

Environments That Support and Sustain Interactive Talk

Classrooms that allow students a variety of ways to communicate in interactive ways support language development (Cazden, 1988; Vygotsky, 1934/1978).

Role of Metalanguage About Language and Literacy Processes. Supportive classroom environments are often held together by the presence of a *metalanguage*, that is, an intentional use of vocabulary to describe structural and language processes expected by the teacher. Students and teachers alike are well able to use and describe these processes as part of their everyday classroom lives, for example, talking about composing a draft, making a prediction about text, sharing a book talk. In this way, teachers talk about literacy expectations for students, explicitly talk about how to use these processes, and problem solve ways through issues with both process and expectation.

Allington and Johnston (2002), in their study of exemplary fourth-grade teachers, found that the single most-striking feature of these classrooms was the nature of the conversations that flowed within them. Teachers and students authentically talked about books, the use of language and literacy processes, and metacognitive processes of reading; the teachers essentially were participating in and modeling this type of talk consistently. Langer (2002) and Applebee, Langer, Nystrand, and Gamoran (2003) found similar patterns in their studies of effective high school English teachers, terming this strategy *shared cognition*.

Schoenbach and colleagues (1999) suggest that metacognitive conversations, that is, conversations a reader has with himself or herself, as well as with peers and teachers, about reading strategies and understandings are critical to successful reading by adolescents.

Reading Aloud by Skilled Readers. Rich and supportive literacy environments include opportunities to hear the reading aloud of skilled readers, observe adults who read often themselves, receive adult support for children's literacy activities, and experience routine use of materials for reading and writing at home and at school (Durkin, 1974; Richardson, 2000; Taylor, 1983; Teale, 1984). Ideal settings are oriented to real-life situations; materials are chosen to give learners the chance to explore and experiment (Loughlin & Martin, 1987; Morrow, 1996). Instruction connected to real-life situations and materials that give the learners the chance to explore and experiment produces an ideal setting for learning. Schools must coordinate programs and environments to support the activities and needs of students (Spivak, 1973).

Reading children's and young adult literature has been shown to have one of the greatest impacts on a child's access to a "literate environment." It provides social interaction and physical inclusion, as well as demonstrations of print materials. Introducing and using literature with young children correlates positively with development of sophisticated language structures, including vocabulary and syntax (Chomsky, 1972). Children are engaging in their most intellectually demanding work when they share ideas and opinions about stories, and share experiences related to stories read or told to them (Dyson, 1987; Sweet, 1993). As children hear stories told and read, they learn the structure as well as the linguistic features of stories or narrative text (Cox & Sulzby, 1984). Children often display this knowledge by "talking like a book" when they pretend to read their favorite stories (Pappas & Brown, 1987).

Storybook reading is most effective for developing children's ability to understand stories when it involves far more than reading aloud the words of an author. It is as much the verbal interaction between adult and child during the read-aloud experience as the read-aloud event itself that provides for a positive learning experience for the child (Morrow, 1988; Morrow, O'Connor, & Smith, 1990; Teale & Sulzby, 1987). Readers construct meaning as they interact with peers and adults in discussing stories (Jett-Simpson, 1989). Whether the reading aloud occurs between a parent and child or a teacher and classroom of children, using interactive strategies such as story-based discussions along with storybook reading helps children construct meaning and understand stories that are read to them (cf. Sweet, 1993).

Duke (2000) asserts that information texts should be included in the read-aloud choices for young children. The children are well able to understand the differences in text structures and strategies needed. Modeling these strategies continually throughout the elementary years supports increased expository text reading in middle and high school.

Ivey (2003) found that 62% of sixth graders indicated a preference for teacher read-alouds for a variety of reasons, including that "the teacher makes it more explainable" (p. 812). Ivey and Broaddus (2001) suggest that read-alouds for adolescents be more strategically and deliberately planned to promote thoughtful reading and content learning. Reading aloud enhances middle schoolers' understanding and increases their inclination to read independently.

Language development has been found to correlate with reading success, and both can be improved by regular use of children's and young adult literature in read-aloud situations both at home and at school (Cullinan, 1987; Galda, Ash, & Cullinan, 2000; Galda & Cullinan, 2003). Bisset (1969) found that students in classrooms that included their own collections of literature read and looked at books 50% more often than did those students whose classrooms housed no such collections. Clearly, it is important to provide students with daily positive experiences involving stories and other literature, such as reading and telling stories through literal, interpretive, and critical discussions; integrating literature into themes being studied throughout the curriculum; and encouraging students to share books they have read, to respond to literature through written and oral language, and to participate regularly in social periods set aside for reading and writing (Hoffman, Roser, & Farest, 1988; Morrow, 1996; Morrow et al., 1990).

> *Language development has been found to correlate with reading success, and both can be improved by regular use of children's and young adult literature in read-aloud situations both at home and at school.*

Classroom Communities

Although we have previously described social interaction at home as a critical component of language and literacy acquisition, we must also stress the importance of social interaction within the learning environments of young children at school. For example, in school situations cooperative and collaborative work that includes social interaction in small groups has been shown to increase both achievement and productivity (Johnson & Johnson, 1987; Slavin, 1983). Cazden (1986) also notes that peer interaction allows students to attempt a range of roles usually unavailable to them by traditional student–teacher structures.

Classrooms can be viewed as a community, similar to the everyday communities students come from. The classroom community has appropriate social structures and expectations for those social structures; often, these evolve from the interactions among the teacher and the students in the classroom as well as from the expectations of "doing school" (Bloome, 1991). Effective classrooms for teaching and learning language and literacy in grades K–12 build and respect community (Allington & Johnston, 2002; Langer, 2002; Pearson, 1996; Pressley, Allington, Wharton-McDonald, Block, & Morrow, 2001; Schoenbach, Braunger, Greenleaf, & Litman, 2003; Taylor, Pearson, Clark, & Walpole, 1999). That is, they have respect for the backgrounds and knowledge each student contributes to the community, using this as a foundation from which to build a "literate" classroom community that fosters an understanding for the purposeful use of literacy in everyday lives. These social constructs are critical to successful literacy learning. Teachers need to understand the language and social structures of the cultures of their students and to respect their role in tandem with the learning typical of "doing school." Clearly, learning is influenced by the social situation and the familiarity of task materials and cognitive operations associated with them (Neuman & Celano, 2001).

> " *The classroom community has appropriate social structures and expectations for those social structures; often, these evolve from the interactions among the teacher and the students in the classroom as well as from the expectations of 'doing school.'* "

Allington and Johnston (2002) note that tailored, collaborative, meaningful problem-solving work dominated the instructional day of the exemplary fourth-grade teachers they studied. Students often worked collaboratively on long-term projects. These teachers fostered personal responsibility for learning by providing choice, goal-setting guidelines, and collaborative independence. Langer (2001) describes the strategy of "shared cognition" demonstrated by exemplary high school English teachers. In similar ways, these teachers expected high school students not merely to work together but to sharpen their understandings with, against, and from one another.

Clearly, vibrant and interactive classroom communities support literacy learning at all levels of development.

TEACHER RESOURCE

Graves, D.H. (1991). *Build a literate classroom*. Portsmouth, NH: Heinemann.

Engagement in the reading task is key in successfully learning to read and developing as a reader.

Learners must be motivated to read for authentic purposes, connected to their own lives in meaningful ways. Cambourne (1988, 1995) describes four essential elements of engagement in learning: (1) Learners must see themselves as potential doers, as must those around them; (2) learners must see learning as personally meaningful, (3) learners must perceive learning as a low-risk endeavor; and (4) learners must have the opportunity to bond with other doers. The knowledge and understanding learners construct in any instructional setting are critically dependent on the learners' degree of engagement with the demonstrations of literacy—its various forms, purposes, authors, and audiences—provided by teachers and texts (Cambourne, 2002; cf. Savery & Duffy, 1995). With reference to literacy learning, students who are not motivated to read will simply not benefit from reading instruction (Guthrie & Wigfield, 2000; Kamil, 2003). Given the well-documented decline in motivation to read among postelementary school students, instructional designs that build on the growing body of engagement research are our best hope to turn that decline around and improve reading achievement for students at all grade levels (Guthrie & Wigfield, 2000; Snow & Biancarosa, 2003).

Motivation and engagement are intricately related in reading. Guthrie and colleagues (1998) describe engagement as "the motivated use of strategies to gain conceptual knowledge during reading" (p. 261). A motivated individual initiates and continues a particular activity, returning to a task with sustained engagement, even as it becomes difficult (Maehr, 1976). Guthrie and Wigfield (2000) see motivation as the critical factor in engagement and note that extensive research shows the strong connection between engagement and achievement in reading (Campbell, Voelkl, & Donahue, 1997; Morrow & Weinstein, 1986; National Academy of Education, 1991; Wang, Haertel, & Walberg, 1990).

During the past eight years, the National Reading Research Center (NRRC) has specifically investigated engagement and motivation. One important finding is how motivation actually mediates the Matthew effect, in which the achievement gap between weaker and more capable readers widens over time (Stanovich, 1986; see chapter 3). The NRRC found that increasing competence builds motivation, and increasing motivation leads to more reading. In fact, motivation and subsequent engagement can actually compensate for factors such as low family income and limited educational background, allowing learners to become agents of their own reading growth (Guthrie & Wigfield, 2000). Conversely, a history of less successful reading experiences leads to a lower sense of self-efficacy and decreased motivation to read, even in self-chosen texts (Allington & McGill-Franzen, 2003). Engagement is clearly a contributing factor to the achievement gap in reading.

In setting forth a research agenda on reading comprehension, the RAND Reading Study Group (2002) concurs that engagement is a mediator of instruction's effect on reading. The group defines engagement as a combination of the reader's intrinsic motivation to read; use of cognitive strategies and background knowledge to make meaning with text; and social interaction in reading, such as discussing the meaning of sections of the text or the theme of a narrative. Readers' perception of their own competence, or lack thereof, is highly related to engagement and, subsequently, to comprehension. Judith Langer's (1999) study of middle and high schools that "beat the odds," that is, produced higher than expected student achievement in reading and writing, showed another important aspect of engagement. In classrooms with engaged readers, the norm is to go beyond achievement of the set learning goals; teachers help students deepen their understandings and generate new ideas based on what they have learned.

Researchers have found several factors that increase students' motivation and engagement. Experiences that afford students the opportunity for success, challenge, choice, and social collaborations are likely to promote motivation (Gambrell, Almasi, Xie, & Heland, 1995; Gambrell, Palmer, & Codling, 1993; Guthrie & Wigfield, 2000; Ivey, 1999b; Morrow, 1996; Ryan & Deci, 2000). The learning environment must enable students to perceive the challenge in the activity as one that they can accomplish. When the task is completed, the students must perceive success (Cambourne, 2002; Ford, 1992; Guthrie & Davis, 2003; McCombs, 1989; Spaulding, 1992). Self-selection of tasks instills intrinsic motivation (Guthrie & Wigfield, 2000; Morrow, 1992). Collaboration with a teacher or with peers in learning tasks finds students intrinsically motivated and likely to accomplish more and develop deeper understandings than if they work alone (Brandt, 1990; Oldfather, 1993). High-performing schools actually cultivate this "shared cognition" beyond individual thinking (Langer, 1999, p. 42).

> 66 *Experiences that afford students the opportunity for success, challenge, choice, and social collaborations are likely to promote motivation.* 99

To be engaged readers, students must recognize the value of reading and their own potential as readers and learners. Literacies found at home and within the community foster desire and purpose to read; they are a means by which students become members of a community of readers and society at large. Schools must build on this background knowledge of literacy. Reading instruction should include diverse texts and diverse opportunities to interact with texts, rather than be limited to certain materials and procedures.

Research on reading engagement from the reader's perspective has found that middle and high school students who are not effective readers lack the critical component of engagement (Greenleaf, Schoenbach, Cziko, & Mueller, 2001; Guthrie & Davis, 2003; Ivey, 1999a). These older students, highly sensitive to contexts for reading, share some characteristics. They do not appear to be motivated to read when they have no personal connections to the text or real purposes for reading. They seem to be disengaged from reading, affectively and cognitively; reading is seen as an entirely school-based activity with no impact on their present or future lives outside of school. They are not fluent or frequent readers—in fact, they may lack a self-identity as readers. They are inexperienced, especially in sustained periods of reading and in engagement with a range of genres.

Engaged reading is conceptual, strategic, and social (Guthrie & Anderson, 1999). Guthrie and Wigfield (2000) have conceptualized a mediated engagement model specific to reading, depicting the reciprocal relationship between engagement and reading outcomes (e.g., achievement, knowledge, and practices). The engagement model draws from research in motivation and education, with support from researchers and teachers alike (Moje, Young, Readence, & Moore, 2000). Although the model richly illustrates key interactions between engagement and valued reading outcomes for all learners, Guthrie and Davis (2003) recommend it especially to create instructional contexts that can foster struggling middle school students' engagement with reading. They recommend classroom practice with the following features, operating together in a coherent, dynamic fashion:

- *Knowledge goals*: Students focus on understanding beyond skill development. They learn strategies such as questioning, activating background knowledge, monitoring comprehension, and synthesizing multiple texts as tools to acquire valued conceptual knowledge.

- *Real-world interactions*: Students have opportunities to learn subject area content in authentic, applied contexts (e.g., naturalistic science projects and historical reenactments). Texts and appropriate reading skills are contextualized within the learning goals established for such real-world interactions.

- *An abundance of interesting texts*: Students have access to a wide variety of texts, including print and electronic formats. Student-generated texts are part of the collection and offer a natural site for learning writing process skills.

- *Autonomy support*: Students have a reasonable degree of choice in texts and learning tasks. They develop ownership and increased responsibility when they are involved in key classroom decisions related to their reading and learning.

- *Strategy instruction*: Explicit strategy instruction, as needed, is provided within the context of real reading. Such instruction includes the processes of modeling, scaffolding, guided practice with feedback, and independent reading to gain fluency in the strategy (Wood, Willoughby, & Woloshyn, 1995).

- *Collaboration support*: Students have regular opportunities to share reading experiences with and learn from one another.

These and other instructional implications from the research on engagement offer critical ways for teachers to support all students in becoming active and effective readers. An engagement model of instruction can help students develop not only skills and strategies but also a reader identity essential to functioning in the literate community.

TEACHER RESOURCES

Christensen, L. (2000). *Reading, writing, and rising up: Teaching about social justice and the power of the written word*. Milwaukee, WI: Rethinking Schools.

Fielding, A., & Schoenbach, R. (Eds.). (2003). *Building academic literacy: An anthology for reading apprenticeship*. San Francisco: Jossey-Bass.

Guthrie, J.T., & Davis, M.H. (2003). Motivating struggling readers in middle school through an engagement model of classroom practice. *Reading & Writing Quarterly*, *19*(1), 59–85.

Wilhelm, J.D. (1997). *"You gotta BE the book": Teaching engaged and reflective reading with adolescents*. New York: Teachers College Press; Chicago: National Council of Teachers of English.

Children's understandings of print are not the same as adults' understandings.

CORE UNDERSTANDING 8

Learning strategies for children, as well as their conceptualizations of the world, differ much from those of adults. Goodman offers this summation:

> In general, it is not understood that children do not view the world or the concepts within the world in the same way as adults do...when children are reading and writing they are making sense out of, or through, print. Eventually readers and writers of English intuitively come to know that written language in English is based upon certain alphabetic principles. However, this knowledge is not a prerequisite for children's learning to read and write. Children perceive written language and provide evidence that they are aware that there is a message in that transaction when they read "brake the car" in response to a stop sign or "toothpaste" in response to a Crest toothpaste label. (as cited in Teale & Sulzby, 1986, p. 5)

Children's understanding of print differs from that of adults. The crucial questions are what understandings are vital (e.g., that print carries a message and it should make sense) at the earliest stages of reading and what more sophisticated conventional understandings children grow into as they learn to read independently. For example, many young learners are not good at learning analytically, abstractly, or auditorily (Carbo, 1987). Therefore, for most young children, it is hard to learn aspects of language and literacy without some understanding of the whole of language, that is, without a concept of the meanings words and sentences convey. How young children begin to develop phonemic awareness and phonic knowledge provides important insight into how children perceive language in ways different from adults.

The aspects of linguistic and metalinguistic awareness—children's "knowledge of wordness" (cf. Clay, 1979; Yaden & Templeton, 1986)—must be included in this discussion. Children must become aware of language as written, then gain more sophisticated concepts about print, including being able to talk about and describe its aspects and processes as they understand them. They will need to know about the parts as well as the whole and that it all makes sense—it carries meaning. This is important to make explicit, as children who fail to see the very nature and purposes of reading are often those who are seen to be at risk of not learning to read successfully.

Current research on the role of phonological awareness in beginning reading is substantive. Goswami (2000) summarizes the current status of understanding of phonological processing at three levels: (1) syllable, (2) onset and rime, and (3) phoneme. Goswami and Bryant (1990) began to describe the development of phonemic awareness as a developmental continuum across these levels (cf. Hansen & Bowey, 1994; McClure, Ferreira, & Bisanz, 1996; Stahl & Murray, 1994).

How do children begin to perceive the individual sounds of language? Research has shown that children might not see this task in the same way that adults do. Bruce (1964) demonstrated that young children have difficulty manipulating phonemes. Others (Ehri & Wilce, 1980; Liberman, Shankweiler, Fisher, & Carter, 1974; Mann, 1986; Rosner, 1974; Treiman & Baron, 1981; Tunmer & Nesdale, 1985) looked at phoneme manipulation from a variety of perspectives, all with similar results. This research shows that young children do not analyze speech into phonemes before they begin to read in the way literate adults have traditionally thought they do. It appears that it is much easier for young children first to identify spoken syllables than to abstract either words or sounds from the stream of speech (cf. Adams, 1990; Goswami, 2000; Moustafa, 1997).

Berdiansky, Cronnell, and Koehler (1969), building on the work of Venezky (1967), found that the complexity of the relationship of sounds in words was in the combination of the letters that produced unique sets of sounds. None of the letter sounds are all that regular within the contexts of words because of the interrelationships within the structure of each word. There are not a small, manageable number of rules, as some suggest. Rather, letter–sound correspondences are represented by a complex web of relationships (Hanna, Hanna, Hodges, & Rudorf, 1966; Moustafa, 1997; Venezky, 1970).

The ability to segment phonemes appears to be a consequence of literacy development or at least grows in tandem with it (Goswami, 2000; Lie, 1991; Mann, 1986; Morais, Bertelson, Cary, & Alegria, 1986; Perfetti, Beck, Bell, & Hughes, 1987; Read, Zhang, Nie, & Ding, 1986; Winner, Landerl, Linortner, & Hummer, 1991). Scholes (1998) found that literate adults use their knowledge of spelling to help them do phonemic-awareness tasks. This, again, supports the notion that young children perceive phonemic knowledge in developmentally different ways.

So what do children do as they are learning to read in this complex system of sounds and symbols? From observations of oral language development, we know that young children are capable of using a variety of sophisticated strategies. They do much the same as they learn written language. Young children become sensitive to rhyme at an early age (Goswami & Bryant, 1990). They do not initially hear individual phonemes; rather, they hear the initial phoneme and the spoken syllable. *Onsets* are any consonants before a vowel in a spoken syllable, and *rimes* are the vowel and any consonants after it (Adams, 1990; Moustafa, 1997; Treiman, 1986; Treiman & Baron, 1981; Treiman & Chafetz, 1987; Wylie & Durrell, 1970).

Young children are competent at analyzing spoken words into onsets and rimes but not into phonemes when onsets or rimes consist of more than one phoneme (Calfee, 1977; Goswami & Bryant, 1990; Liberman et al., 1974; Treiman, 1983, 1985). Stahl and Murray (1994) found a strong connection between early reading and the ability to separate an onset from a rime in a consonant-vowel-consonant (CVC) pattern. They concluded that onset–rime awareness is one of the first steps in acquiring the alphabetic principle.

Young children develop an awareness of syllables early and can do so without instruction (Morais et al., 1986; Winner et al., 1991). Those who are beginning to read make analogies between familiar and unfamiliar print words to pronounce unfamiliar print words. Children make these analogies at the onset–rime level rather than at the phonemic level (Goswami, 1986, 1988).

When designing instructional experiences, teachers must consider the factors that support children's learning about print and that are appropriate to children's current understandings.

TEACHER RESOURCES

Goodman, Y., Reyes, I., & McArthur, K. (2005). Emilia Ferreiro: Searching for children's understandings about literacy as a cultural object. *Language Arts, 82*(4), 318–323.

Wilde, S. (1997). *What's a schwa sound anyway? A holistic guide to phonetics, phonics, and spelling.* Portsmouth, NH: Heinemann.

Children develop phonemic awareness and knowledge of phonics through a variety of literacy opportunities, models, and demonstrations.

CORE UNDERSTANDING 9

Much time and effort has been invested in investigations and consequent discussions about how children learn to apply the alphabetic principle—those understandings of print that are the critical difference between oral and written language—in order to read and write. The importance of the development of early word identification skill is evident (Juel, 1991; National Institute of Child Health and Human Development [NICHD], 2000; Pearson, 1993; Stanovich, 1991; Snow, Burns, & Griffin, 1998). Unfortunately, these discussions have become as much political as educational, with policy and instructional decisions often made more on rhetoric than on research (Cunningham, 1992).

Currently, the debate has come to focus primarily on two factors: (1) the place of phonemic awareness (discerning that spoken language is composed of separate speech sounds; the ability to segment the speech stream of a spoken word), and (2) the place of phonics (the teaching of particular parts of language, specifically rules for phoneme–grapheme relationships) in early reading instruction. Many studies point to phonemic awareness as a predictor of early reading success (cf. Adams, 1990; Blachman, 2000; NICHD, 2000; Snow et al., 1998); however, it is clearly but one factor important to the development of effective reading strategies to read for meaning (Pearson, 2000; Pressley, Allington, Wharton-McDonald, Block, & Morrow, 2001; Strickland, 1998; Taylor, Pearson, Clark, & Walpole, 1999; Weaver, 1998). Also, research supports that a basic knowledge of letter–sound relationships (phonics) is a necessary but not a sufficient strategy used by successful readers (Camilli, Vargas, & Yurecko, 2003; "IRA Takes a Stand," 1997). The questions are thus how much, how, when, and under what circumstances phonemic awareness and phonic knowledge should be included in instruction to make it effective. Furthermore, all stakeholders need to stand back and consider whether we are asking the right questions in regard to what children need to know, based on what we now know.

Perspectives at the Heart of the Debate

The passionate debates that have arisen on the role of phonemic awareness and phonics in instruction make it even more critical for teachers to understand broadly and deeply the aspects of the alphabetic principle as it pertains to the teaching and learning of reading. Although there are several perspectives from which to view reading, most commonly reading is seen as either a process of decoding or a process of constructing meaning (see chapter 1).

Currently, policy decisions at any level (federal, state, or local) about reading instruction, particularly on phonemic awareness and phonics instruction, have followed the recommendations of two major syntheses of research: *Preventing Reading Difficulties in Young Children* (Snow et al., 1998) and the National Reading Panel (NRP) report (NICHD, 2000). Snow and colleagues (1998) highlight the use of systematic phonics instruction, particularly for those children at risk of failing to learn to read. They recommend that beginning reading instruction should be designed to provide explicit instruction and practice with sound structures that lead to phonemic awareness, familiarity with spelling–sound correspondences and common spelling conventions and their use in identifying printed words, sight recognition of frequent words, and independent reading, including reading aloud in a wide variety of well-written and engaging texts. They also recommend that explicit instruction on comprehension strategies be included throughout the early grades.

The NRP Report of the Subgroups for Phonics Instruction (NICHD, 2000) supports systematic instruction for phonics. The report states that a variety of phonics programs have proven effective with children of different ages, abilities, and socioeconomic backgrounds; however, the panel suggests caution is needed in giving a blanket endorsement to all kinds of phonics instruction. The panel emphasizes that the goal of phonics instruction as a means to an end and that the role of the teacher needs to be better understood and defined beyond the boundaries of a particular curriculum design. One critique of the panel's report is that it does not provide a definition of reading, and to many this infers that reading is made up of a series of isolated skills and strategies (Yatvin, 2002; Yatvin, Weaver, & Garan, 2003).

Many reviews, interpretations, and critiques of both reports have been published. Although the research findings will be integrated throughout this discussion, it is our intent to provide an overarching synthesis of the literature surrounding the place of phonemic awareness and phonic knowledge in the teaching and learning of word identification to support strategic, meaning-based reading.

As knowledge of the reading process continues to emerge, it often leads to more questions to pursue to better understand the processes of becoming literate. As Weaver, Gillmeister-Krause, and Vento-Zogby (1996) note,

> [Those who believe reading is a construction of meaning] point out that too much attention to phonics can detract from the construction of meaning, while [those who believe reading is decoding] cite correlations between tests of phonemic awareness and scores on standardized tests as evidence that phonemic awareness and phonics must be taught early to promote reading achievement—that is, high standardized test scores. Another major difference: Researchers who have studied emergent literacy (e.g., Harste, Woodward, & Burke, 1984) point out that phonics knowledge is gained in the process of becoming a reader and a writer, while those who have examined correlations between phonemic awareness and reading test scores note that phonemic awareness is a requisite to becoming an *independent reader* (e.g., Beck & Juel, 1995). Note, however, that the two ideas are compatible: Independent readers may have developed phonemic awareness in the process of becoming readers and writers; and, in fact, there is substantial evidence that this happens (Mann, 1986; Morais, Bertelson, Cary, & Alegria, 1986; Moustafa, 1995; Winner, Landerl, Linortner, & Hummer, 1991). (n.p.)

Regarding correlational research, we must make the following caveat: *Correlation* simply means that the two things are observed to occur together; it says nothing about whether one causes the other—for example, whether phonemic awareness leads to independent reading, whether learning to read results in phonemic awareness, or whether they interact and support each other's development (Weaver et al., 1996; Moustafa, 1995, 1997). Correlation is not causation; thus, interpretations of research data must be careful in their generalizations. One critique of the NRP report, particularly in the case of the subgroup report on phonic knowledge, is just that—it has inconsistently defined and included research findings that are based on correlational results to support (or not support) aspects of teaching and learning to read (Allington, 2005; Krashen, 2001, 2002; Yatvin, 2002).

The NRP report (NICHD, 2000), based solely on meta-analyses of narrowly defined research studies (see chapter 1), has fueled discussion across the profession of both this type of research methodology and the relativity of effect sizes. McCartney and Rosenthal (2000) remind us that a small effect size is not necessarily inconsequential for informing educational practice any more than a large effect size is always of consequence (cf. Camilli et al., 2003). They say, "There are no easy conventions for determining practical importance. Just as children are best understood in context, so are effect sizes" (p. 173).

Research in linguistics, cognitive and developmental psychology, anthropology, sociology, and education has shown that when dealing with print, several levels of information are available to assist the reader to make sense of the text. These levels include graphophonic, semantic, syntactic, and pragmatic (see chapter 2 and Core Understanding 5). In this way, reading is much more complex than consideration of only the "visible" or print levels (Moustafa, 1995). At least, it appears that phonemic awareness and phonic knowledge develop simultaneously as children have many varied experiences with print, supported and guided by a knowledgeable other.

Systematic Instruction: Definitions

The term *systematic instruction* appears to be one of the most important factors at the heart of the debates around early reading instruction. Those advocating a phonics-centered approach emphasize that explicit systematic phonics lessons are necessary for learning to read and write (Adams & Bruck, 1995; Beck & Juel, 1995; Chall, 1967/1983; Ehri, 1991; Foorman, Francis, Fletcher, Schatschneider, & Mehta, 1998). Stahl (1998) describes these lessons as involving direct instruction (often in teacher-scripted, whole-class lessons) and learner practice in materials crafted to emphasize specific phonics concepts.

Strickland (1998) offers an alternative definition: "Instruction is systematic when it is planned, deliberate in application, and proceeds in an orderly manner. This does not mean a rigid progression of 'one size fits all' instruction. Rather, it means a thoughtfully planned program that takes into account learner variability" (p. 51). In this definition, teachers are able to consider their knowledge of the individual learner, differentiating instruction as needed to meet the diverse needs of students.

Pearson (1996) clarifies the term *explicit instruction*:

Explicit instruction bears a family resemblance, albeit a weak one, to one of its intellectual predecessors, direct instruction, because of a common emphasis on clarity and systematicness on the presentation of skills and strategies. But the resemblance ends there.... Explicit instruction is less likely to employ skill decomposition (breaking a complex skill down into manageable pieces), which is a staple of direct instruction, as a strategy for dealing with the complexity of important strategies. Instead, it is more likely to employ "scaffolding" as a tool for coping with complexity. Second, explicit instruction is more likely than direct instruction to rely on authentic texts rather than special instructional texts in both initial instruction and later application. (p. xvii)

(See Core Understanding 11 for further discussion.)

Clearly, the profession sees systematic instruction through a range of theoretical lenses; explicitness is also defined by these theories. However, it is important to emphasize that one of the most important, if not the most important, factors of effective teaching is the ability of the teacher to make well-grounded and appropriate instructional decisions and reflect on their success with students (Taylor et al., 1999).

Phonemic Awareness

Phonemic awareness, in its simplest definition, is the ability to segment, delete, and combine speech sounds into abstract units. Although children will be able to hear phonemes, they may not be able to conceptualize them as units. This concept is even more complex than this description would suggest. Phonemic awareness must be based on a growing understanding of the alphabetic principle of English; there is sufficient evidence that many children basically understand this concept before they have been taught—and mastered—the set of letter-to-sound correspondences (Adams, 1990).

The International Reading Association (IRA; 1998) states in *Phonemic Awareness and the Teaching of Reading*,

> On the positive side, research on phonemic awareness has caused us to reconceptualize some of our notions about reading development. Certainly, this research is helping us understand some of the underlying factors that are associated with some forms of reading disability. Through the research on phonemic awareness we now have a clearer theoretical framework for understanding why some of the things we have been doing all along support development (for example, work with invented spelling)....
>
> On the negative side, we are concerned that the research findings about phonemic awareness might be misused or overgeneralized. We are very concerned with policy initiatives that require teachers to dedicate specific amounts of time to phonemic awareness instruction for all students, or to policy initiatives that require the use of particular training programs for all students. Such initiatives interfere with the important instructional decisions that professional teachers must make regarding the needs of their students. (n.p.)

Data that influence the interest in phonemic awareness (sometimes shortened to PA) include the following:

• Poor readers have lower phonemic awareness than do good readers. (Juel, 1994).

- Very young children differ in phonemic awareness (Chaney, 1992).

- Phonemic awareness can be improved by training (Ball & Blachman, 1991; Cunningham, 1990; Hatcher, Hulme, & Ellis, 1994; Lundberg, Frost, & Petersen, 1988).

- Phonemic awareness is supported by the use of invented spelling by emergent readers and writers (Henderson & Beers, 1980; Invernizzi, 1992; Morris & Perney, 1984; Schlagal, 1992; Zutell, 1979).

- Phonemic awareness training that is not combined with reading or letters has less effect on reading (Bus & van IJzendoorn, 1999; NICHD, 2000).

- Snow and colleagues (1998) found phonological awareness—the ability to attend broadly and explicitly to the phonological structure of spoken words, including phonemic awareness—is an important predictor of success in beginning reading tasks and is a critical instructional component in preventing reading difficulties in young children.

- The National Reading Panel reviewed 52 published studies and found that teaching children to manipulate the sounds in language helps them learn to read (NICHD, 2000). The panel suggested that no more than a total of 18 hours of focused training, based early in the instructional curriculum, is the most beneficial.

Several research reviews have provided contrasting views of the importance of phonological and phonemic awareness. Troia (1999) reviewed the methodological rigor of 39 published studies on phonemic awareness training. All the studies demonstrated at least one fatal flaw, and only seven met two thirds or more of the evaluative criteria. Of the seven best studies, none investigated the effectiveness of phonemic or phonological awareness in classrooms. Bus and van IJzendoorn (1999) reviewed the findings of 32 published studies on phonological awareness training. They found the studies varied widely in their findings. Swanson, Trainin, Necoechea, and Hammill (2003) found that their meta-analysis of rapid naming, phonological awareness, and reading studies "is consistent with the current literature suggesting that isolated processes, such as phonological coding, do play a modest part in predicting real-word reading and pseudoword reading"; but they continue, "our study highlights additional processes as playing equally important roles in reading" (p. 432). They suggest the importance of phonological awareness may have been overstated in the literature.

The research of the last two decades emphasizes that phonemic awareness plays a critical role in the development of the ability to decode and to read for meaning (Adams, 1990; Juel, 1988, 1991; cf. NICHD, 2000; Snow et al., 1998; see also Core Understanding 8). The weight of evidence, irrespective of mode of instruction, suggests that phonemic awareness is a necessary but not sufficient condition for the development of decoding and reading. Allington (1997) notes that although a convergence of evidence emphasizes the importance of phonemic awareness in learning to read an alphabetic language, the evidence also indicates that most children (80–85%) acquire this awareness by the middle of first grade as a result of typical experiences at home and at school. Both Juel (1988, 1991) and Adams (1990) have documented the success of teaching phonemic awareness, especially when teachers encourage students to use invented spellings. Context appears to be critical to the efficacy of phonemic awareness as a predictor of success; the impact of increased performance in isolated phonemic awareness tasks on tests of reading comprehension is considerably less (Tunmer, Herriman, & Nesdale, 1988). If, for example, a child is able to produce invented spelling in which most or all phonemes are represented, phonemic awareness has been demonstrated, thus obviating the need for any training in it.

Some students may need more explicit instruction in phonemic awareness, but in general the following types of instruction support development of phonemic awareness:

- *Language play*: Games that emphasize rhyming and thinking about the structure of words particularly exploit children's tendency to first unconsciously analyze and discriminate sounds at the onset–rime level rather than the individual phonemic level (Snow et al., 1998).

- *Sociodramatic play*: This type of thematic activity gives children the opportunity to integrate and extend their understanding of language, stories, and new knowledge spaces (Levy, Wolfgang, & Koorland, 1992; cf. Snow et al., 1998).

- *Reading aloud*: Reading aloud models what language sounds like and how one reads, and it helps children to foster their appreciation and comprehension of text and literary language (Galda, Ash, & Cullinan, 2000; Galda & Cullinan, 2003; Snow et al., 1998).

- *Opportunities to help children notice and use letters and words*: Knowledge is further fostered through the use of alphabet centers and word walls (Fountas & Pinnell, 1996). Such opportunities help children to become familiar with letter forms, to learn to use visual aspects of print, to notice and use letters and words that are embedded in text, to acquire a growing inventory of known letters and words, to link sounds and letters and letter clusters, and to use what they know about words to learn new words (Adams, 1990; Cunningham, 1990; Fountas & Pinnell, 1996; IRA, 1998; Pressley et al., 2001; Taylor et al., 1999; Read, 1975; Schickedanz, 1986).

- *Invented spelling*: These experiences provide a medium through which both phonemic awareness and phonic knowledge develop (Adams, 1990; Clarke, 1988; Juel, 1991; Snow et al., 1998; Wilde, 1992; Winsor & Pearson, 1992).

- *Language experience*: Dictation of children's own oral language—in the form of stories and experiences—becomes the texts from which children read; modeling and demonstration of particular phonemic awareness and phonic knowledge occur as the teacher takes dictations (Adams, 1990; Allen, 1976).

- *Reading for meaning*: To develop such decoding proficiency, teachers need to provide many models of reading aloud; to demonstrate and problem-solve using phonemic awareness while reading aloud; and to offer manageable, connected texts for beginning readers to apply their phonemic awareness successfully (Gough, as cited in Pearson, 1993; IRA, 1998; Pressley et al., 2001; Taylor et al., 1999).

- *Rich experiences with language, environmental print, patterned stories, and Big Books*: These provide a broad range of experiences to model, demonstrate, and explicitly teach phonemic awareness (Adams, 1990; IRA, 1998; Juel, 1991; Pearson, 1993; Pressley et al., 2001; Taylor et al., 1999).

Phonics, in General

Phonic knowledge (including but going beyond phonemic awareness) can be taught through a wide variety of methods: intensive, explicit, synthetic, analytic, embedded. All methods of phonics instruction focus on the learner's attention to the relationships between sounds and symbols as an important strategy for word recognition. There continues to be insufficient evidence that one form of phonics instruction is strongly superior to another (Allington, 1997; Cunningham & Allington, 2003; Stahl, McKenna, & Pagnucco, 1994; cf. Yatvin et al., 2003).

The continued intensity of the debate led IRA, long maintaining that no single approach to reading instruction can be dictated as being best for every student, to issue a position statement (1997) asserting three basic principles regarding phonics and the teaching of reading:

1. *The teaching of phonics is an important aspect of beginning reading instruction*. This statement only suggests there is nearly unanimous regard for its importance, not unanimity as to methodology.

2. *Classroom teachers in the primary grades do value and do teach phonics as part of their reading program*. Effective teachers make appropriate instructional decisions for the inclusion of phonics based on their knowledge of children and children's language development. The position statement concludes that "programs that constrain teachers from using their professional judgment in making instructional decisions about what is best in phonics instruction for students simply get in the way of good teaching practices" (n.p.).

3. *Phonics instruction, to be effective in promoting independence in reading, must be embedded in the context of a total reading/language arts program*. Specific instruction in phonics takes on meaning for learners when it is within meaningful contexts of language use (e.g., interesting and informative books, nursery rhymes, poetry, and songs) that provide patterns and structures to support their understanding.

Although these recommendations are focused on young children just beginning to read, other recommendations have focused on the effectiveness of continued phonics instruction with upper elementary and adolescent readers. In its statement on adolescent literacy, the National Council of Teachers of English (NCTE; 2004) asserts that most adolescents do not need further instruction in phonics or decoding skills (cf. Ivey & Baker, 2004). More typically, older readers who are identified as "struggling" lack experience reading extended, coherent text (Allington, 2001; Schoenbach, Greenleaf, Cziko, & Hurwitz, 1999). In cases where older students need help to construct meaning with text, teachers should target and embed instruction in authentic reading experiences. This approach seems a more productive response, given that the research summarized in the NRP report (NICHD, 2000) notes that the benefits of phonics instruction are strongest in first grade and are diminished for students in subsequent grades.

Several key studies have been used to frame the debate over phonics. These fall into two general categories: those that assert the primacy of phonics instruction in learning to read and those that show phonics instruction as but one of many factors in learning to read.

Studies That Assert the Primacy of Phonics Instruction in Learning to Read. Among those that highlight the primacy of phonics instruction is Chall's (1967/1983) work, which suggests that systematic phonics instruction is a valuable component of beginning reading instruction within the complementary context of connected and meaningful reading (cf. Adams, 1990). Others point out, though, that Chall's findings of a positive correlation between systematic phonics instruction and higher scores on tests of reading and spelling "achievement" only holds through the primary grades; beyond grade 4, the correlation ceases (Purcell-Gates, McIntyre, & Freppon, 1995; Shannon, 1996).

Adam's (1990) review of research concludes that phonemic awareness and phonic knowledge instruction is a critical factor for success in early reading. Although many praise her work for its thoroughness, many who view reading as a construction of meaning find this perspective to be lacking particularly in regard to the sociocultural contexts of literacy.

Foorman (1995) and her colleagues (Foorman et al., 1998) have continued to conduct studies that look at how children with training in phonemic awareness and phonic knowledge fare, most recently in comparison to children participating in a whole language curriculum. Although their findings show that children in whole language classrooms do not fare as well as their peers in the trained group, critiques focus on the lack of definition of the whole language curriculum.

Studies That Show the Importance of Many Factors in Learning to Read. Among the studies that highlight phonics instruction as but one factor in learning to read is Bond and Dykstra's (1967/1997) work. The authors concluded that no one approach is so much better in all situations that it should be considered a best method. Even more generally and probably more important for instructional considerations, they found that no matter what the program, the quality of teaching made the difference in the instruction. The implication is that to improve reading instruction, both programs and classroom delivery must be improved (Adams, 1990).

Stebbins, St. Pierre, Proper, Anderson, and Cerva (1977) focused on a wide variety of models but found that no one model proved to be more effective than others on conceptual measures. Advocates of strong systematic phonics instruction continue to find data about one of the sites using the Distar program—a highly structured and highly focused systematic teaching of the alphabet—as consistently showing the best reading achievement. However, much debate continues over the validity of these results (House, Glass, McLean, & Walker, 1978).

Anderson, Hiebert, Scott, and Wilkinson (1985) support repeated opportunities to read over continuing phonics instruction beyond the basics. They state,

> Phonics instruction should aim to teach only the most important and regular of letter-to-sound relationships...once the basic relationships have been taught, the best way to get children to refine and extend their knowledge of letter-sound correspondences is through repeated opportunities to read. If this position is correct, then much phonics instruction is overly subtle and probably unproductive. (p. 38)

Schweinhart, Weikart, and Larner (1986) looked at three programs for emergent readers: (1) Distar, (2) whole language, (3) and traditional. Whole language appeared to give children important first knowledge about reading, whereas the most-structured of programs, Distar, appeared to severely limit the long-term social potential of its participants. Although this study showed diverse curriculum models can be equally effective, it also showed the vital importance of social interaction in successful teaching and learning.

Wharton-McDonald, Pressley, and Hampston (1998) found that the most effective first-grade teachers in their study taught decoding skills explicitly and provided their students with many opportunities to engage in authentic reading. However, systematic phonic instruction in isolation only, along with sheer opportunity to practice through reading connected text, may not be the optimal path toward a rich repertoire of word-recognition strategies; rather, the data suggest that it is what teachers do to promote application of phonics knowledge during the reading of connected text that matters most. What distinguished the most accomplished teachers and the majority of teachers in the most effective schools from their peers was their use of coaching to help students learn how to apply word-recognition strategies to real reading. Although more research is needed to unpack the specifics of these coaching and application strategies, our results suggest that conversations about systematic phonics instruction and opportunity to practice need to be broadened to include on-the-job coaching during everyday reading (cf. Pressley et al., 2001; Taylor et al., 1999).

Among other studies relevant to phonics instruction is Cantrell's (1999) work. The author studied eight primary multiage classrooms, four that focused on reading for meaning and skills taught in context and four that did not promote meaning-centered reading and taught skills out of context. Children in classrooms that taught skills in context did better than children in classrooms where skills were taught out of context on every measure of reading achievement including word analysis (phonics), fluency, comprehension, and spelling.

Juel and Minden-Cupp (2000), in their study of four first-grade classrooms, found that a combination of explicit phonics instruction combined with work with onset and rime was very effective. They found that teachers effective in teaching reading differentiated instruction based on the needs of their students. The children who entered first grade with low literacy skills did benefit from a heavy dose of phonics first and fast, while also including a wide range of in-context reading and writing experiences. The phonics instruction reflected the teachers' knowledge of both the hands-on nature of activities that focus the attention of young children and of the active child decision making involved in compare-and-contrast activities that can facilitate cognitive growth. They agree with Duffy and Hoffman (1999) that "improved reading is linked to teachers who use methods thoughtfully, not methods alone" (pp. 31–33).

66 Systematic phonics instruction in combination with language activities and individual tutoring may triple the effect of phonics alone. 99

Dahl, Scharer, Lawson, and Grogan (1999) studied nine first-grade teachers who met a set of explicit criteria that defined the parameters of a whole language classroom. They found (a) the content of phonics instruction in these classrooms focused on phonics skills taught with an emphasis on their application strategically; (b) instruction in phonics occurred across a range of teaching and learning events throughout the day where children could apply phonics skills and strategies to the point of personal use; (c) teachers differentiate phonics instruction developmentally, based on the individual progress of their students; and (d) while the students in this study had diverse abilities, all learners made impressive gains in encoding and decoding, in and out of context.

Of particular note, Camilli and colleagues (2003), in their attempt to replicate the NRP findings (NICHD, 2000), found that systematic phonics instruction in combination with language activities and individual tutoring may triple the effect of phonics alone. Camilli and others believe an approach that recognizes the complexity of reading (rather than looking at only effect sizes in one aspect) has the potential to improve estimates of average effect sizes in all substantive areas the NRP considered.

In a longitudinal study of one kindergarten class, Xue and Meisels (2004) found that different approaches made different contributions to children's literacy development in kindergarten. In particular, they looked at the use of both an integrated language arts curriculum and phonics instruction, finding them to be moderately correlated with each other. On average, higher levels of integrated language arts and phonics instruction were associated with greater gains. Children also displayed more optimal approaches to learning in classrooms where integrated language arts and phonics instruction occurred more often.

Considering Methodology of Research and Interpretation of Outcome. It is important to acknowledge the important contribution of each of these studies as we continue to ponder how children learn to read. However, we must consider each with a careful and critical eye toward methodology and interpretation of outcome.

Although no disagreement exists about sound–symbol relationships as critical aspects of reading, and thus of learning to read, it is important to distinguish between the alphabetic principle of English (i.e., a sound–symbol relationship) and the phonetic principle (i.e., a high consistency between sound and letter patterns, such as in Spanish—which is phonetic—but not in English).

Some interesting research to consider in light of this distinction follows (c.f. Moustafa, 1995):

- Clymer (1963/1996) discovered that traditional phonics generalizations are not all that reliable. For example, of the 31 vowel generalizations Clymer tested, only half of them worked at least 60% of the time.

- Read (1986) found that the "creative spelling" of 4-year-olds followed particular developmental patterns that reflected their emerging knowledge and understanding of written language rules. These patterns paralleled real language development; children re-created the general rules of the language through their approximations and interactions with sophisticated users of print (cf. Adams, 1990; Weaver, 1994, for thorough discussions).

Weaver and colleagues (1996) see four major points of agreement about the teaching of phonics even among such varying perspectives:

1. Children should be given some explicit, direct help in developing phonemic awareness and a functional command of phonics.

2. Such direct teaching does not need to be intensive and systematic to be effective.

3. Indeed, worksheets and rote drills are not the best means of developing phonics knowledge (e.g., Cunningham, 1990).

4. Phonemic awareness and phonics knowledge also develops without instruction, simply from reading and writing whole, interesting texts. (n.p.)

Sweet's (1993) early summary remains true today: She calls for a balance of activities designed to improve word recognition, including phonics instruction and reading meaningful text, saying it is necessary for creating effective beginning reading instruction. The focus is on providing for the child what he or she needs when he or she needs it, rather than relying on a set curriculum to meet the assumed needs of every child. No one teaching method is a panacea, as some children continue to have difficulty in developing phonemic awareness and phonics knowledge no matter how they are taught (Freppon & Dahl, 1991). However, teaching phonics knowledge in context and through discussion and collaborative activities seems to be more effective with more children than other means.

Also, some studies show that children in classrooms where skills are taught in the context of reading and writing whole texts get a better start on becoming proficient and independent readers, beyond simply becoming word callers (e.g.,

Cantrell, 1999; Dahl et al., 1999; Freppon & Dahl, 1991; Kasten & Clarke, 1989; Ribowsky, 1985; Stice & Bertrand, 1990).

Struggling Readers

What about beginning readers who struggle? Much of the research on the role of phonemic awareness and phonics instruction points to the need for more direct, systematic, explicit teaching of this aspect of the reading process for such beginning readers (e.g., Delpit, 1986, 1988). Snow and colleagues (1998) propose exactly this for all children as they begin to read, but particularly for children at risk for failure to learn to read. (See also discussion in chapter 3.)

However, equally substantive studies point to the increased benefit of contextual literacy experiences—storybook reading, in particular, but also other meaningful interactions with print—for struggling readers at beginning stages (Neuman, 1999; Purcell-Gates et al., 1995). At the same time, research shows that by fourth grade, the relationship between phonic knowledge and successful reading no longer shows a strong correlation (Chall, 1983). When considering older readers who struggle, Ivey and Baker (2004) propose two critical questions: Does the chosen instruction help students to read better? Does it make students want to read more? They find no evidence to suggest that focusing on sound-, letter-, or word-level instruction will benefit older readers in any way. What does this imply for instruction?

Instruction for cultural, ethnic, and linguistic minority students that is primarily skills-based may limit children's learning by failing to develop their analytical skills or conceptual skills or by failing to provide purposes for learning (Knapp & Shields, 1990). Thompson, Mixon, and Serpell (1996) suggest that instructional methods for teaching reading to these children emphasize construction of meaning (Au, 1993; O'Connell & Wood, 1992); language development (Heath, Mangiola, Schecter, & Hull, 1991; Ovando, 1993; Tharp, 1989); and higher order thinking skills, including metacognitive and prior knowledge strategies (Chamot, 1993; Crawford, 1993; Cummins, 1986; Pogrow, 1992). Delpit (1988) and Gay (1988) believe it is important to offer a balance within a curriculum for minority students that provides explicit instruction in "the language of power" within a meaningful context that acknowledges all students are capable of critical, higher order thinking.

Alvermann (2002) suggests that literacy instruction for adolescents should focus on individual interests and use diverse reading materials. Students who struggle with school reading and writing tasks may read and write for their own purposes successfully outside of school (Knobel, 2001).

The literature clearly supports a combination of a wide variety of teaching strategies focused on all aspects of the reading process as critical to the support of struggling readers. While they may need more explicit or differently designed instruction to support their learning needs, they do not need a focused reliance on instruction in phonic knowledge and phonemic awareness activities.

TEACHER RESOURCES

Cunningham, P. (2000). *Phonics they use: Words for reading and writing* (3rd ed.). New York: Longman.

Dahl, K.L., Sharer, P.L., Lawson, L.L., & Grogan, P.R. (1999). Phonics instruction and student achievement in whole language first-grade classrooms. *Reading Research Quarterly, 34*(3), 312–341.

Moustafa, M. (1997). *Beyond traditional phonics: Research discoveries and reading instruction*. Portsmouth, NH: Heinemann.

Savage, J.F. (2004). *Sound it out! Phonics in a comprehensive reading program* (2nd ed.). Boston: McGraw-Hill.

CORE UNDERSTANDING

Readers learn productive strategies in the context of real reading.

To be effective at making meaning, readers need to learn appropriate strategies for orchestrating the information provided at all levels by the four cueing systems (see Core Understanding 5). Research based in miscue analysis and running records (e.g., documentation of the kinds of errors readers make and their impact on meaning making) continues to provide insight into the kinds of strategies effective readers choose to employ (Clay, 1985; Goodman, 1965; Goodman, Watson, & Burke, 1987). Strategies may include the use of cues to construct meaning of the text via words, structures, meanings, and purposes in the text; knowing what to do before, during, and after reading a particular piece; knowledge of the similarities and differences among different text structures; and the use of self-monitoring strategies (Does it make sense? What do I do if it does not? What do I know that can help me to understand this text?).

Recent work in retrospective miscue analysis with older readers adds the empowering element of learner response to the reading process. The learner–teacher conversation about strategies employed in reading a specific text provides an opportunity to build on the reader's current strengths and develop greater proficiency (Goodman & Marek, 1996; Moore & Aspegren, 2001).

Much research and scholarship on the process of reading comprehension has been grounded in studies of good readers. And we know quite a lot about what these readers do when they read (Duke & Pearson, 2002). In general, expert readers are active, purposeful, strategic, and metacognitive. Sweet (1993) describes such readers as using strategies to construct meaning before, during, and after reading. Strategies also include plans for solving problems they encounter in their reading experiences. A strategic reader (Paris, Lipson, & Wixon, 1983; Paris, Wasik, & Turner, 1991) is the problem solver who draws from his or her toolbox of metacognitive strategies to repair virtually any comprehension failure that might arise (Pearson, 1993). Reading strategies that have been identified as critical to learning from text include the following:

- *Inferencing*: The process of reaching conclusions based on information within the text, the cornerstone of constructing meaning. Inferencing includes making predictions using prior knowledge combined with information available from text (Cooper, 1993; Sweet, 1993).

- *Predicting*: Frequently setting forth an expectation of what is to come, based on understanding of the text so far. Efficient readers regularly check and either confirm or revise these predictions as the text provides new information (Duke & Pearson, 2002).

- *Reading selectively*: Making decisions about what to read carefully and what to skim, what not to read, what to reread (Duke & Pearson, 2002).

- *Identifying important information*: The process of finding critical facts and details in narrative (e.g., stories) or expository (e.g., informational) text. Because of text structures, the type of information to seek is different. Knowing strategies for approaching each type of text is critical to successful meaning making (Beck, Omanson, & McKeown, 1982; Duke & Pearson, 2002). Good readers appear to use text structure more than poor readers do (Englert & Hiebert, 1984; McGee, 1982; Meyer, Brandt, & Bluth, 1980; Taylor, 1980).

- *Monitoring*: A metacognitive or self-awareness process. Efficient readers know how to adjust their speed or process as needed. They also know when they have a problem, and they have a variety of strategies at hand to "fix" it (Duke & Pearson, 2002; Pressley, 2002).

- *Summarizing*: A process that involves determining significant information in a long passage of text and creating a synthesis that accurately represents the original (Dole, Duffy, Roehler, & Pearson, 1991).

- *Question generating*: A process that involves readers asking themselves questions they want answered from reading that require them to integrate information while they read (Baumann, 1984; Palincsar & Brown, 1984; Pressley, Gaskins, Wile, Cunicelli, & Sheridan, 1991; Pressley, Schuder, & Bergman, 1992; Rinehart, Stahl, & Erickson, 1986). As good readers construct meanings with text, they continually question and revise these meanings (Duke & Pearson, 2002).

When modeling these strategies, teachers must treat them as a set of ways for constructing meaning instead of as independent activities that are isolated from the literacy context. And when students receive coaching or supportive instruction in relevant strategies as they read, they both expand their repertoire of strategies (e.g., in word recognition) and develop control of the strategies for greater independence as readers (Taylor, Pearson, Clark & Walpole, 1999; Taylor,

Peterson, Rodriguez, & Pearson, 2002). Increasingly competent and independent strategy use is a hallmark of competent reading; it is also an important link to motivation and ongoing growth as a reader (Alexander & Murphy, 1999; Guthrie & Wigfield, 2000).

A number of studies point to the importance of embedding strategy instruction in rigorous content area learning. Langer's (2001) research studied middle and high school English teachers whose students were outperforming expectations, or "beating the odds." Although she found that teachers variously employed separate, simulated, or integrated approaches to skill and strategy instruction, all of the successful teachers used the three systematically, and none of them relied primarily on separate or isolated skill instruction. Instead, these teachers provided separated or simulated activities to help students "mark" a skill for future use (Langer, 2000). Students were then able to integrate the skill or knowledge into larger, more meaningful experiences of the curriculum. In contrast, in the more typical classrooms where students were not beating the odds, separate, freestanding skill instruction was the norm. In addition, when readers learn strategies in the context of in-depth content learning, they are more likely to understand the strategies as purposeful tools that they can and will use to support their understanding of new texts (Greenleaf, Schoenbach, Cziko, & Mueller, 2001; Guthrie et al., 1998; RAND Reading Study Group, 2002).

If students are to learn effective reading strategies in the context of real reading, it follows that they need opportunities to read many and diverse types of texts to gain experience, build fluency, and develop a range as readers (Greenleaf et al., 2001, as cited in National Council of Teachers of English [NCTE], 2004). (See also Core Understanding 12.) Classroom contexts that support comprehension development offer large amounts of time spent in real reading, experience reading texts purposefully, and experience reading the range of text genres students are expected to comprehend (Duke & Pearson, 2002). Learning a strategy fully involves repeated opportunities to use it in reading actual texts; over time and across a range of reading experiences, readers build competence in and conscious control over powerful strategies (Allington & McGill-Franzen, 2003; Duke & Pearson, 2002; Kamil, 2003). Clay (1991) describes this process as the construction of inner control, in which the reader takes on the responsibility of learning to read by reading.

Apprenticeship offers a useful metaphor for how powerful reading strategies are acquired in the context of actual reading. A number of middle and high school content area teachers are using Reading Apprenticeship (Schoenbach, Greenleaf, Cziko, & Hurwitz, 1999), an instructional framework informed by work on cognitive apprenticeship (Applebee, 1996; Resnick, 1990; Rogoff, 1990), to demystify the reading processes involved in understanding discipline-based texts and to make these texts accessible to students. As students grapple with challenging texts, they have access to the teacher's and one another's processes for constructing meaning, checking understandings, revising predictions, applying schema, and developing new ones—the myriad reading strategies expert readers in a discipline have at their disposal and can scaffold for their students to take up and master. Teachers are actually apprenticing students into discipline-based ways of thinking, talking, reading, and writing with actual texts (Schoenbach, Braunger, Greenleaf, & Litman, 2003).

Part of the process of learning and eventually controlling powerful reading strategies is metacognitive. As with the strategies themselves, this faculty is best developed in actual engagement with texts. Think-alouds, modeled by the teacher and practiced by the student with authentic text, build metacognitive strategies and improve comprehension (Duke & Pearson, 2002). In Reading Apprenticeship classrooms, conversations about metacognition (how we read, why we read, different strategies in use by students with a given text) lead to conscious, individual metacognition by students as they work with new texts (Greenleaf et al., 2001). In the beating-the-odds schools and classrooms, teachers provided instruction not just in how to accomplish a literacy task but also in how to do it well and monitor one's processes while so engaged (Langer, 2001). To orchestrate the multiple strategies that good readers use as they interact with text, learners need many opportunities to learn and apply those strategies with actual texts. Pressley (2002) describes "metacognitively sophisticated readers" (p. 305) as reading a lot and knowing that strong comprehension requires both knowledge of the strategies they have and can use and moment-to-moment awareness of their reading process as they read.

Readers must learn to recognize the differences within text structures (e.g., poetry, nonfiction, narrative texts). Opportunities to interact with many types of texts, in tandem with explicit instruction in problem-solving strategies for making sense of each type of text, must be provided. Reading instruction across curricular areas (e.g., science, social studies) can provide learners with an understanding of authentic uses for these strategies throughout reading experiences.

Teaching skills and strategies in the context of real reading provides students with opportunities to make sense of what they are reading as well as to experience the how-tos of reading within authentic purposes. Some instructional approaches that emphasize this process are the following:

- *Retellings*: Learners have the opportunity to retell stories or other texts they have read and to relate them to personal experiences. Teachers can use these literacy learning and assessment activities to model good retelling, scaffold the student's understanding of text structure, and build improved comprehension (Beers, 2003; Braunger, 1996; Brown & Cambourne, 1990; Morrow, 1990).

- *Transactional strategies instruction*: Students learn comprehension-monitoring and problem-solving strategies as they read real texts. Teachers encourage personal meanings and emphasize personal enjoyment (Pressley et al., 1992).

- *Reciprocal teaching*: Students use questioning, predicting, clarifying, and summarizing while reading a challenging text interactively in a small group

(Palincsar & Brown, 1984). The purpose of the instructional conversation is not practice with the strategies but a shared understanding of the text. Strategies are only a means to the end (Snow, Burns, & Griffin, 1998).

- *Scaffolded reading experience*: Instructional support before, during, and after reading a text bridges the gap between students' independently achieved comprehension and the deeper understanding set as a goal (Fournier & Graves, 2002; Graves & Graves, 2003).

- *Concept-oriented reading instruction*: Long-term inquiry units combine science and language arts for upper elementary students. Framework elements include opportunities to observe and personalize relevant events and objects, search-and-retrieve processes on subtopics of individual interest, comprehension and integration strategies learned in the context of reading a variety of texts, and synthesis and sharing of findings (Guthrie et al., 1996).

These approaches illustrate ways to incorporate strategy instruction in purposeful reading of authentic texts. The strategies serve the reader in constructing meaning.

TEACHER RESOURCES

Buehl, D. (2001). *Classroom strategies for interactive learning* (2nd ed.). Newark, DE: International Reading Association.

Goodman, Y.M. (1996). I never read such a long story before. In S. Wilde (Ed.), *Notes from a kidwatcher: Selected writings of Yetta M. Goodman* (pp. 53–65). Portsmouth, NH: Heinemann.

Langer, J.A. (2000). *Guidelines for teaching middle and high school students to read and write well: Six features of effective instruction.* Albany: National Research Center on English Learning and Achievement, State University of New York.

National Council of Teachers of English (NCTE). (2003). *Features of literacy programs: A decision-making matrix.* Retrieved September 10, 2004, from http://www.ncte.org/about/over/positions/category/read

---

Students learn best when teachers employ a variety of strategies to model and demonstrate reading knowledge, strategy, and skills.

Students need a wide variety of experiences with texts to gain sophistication in reading. In addition, teachers need to employ a wide variety of teaching strategies to provide the appropriate scaffolds for individual learners. Effective teachers of reading make the instructional decisions concerning how they will provide experiences and opportunities for students to learn to read. The importance of teaching strategies is their eventual uptake by students as internalized, self-regulated learning strategies; thus, effective teachers keep their focus on student agency and empowerment.

Teaching decisions are based on teachers' knowledge and choices. Their knowledge of current best practice in literacy instruction and of each learner's abilities and needs inform their choices regarding the type of instructional setting necessary for an experience (small group, whole group, partner work, individual work) and the need for implicit or explicit instruction in a particular situation.

Darling-Hammond (1999) suggests that the quality of a state's teaching force is a much more powerful predictor of student achievement levels across content areas than other factors, including student demographic characteristics and measures of school resources.

Research About Effective Reading Teachers

Bond and Dykstra (1967/1997) found that the most important variable in the success of beginning readers was the quality of the teacher. Several recent research studies have focused on the attributes of exemplary teachers of reading. Allington and Johnston's (2000, 2002) study of exemplary fourth-grade teachers utilized three types of study: (1) observational, (2) interview, and (3) survey and case study. Thirty teachers in five states were studied, representing diverse communities and populations. Four categories of findings from this work include as essential elements of effective classroom instruction (1) the nature of classroom talk, (2) the nature of the organization and use of curriculum materials, (3) the nature and organization of instruction, and (4) the nature of evaluation (cf. Allington, 2002; Allington & Johnston, 2000, 2002; Allington, Johnston, & Day, 2002).

Langer's (2002) five-year study asked two questions: What kind of middle and high school English instruction is enabling students to develop the kinds of literacy needed for the 21st century? What kinds of instruction (programs) are enabling these teachers to instruct so effectively? (cf., Applebee, Langer, Nystrand, & Gamoran, 2003; Langer, 2001). The study included 25 schools over a wide range of economic and cultural communities, 44 teachers, and 88 classes. Of the 25 schools, 14 were beating the odds; that is, students were engaged in learning and were thinking, writing, and conversing about the literature they were reading. And they were performing better on the state-administered reading and writing tests than were students at schools rated as comparable by state criteria. Six categories of findings from this study include (1) approaches to skills instruction (separated, simulated, and integrated), (2) approaches to test preparations (integrated throughout the curriculum, not only taught as separate), (3) connecting learnings (across the curriculum, across the school, across time, both in and outside of school), (4) enabling strategies (strategic awareness, teaching students strategies, content as well as intentional ways of thinking and doing), (5) conceptions of learning (what counts as knowing, what counts as evaluation; moving students more deeply as well as broadly across concepts and content—a generative approach to learning), and (6) classroom organization (collaborative, cooperative, envisioning; learning as a social activity).

Pressley, Allington, Wharton-McDonald, Block, and Morrow's (2001) study comprises a survey of 30 teachers and case studies of 5 exemplary first-grade teachers. In their findings, the researchers list the following practices as distinguishing first-grade classes with high achievement: instructional balance that integrated skills instruction with holistic activities; instructional density revealed through a great deal going on—in particular, a lot of instruction aimed at achieving multiple goals; scaffolding, where the teacher was able to provide just enough support to enable a student to begin to make progress on a task but not so much as to be doing the task for the student; encouragement of self-regulation; integration of reading and writing; high expectations; and good classroom management (cf. Pressley, Rankin, & Yokoi, 1996; Wharton-McDonald, Pressley, & Hampston, 1998).

A Center for the Improvement of Early Reading Achievement study by Taylor, Pearson, Clark, and Walpole (1999) of 14 elementary schools across urban, suburban, and rural contexts lists the following key findings: The most accomplished teachers were experts at classroom management, organized for high instructional density, and managed to engage virtually all students in the work of the classroom. Small-group instruction was used, averaging 60 minutes a day of small, ability-grouped instruction supported by a schoolwide collaborative model. Independent reading 27–28 minutes a day was an important aspect of the most effective and moderately effective schools. The most effective teachers implemented coaching (e.g., scaffolded instruction). Phonics instruction was explicit and coupled with authentic reading activities—the data suggest that it is what teachers do to promote application of phonic knowledge during the reading of connected text that matters most. Teachers encouraged higher level questions and response to text, and their high expectations for student learning were clear. Finally, reading was an instructional priority.

Results of the Studies

These studies agree that effective and powerful instruction from knowledgeable teachers is the key to successful reading achievement across the K–12 years (cf. Bond & Dykstra, 1967/1997). Based on these studies and several recent syntheses of research and practice in the teaching of reading, exemplary teachers of reading are known to demonstrate the following critical qualities of knowledge and practice. Such teachers

- understand reading and writing development (International Reading Association [IRA], 2000; Snow, Burns, & Griffin, 1998);
- believe that all students can learn to read and write, maintaining high expectations for all (IRA, 2000; Morrow & Asbury, 2003; Pressley et al., 2001; Taylor et al., 1999; Wharton-McDonald et al., 1998);

- engage students much of the time in reading and writing, relating reading instruction and activities to students' background knowledge and experience (Allington & Johnston, 2000, 2002; IRA, 2000; Langer, 2002; Pressley et al., 2001; Snow et al., 1998; Taylor et al., 1999);

- demonstrate effective classroom management techniques appropriate for the developmental levels of students that focus on positive, respectful, reinforcing, participatory, and cooperative environments for learning (Allington & Johnston, 2000, 2002; Langer, 2002; Morrow & Asbury, 2003; Taylor et al., 1999; Pressley et al., 2001; Wharton-McDonald et al., 1998);

- offer a variety of appropriate, engaging, and accessible materials and texts for students to read, including children's and adolescents' literature (Allington & Johnston, 2000, 2002; IRA, 2000; Morrow & Asbury, 2003; Morrow, Tracey, Woo, & Pressley, 1999; Pressley et al., 2001; Snow et al., 1998);

- know a variety of instructional philosophies, methods, and strategies; when to use each and how to combine them into an effective instructional program (IRA, 1999, 2000; Langer, 2002; Morrow & Asbury, 2003; Morrow et al., 1999; Pressley et al., 2001; Snow et al., 1998); and are supported in making these individual classroom decisions (Flippo, 1998, 2001; Langer, 2002; Morrow, Gambrell, & Pressley, 2003);

- balance skills instruction with more holistic teaching as appropriate for developmental levels (Baumann, Hoffman, Moon, & Duffy-Hester, 1998; IRA, 1999; Pressley, 1998; Pressley et al., 2001; Taylor et al., 1999; Wharton-McDonald et al., 1998);

- provide a comprehensive program of skills development in phonemic awareness, phonics, vocabulary, comprehension, and fluency (Morrow & Asbury, 2003; National Institute of Child Health and Human Development [NICHD], 2000; Pressley et al., 2001; Snow et al., 1998);

- use flexible grouping strategies to tailor instruction to individual students (IRA, 2000; Morrow & Asbury, 2003; Morrow et al., 1999; Pressley et al., 2001);

- provide a classroom environment where there is *instructional density*, that is, a lot of instruction going on that achieves multiple goals; transform classroom routines into instruction (Allington & Johnston, 2000, 2002; Langer, 2002; Pressley et al., 2001; Taylor et al., 1999; Wharton-McDonald et al., 1998);

- provide scaffolded instruction to coach students to improve their use of various strategies (Allington & Johnston, 2000, 2002; IRA, 2000; Pressley et al., 2001; Taylor et al., 1999; Wharton-McDonald et al., 1998);

- focus on classroom talk as a critical factor to the social construct as well as the learning objectives of the classroom (Allington & Johnston, 2000, 2002; Applebee et al., 2003);

- demonstrate metacognitive strategies rather than only directly teaching specific skills (Allington & Johnston, 2000, 2002; Langer, 2002; Snow et al., 1998; Taylor et al., 1999);

- focus on helping students internalize these strategies to support their growing independence as readers and problem solvers, encouraging self-regulation (Allington & Johnston, 2000, 2002; Langer, 2002; Taylor et al., 1999; Wharton-McDonald et al., 1998);

- provide connection and integration across the curriculum for using reading as well as all language processes (Allington & Johnston, 2000, 2002; Langer, 2002; Morrow & Asbury, 2003; Pressley et al., 2001);

- monitor student progress, encouraging continual improvement and growth (Allington & Johnston, 2000, 2002; IRA, 2000; Langer, 2002; Snow et al., 1998; Taylor et al., 1999);

- know early intervention techniques and intervene as early as possible (IRA, 1999; Snow et al., 1998);

- involve families and communities in actively supporting students' reading development (Snow et al., 1998); and

- collaborate effectively with colleagues and administrators in appropriate professional development activities, both in design and participation (Langer, 2002; Morrow et al., 1999; Pressley et al., 2001; Taylor et al., 1999).

For the purposes of supporting Core Understanding 11, our review of literature will focus on the categories of emerging instructional models, scaffolded instruction, organizing for instruction, the role of texts in instruction, effective teaching strategies, and learning goals (fluency, comprehension, vocabulary, response to text, and questioning).

An Instructional Model Appropriate to Support Effective Reading Instruction

It is important to understand the elements of different theories and how they become evident in daily classroom practice. What teachers believe about how students acquire and learn language becomes transparent through their instructional stance and consequent instructional decisions; thus the differences found across classrooms. The debate continues over the efficacy of different types of instruction, variously labeled, for example, *direct instruction, explicit instruction, models,* and *demonstrations.* Direct instruction, by itself, holds a wide variety of connotations for educators: Those trained in special education often equate this term with the Distar method (Gersten & Carnine, 1986), whereas many educators trained in current cognitive learning theory define direct instruction as a method using cognitive strategies to directly teach students (cf. Schoenbach, Braunger, Greenleaf, & Litman, 2003). (See Core Understanding 9 for further discussion.)

Much research validates the importance of explicit instruction for the processes and strategies acknowledged by current research (cf. Pressley, 1998, 2000). This strategy suggests that teachers who take the time to model, explain differences, show significance, and guide students in their acquisition and their learning can make an important impact on students' successful learning (Allington & Johnston, 2000, 2002; Langer, 2002; Pressley et al, 2001; Taylor et al., 1999). Our new understandings of how we learn occasion the need to rethink our teaching strategies to move beyond traditional labels and terminology. For the purposes of this book, the term *explicit instruction* will conform to Pearson's definition (see Core Understanding 9).

Although recent syntheses of best practice focus on the importance of a practitioner knowledgeable about a variety of philosophies, theories, and methods and how to implement them (e.g., IRA, 1999), teachers must be careful to avoid simply selecting a random array of the "best" teaching and learning activities from various approaches to literacy instruction as a means of meeting the diverse needs of learners. Rhodes and Dudley-Marling (1996) see a problem with this approach: When choosing activities regardless of their theoretical basis, teachers risk involving students in significant contradictions on the role of readers in making meaning. This type of "eclecticism," they argue, assumes that readers learn to read "once and for all, by whatever means" (p. 28), which ignores the social aspects of literacy. Effective teachers of reading are clear as to the assumptions they convey in regard to how people learn to read and what it means to read (Langer, 2002; Pressley et al., 2001; Taylor et al., 1999). Particularly in the current climate of federal and state legislative mandates on curriculum choice, teachers need to be grounded in and articulate about a solid theoretical understanding for the way in which they are working in order to create instructional plans and learning experiences that honor their beliefs and fit within the context of legislative and curricular program mandates.

Caine and Caine (1997) contend that current learning theory shows the need for a variety of teaching strategies but, most important, emphasizes the needs of individual students. A variety of experiences both in and out of school and a focus on critical thinking are also salient features of emerging theories. Morrow and Asbury (2003) suggest,

> A rich model of literacy learning encompasses both the elegance and the complexity of reading and language arts processes.... Such a model acknowledges the importance of both form (phonemic awareness, phonics, mechanics, and so on) and function (comprehension, purpose, and meaning), and recognizes that learning occurs most effectively in a whole-to-part-to-whole context. (p. 48)

Many researchers agree that no single method or single combination of methods exists that can successfully teach all students to read. This consensus has been consistent over time and developmental level (Adams, 1990; Bond & Dykstra, 1967/1997; Foorman, Francis, Fletcher, Schatschneider, & Mehta, 1998; Hoffman et al., 1994; IRA, 1999, 2000; Snow et al., 1998; Stallings, 1980, 1995). Current research highlights the pros and cons of a variety of instructional models. We will present the most prominent studies in the following sections.

Direct Instruction or Scripted Lessons. Taylor and colleagues (1999) found a negative relationship between a highly teacher-directed stance toward instruction and student reading growth in grades 2–6. Telling students is less effective than coaching students to come up with their own response. Ryder, Sekulski, and Silberg (2003) found that highly scripted, teacher-directed methods of teaching reading in first through third grade were not as effective as methods that allowed a more flexible approach; urban teachers in particular expressed great concern over the lack of sensitivity to the issues of poverty, culture, and race found within this approach. After three years of direct instruction, students scored significantly lower on overall reading achievement and comprehension. Moustafa and Land (2002) found scripted reading instruction was less effective than reading instruction where teachers were allowed to exercise their professional knowledge and match instruction to instructional needs. Moustafa and Land also suggest that veteran teachers are much more able to negotiate adaptations to scripted texts to meet the individual needs of their students. This conclusion contradicts the notion that scripted programs can support weak, undertrained, or beginning teachers.

Many effective reading teachers describe that the instruction they deliver to struggling readers differs only in length and intensity, *not* in format, design, or philosophical underpinnings about how young people learn, specifically how they learn to read (Pressley et al., 2001).

Cognitive Apprenticeship. Some researchers have adopted the metaphor of *cognitive apprenticeship*, based on studies of novice and expert performance on a variety of mental tasks (Resnick, 1990; Rogoff, 1990), to describe a type of teaching designed to assist students in acquiring more proficient cognitive processes for such valued tasks as reading comprehension, composing, and mathematical problem solving (Schoenbach et al., 2003). In an apprenticeship approach, teachers act as mentors to student apprentices, modeling and demonstrating the how-tos of a cognitive task in very explicit ways. They scaffold knowledge and skill in meaningful ways, allowing for extensive practice and application in the task. (See Core Understanding 10 for a description of Reading Apprenticeship.)

Balanced Approaches. Fisher and Adler (1999) found that successful early reading programs for high-poverty schools focused on a balance of instruction and application into authentic literacy events. Sacks and Mergendoller (1997) found that low-level kindergarteners made the most improvement in classrooms with contemporary meaning-emphasis instruction (cf. Anderson, Wilkinson, & Mason, 1991; Cantrell, 1999; Milligan & Berg, 1992). Pressley and colleagues (1996) describe a balanced approach as extremely complicated: "Effective curricular balance can be thought of as juggling hundreds of balls in the air, each carefully coordinated with the other, the particular balance of the balls varying from child to child and from situation to situation throughout the school day" (p. 39). Au and Raphael (1998) suggest five teacher roles in a model of balanced instruction: explicit instructing, modeling, scaffolding, facilitating, and participating. Rankin-Erickson and Pressley (2000) found whole language and skills instruction were complementary (cf. Wharton-McDonald et al., 1997; Morrow et al., 2003; Pressley, 1998).

Engagement Model. Guthrie and Davis (2003) emphasize that cognitive strategy instruction is ineffective if isolated from rich content designed to engage learners, particularly adolescent readers, in using the strategy (cf. Guthrie, Schafer, Von Secker, & Alban, 2000). They suggest that teachers can use six classroom practices to provide support for engaged reading:

1. Construct rich knowledge goals as the basis for reading instruction.

2. Use real-world interactions to connect reading to student experiences.

3. Afford students an abundance of interesting books and materials.

4. Provide some choice among materials to read.

5. Give explicit instruction for important reading strategies.

6. Encourage collaboration in many aspects of learning.

Scaffolding Instruction

The role of *scaffolding*—the careful use of guidance and support—is critical as a way for teachers to structure their instructional interactions with learners (Applebee & Langer, 1983; Bruner, 1975). Modeling as a scaffold of support can occur as part of the everyday literacy experience (e.g., when reading a story aloud to students also engaging them in the meaning of story and conveying a purpose for reading) or as an explicit modeling to demonstrate to students how to approach a task (e.g., how to use a table of contents) (Roehler & Duffy, 1991). To be effective, such modeling practices must be seated within whole literacy events lest they easily become instances of isolated skills teaching. IRA (2000) suggests that effective reading teachers scaffold, or coach, learners as they grow and develop as readers.

Pressley and colleagues (2001) list effective scaffolding as a common instructional technique of the exemplary first-grade teachers they studied. The RAND Reading Study Group (2002) highlights the importance of scaffolded learning for adolescent learners, particularly in literacy learning. They note that careful and slow fading of this scaffolding is important.

Particularly in the case of English-language learners (ELLs), Walqui (2003) describes scaffolding as moving sequentially from structure to process and as having six central features:

1. *Continuity*: Tasks are repeated, with variations, and are connected to one another (e.g., as part of projects).

2. *Contextual support*: Exploration is encouraged in a safe, supportive environment; access to means and goals is promoted in a variety of ways.

3. *Intersubjectivity*: Mutual engagement and rapport are established; there is encouragement and non-threatening participation in a shared community of practice.

4. *Contingency:* Task procedures are adjusted depending on actions of learners; contributions and utterances are oriented towards each other and may be co-constructed.

5. *Handover/takeover:* There is an increasing role for the learner as skills and confidence increase; the teacher watches carefully for the learner's readiness to take over increasing parts of the action.

6. *Flow:* Skills and challenges are in balance; participants are focused on the task and are "in tune" with each other. (p. 6; cf. van Lier, 1996, 2004)

Clearly, appropriate use of scaffolding as an instructional strategy is critical to successful teaching. (See chapter 2 for a foundational discussion of scaffolding as a cognitive process.)

Allington and Johnston (2000, 2002) consider the talk within the classroom to be a key strategy found in the practice of the exemplary fourth-grade teachers they studied; much of the talk represents scaffolding by the teacher for students as well as by the students themselves. Applebee and colleagues (2003) studied discussion-based approaches within secondary English instruction; their findings mirror the importance of the teacher providing scaffolded instruction, as well as the need for students to participate within such structures for the scaffolds to take effect. The social dynamic of talk is critical to effective literacy learning.

Organizing for Instruction: Using Flexible Patterns of Grouping

Effective reading teachers provide a classroom organization that is predictable, where students know the expectations. They create participation structures where students have the opportunity to experience reading individually, with the teacher in small and large groups, and with peers in small and large groups.

Whole-class instruction used exclusively clearly fails to meet the needs of individual students, especially those with learning disabilities (Schumm, Moody, & Vaughn, 2000; Taylor et al., 1999). Lou and colleagues (1996) found conclusive results favoring ability grouping over no grouping at all with positive findings related to achievement, attitude, and self-concept. However, much research has been critical of the long-term effects of ability-focused grouping procedures used consistently over time.

Taylor and colleagues (1999) found that those schools beating the odds focused on small-group instruction in reading interventions. Eighty-three percent of the teachers in the most effective schools agreed that small-group instruction was an important factor in improving struggling readers' achievement. These groups were flexible. Flexible patterns of grouping students are key for effective instruction (Flood, Lapp, Flood, & Nagel, 1992; Opitz, 1998; Wilkinson & Townsend, 2000), as indicated in the following findings:

- Long-term ability grouping can create serious problems for students who are social in nature but cognitive in effect (Allington, 1980; Barr, 1989; Hiebert, 1983; Indrisano & Paratore, 1991; Shannon, 1985).

- Supportive patterns provide a variety of opportunities for social interaction: working individually, working in cooperative groups, working in pairs or small groups to develop questions, meeting in small groups to read to each other, reading aloud to the teacher on an individualized basis, and listening as a whole group to a read-aloud piece of literature and then working individually (Au, 1991; Cunningham, Hall, & Defee, 1991).

- The most appropriate grouping pattern for each instructional experience can be determined only by analyzing student strengths and needs and matching this information with the choices available to the teacher and student. There must be a successful interaction of three sets of variables to ensure student success: (1) choosing the most appropriate basis for grouping, (2) choosing the most effective format, and (3) choosing the most appropriate materials (Flood et al., 1992; cf. IRA, 2000; Taylor et al., 1999).

Wilkinson and Townsend (2000) suggest that ability grouping can be used successfully if three conditions are met:

1. Teachers view ability as incremental and malleable rather than fixed.

2. Teachers ensure a close fit between teachers, texts, and students.

3. Teachers use ability grouping as only one of many arrangements to group students for instruction and other activities.

Tutoring and small-group instruction have become a favored secondary prevention approach for students struggling with reading (Al Otaiba & Fuchs, 2002; Pinnell, Lyons, DeFord, Bryk, & Seltzer, 1994; Slavin, 1990; Vadasy, Jenkins, & Pool, 2000; Wasik, 1998).

Role of Texts in Teaching and Learning to Read

Texts can be considered to be considerate or inconsiderate (Armbruster, 1984)—that is, texts can be written in ways that support readers in their ability to successfully negotiate a text.

Texts for Beginning Readers. Hiebert (1998) analyzed texts historically used in beginning reading, finding that their common attribute was a focus on word features. Currently, however, perspectives such as those represented by cognitive science, reader response, and sociocultural frameworks have drawn attention to their influence on text choice, particularly at the beginning level. Texts must be considered as a whole: their content, text structure, and illustrations, as well as purposes for reading. This criterion is true across K–12 curricular text choice.

Traditional formats for determining the readability of a text to assign a grade-level designation have not been able to account for variations within the first grade (Klare, 1984) or to consider features of text support associated with predictable texts (Rhodes, 1981; cf. Hoffman, Roser, Salas, Patterson, & Pennington, 2000). Clay (1991b) feels teachers fail their students if they attend only to levels of text, noting the critical issue is the interaction between the child and the teacher that accompanies a particular reading.

Fountas and Pinnell (1996, 1999) suggest analyzing authentic texts (children's and adolescents' literature as well as "little books" published as components of beginning reading curricula) by their features of text. In general, the features important to support beginning readers emphasize the naturalness of language, a close picture–text match, predictability of text structure, number and frequency of high-content words essential to meaning, and potential for readers to cross-check data for meaning. Specifically, Fountas and Pinnell (1999) list these characteristics to consider when analyzing texts:

- *Book and print features* include the length, type of print, the layout, punctuation, and illustrations.

- *Content, themes, and ideas* focus on the content (familiarity or technical nature), the general sophistication of the themes represented in the story or event, and the complexity of the ideas presented in the text.

- *Text structure* considers the type of text, narrative or expository, and its success at communicating the story or information.

- *Language and literary features* include perspective of author and/or characters, language structure, literary language/devices, vocabulary, and words. (pp. 18–19)

Hoffman and colleagues (2000) analyzed the use and accuracy of the Fountas and Pinnell (1996, 1999) system and the Scale for Text Accessibility and Support–Grade 1 (Hoffman et al., 1994; Hoffman et al., 1998), a similar analytic structure for text leveling for beginning reading instruction, and found these systems to be largely accurate in their support of beginning reading development.

Use of decodable texts in beginning reading instruction. One of the loudest controversies in beginning reading instruction centers on the value of *decodable texts*, that is, texts that contain only words that have been explicitly taught to children. Research against this practice as the sole focus of beginning reading instruction includes the following studies:

- Rhodes (1979) found that children read and comprehended stories with natural language better than stories with contrived (decodable) language (cf. Bridge, Winograd, & Haley, 1983).

- Tatham (1970) found that children obtained significantly higher comprehension scores on reading materials with natural language patterns.

- Hiebert (1998) suggests that while phonetically regular text is presumed to facilitate acquisition of word-recognition skills, numerous questions remain about the kind and amount of phonics information that beginning readers need and the effects of a diet of phonetically regular texts on children's comprehension of and engagement with text.

The practice of using decodable text as the sole focus of beginning reading instruction is supported by the following studies:

- Foorman, Fletcher, Francis, Beeler, and Winikates (1997) suggest that for a period during beginning reading instruction, all students benefit from practicing letter–sound connections in decodable text.

- Beck (1997) acknowledges gaps in the research literature but suggests that teachers can reach an "educated conclusion" on the appropriate level of decodability by taking into account principles of learning with research on code-emphasis programs finding that 70–80% decodable text would help beginning readers to map speech to print.

Jenkins, Peyton, Sanders, and Vadasy (2004) asked the question, "Do decodable texts add value to supplemental reading tutoring for struggling beginning readers?" (p. 79). Their results show broad effects from tutoring in phonics and word study and storybook reading, but no reliable effects for differing levels of text decodability. They surmise that decodable texts may exert more influence in the earliest stages of reading acquisition. However, if the benefits in decodable text disappear by the end of first grade, they are short lasting. Their results suggest that if decodable texts contribute to reading achievement, even substantial differences in text decodability may not always "power through" other tutorial and background factors. They suggest a case for the use of decodable text:

- It may facilitate alphabetic insight.

- It may exemplify specific graphophonemic connections and may help students to anchor those connections in memory.

- It may enhance motivation and build confidence because the majority of the text yields to a decoding strategy.

Hiebert (1998) suggests that the difference of opinion among educators concerning decodable text is not so much whether decodable texts are ever useful, but how much and for whom to use such texts. She sees numerous questions about texts that support the acquisition of a metacognitive stance toward the linguistic systems of written English: What is the role of illustrations, the density of the text and language structure, and the expectation of vocabulary knowledge in a text that support the reader's understanding of both process and comprehension?

Use of high-frequency words in texts for beginning reading. Simplifying the text to the lowest denominator of high-frequency words does not facilitate the task of learning to read in the manner that the generation of educational psychologists advocating this type of text believed (Hiebert, 1998).

Use of literature as texts in reading instruction. Literature models natural and expected language structures of English and of often used texts (Fisher, Flood, & Lapp, 2003; Moss, 2003; Roser & Keehn, 2002; Roser & Martinez, 2000). Predictable texts (Holdaway, 1979; Martin & Brogan, 1971) provide scaffolds for beginning readers to predict both meaning and word identification of familiar stories.

Block and Mangieri (2002) found that teachers who had a high knowledge of children's and young adult literature and recreational reading activities were lifelong readers themselves. The teachers provided students with a rich and wide array of pleasurable experiences with books and engaged students in books of diverse content, styles, and formats (cf. Galda, Ash, & Cullinan, 2000; Galda & Cullinan, 2003).

Use of expository texts in reading instruction. Duke (2000) found a lack of access and use of expository texts in primary grades. She recommends that beginning readers should be taught specific strategies for reading nonfiction texts and narrative texts.

Texts for Older Readers. Fountas and Pinnell (2001) remind us that a teacher's purpose in preparing instruction and selecting texts must move beyond simply learning more about reading, particularly in the case of upper elementary and adolescent readers. Text selection is critical to engaging students in purposeful reading (cf. Guthrie & Davis, 2003; Schoenbach, Braunger, Greenleaf, & Litman, 1999). Fountas and Pinnell suggest the following list of factors to consider when matching books to the needs of readers:

- readers' present strategies
- readers' interest and background knowledge
- text complexity in relation to readers' current skills
- the language of the text in relation to readers' experience
- the content of the text in relation to readers' background knowledge
- the appropriateness of the content to the age group
- the representation of gender, racial, ethnic, and socioeconomic groups in positive ways
- teacher's assessment of the learning opportunities inherent in a text and their match to your instructional goals
- the quality of text: language, illustrations, layout, and writing style (p. 223)

Knowledge of text structure in fluent reading. The RAND Reading Study Group (2002) found the relationship of a reader's knowledge of text structure to comprehension was key to successful reading. The demands on the reader to understand and use this relationship increase as students move through school.

Use of a wide range of genres across the curriculum. Brozo and Hargis (2003) suggest the use of novels in content area instruction to provide more readable alternatives to the traditional textbook formats often found in the upper grades, through middle and high school. Their reading apprenticeship model suggests that students must be apprenticed to read as historians, scientists, and so forth. The RAND Reading Study Group (2002) highlights the significance of reading more expository texts from the very beginning of schooling.

Hiebert (1998) suggests that the texts we need for effective reading instruction, particularly for beginning readers, must come in the form of multiple-criteria texts. Texts must offer a variety of scaffolds for young readers rather than focusing on only one (e.g., decodable texts). These texts would provide scaffolds to support the development of a variety of knowledges, skills, and strategies critical to effective meaning making in reading.

Learning Goals

In the teaching and learning of reading, instruction focuses on the following learning goals: comprehension, including vocabulary instruction, metacognitive strategies to monitor meaning, discussion and response to text, and questioning strategies to support comprehension; fluency; and word identification. These goals are interconnected in a seamless manner where students are guided to integrate the cues and knowledge gained from each aspect of the reading process.

Comprehension. Research continues to grow in support of the explicit teaching of a range of comprehension strategies that influence how readers make meaning from a text (Brown & Coy-Ogan, 1993; Brown, Pressley, Van Meter, & Schuder, 1996; Collins, 1991; Keene & Zimmermann, 1997; Pressley, 2000; Wilhelm, 2001).

Vocabulary. Word knowledge grows over the school years (Johnson & Anglin, 1995; Roth, Speece, Cooper, & De la Paz, 1996). Nagy and Scott (2000) describe vocabulary development as understanding how schoolchildren add words to their reading and writing vocabularies and how they learn the meanings of new words.

Vocabulary knowledge strongly influences reading comprehension (Anderson & Freebody, 1981; Davis, 1944). Nagy and Scott (2000) propose a perspective beyond a reductionist perspective, traditionally a focus on simply learning the definitions, or meanings, of words. They see a complexity in word knowledge where vocabulary is embedded in authentic, meaningful, and integrated contexts. Learners can gain information about words from context and word parts as well as definitions. The ability to consider a variety of sources of information can assist readers in becoming more aware of the subtle differences in many word meanings.

Nagy and Scott (2000) describe five aspects of this complexity:

1. *Incrementality*: Knowing a word is a matter of degrees, not all-or-nothing.

2. *Multidimensionality*: Word knowledge consists of several qualitatively different types of knowledge.

3. *Polysemy*: Words often have multiple meanings.

4. *Interrelatedness*: One's knowledge of any given word is not independent of one's knowledge of other words.

5. *Heterogeneity*: What it means to know a word differs substantially depending on the kind of word. (p. 270)

Metacognitive strategies. The RAND Reading Study Group (2002) notes the importance of adolescent readers becoming self-initializing in regard to strategy use. Readers are aware of ways to improve their reading, including their conscious control of strategies as they read (Alexander & Murphy, 1998). (See Core Understanding 10 for further discussion.)

Discussion and response to text. The context within which any teaching strategy is employed is critical to success. Given that reading is a socially constructed event, carried out via interactions with others within a particular social group, the discussions involved in response to any text are vital to students' success as readers. Those who participate in discussions are active learners who engage in the construction of knowledge (Gambrell, 1996). Thus, the primary goal of instruction through discussion is to help students construct personal meanings in response to new experiences rather than to simply learn the meanings others have created (Poplin, 1988). Discussions—of ideas generated by the reading and of ideas generated about the process of reading—support learning through the social interactions of students to construct knowledge.

When students are encouraged to verbalize their ideas and questions, cognitive development is supported. They learn how to realize uncertainties in their understandings, explain and justify their positions, seek information to help them resolve the uncertainty, and learn to see alternative points of view (Almasi, 1995; Brown & Palinscar, 1989; Doise & Mugny, 1984; Johnson & Johnson, 1979; Mugny & Doise, 1978). Student interaction in discussions promotes the ability to think critically and to consider multiple perspectives (Almasi, 1995; Applebee et al., 2003; Green & Wallet, 1981; Hudgins & Edelman, 1986; Prawat, 1989; Villaume & Hopkins, 1995) and develops the ability to confirm, extend, and modify individual interpretations of texts (Eeds & Wells, 1989; Leal, 1992). Discussion promotes deep understanding of text (Eeds & Wells, 1989; Morrow & Smith, 1990; Nystrand, 1997; Palincsar, 1987; Palincsar & Brown, 1984).

Students who talk about what they read are more likely to be motivated to read (Guthrie, Schafer, Wang, & Afflerbach, 1995; Morrow & Weinstein, 1986). Student participation in discussions increases self-esteem while fostering positive attitudes, quality communication skills, and friendships among students of different backgrounds (Almasi, 1995; Eeds & Wells, 1989; Goatley & Raphael, 1992; Philips, 1973; Slavin, 1990). The quality of the discourse in discussions is more complex than the dialogue of students who participate in more traditional teacher-led recitations (Almasi, 1995; Applebee et al., 2003; Eeds & Wells, 1989; Leal, 1992; Sweigart, 1991).

Response to literature through discussion can be implemented in a variety of ways. Group discussions of texts are influenced by the following:

- *Text type*: Texts that support both reading ability and interest provide a solid foundation for successful discussion (Horowitz & Freeman, 1995; Leal, 1992).

- *Group size*: Small group is preferable—large enough to ensure diversity of ideas, yet small enough so that each student has an opportunity to fully participate (Davidson, 1985; Morrow & Smith, 1990; Palincsar, Brown, & Martin, 1987; Rogers, 1991; Sweigert, 1991; Wiencek & O'Flavahan, 1994).

- *Leadership*: Clearly, students profit from their own agendas during discussion; however, it appears that they also profit from teacher guidance. Teachers play a significant role in guiding students toward higher level discussions as they engage in modeling behavior, providing frameworks for approaching texts and posing interpretive questions (McGee, 1992; O'Flavahan, Stein, Wiencek, & Marks, 1992).

- *Cultural background of participants* (Heath, 1983; White, 1990): Learning that focuses on cooperation and interaction has been found to be highly effective in improving achievement among African American students (Strickland & Ascher, 1992), native Hawaiian students, and Hispanics (Wong Fillmore & Meyer, 1992).

Teachers can support collaborative discussion in the following ways:

- Pair students with a buddy to interact and problem solve. Discussion becomes more productive as students gain in social skills.

- Form a cooperative learning group of students with varying abilities to read, discuss, or respond to a piece of text. More formal approaches include literature circles (Short, Harste, & Burke, 1996) and Book Clubs (Raphael, Florio-Ruane, & George, 2001; Raphael & McMahon, 1994).

- Use story retellings as a beginning framework for discussion of texts. This approach is particularly successful for students who come from cultures with a rich oral tradition (Thompson, Mixon, & Serpell, 1996).

- Use the discussion structure of the prominent culture in discussions of texts whenever possible. For example, Au (1993) uses the Hawaiian "talk-story" structure to provide native Hawaiian students with a familiar discussion format.

- Focus courses for adolescents around one or more central topics of conversation. This focus provides support for students' knowledge and understanding to develop cumulatively as they revisit main issues and concepts from new perspectives (Applebee, Burroughs, & Stevens, 2000).

Written response to what is read is also essential. Writing provides scaffolds and models for students as they write about their thoughts, feelings, and ideas. Students can document what they have read and their responses to it in literature logs. Following simple formats, young children can compose significant artifacts of their growing sophistication as readers. In addition, children can respond to reading through drama, dance, and art.

Questioning strategies. Once thought of as a hierarchical set of levels through which to move, questioning is now viewed as a complex cognitive process. Not only must teachers move students—even those at early and emergent stages of reading—beyond literal levels of recall to levels of synthesis, evaluation, comparison–contrast, and problem solving, they must also teach students to ask a wide variety of questions rather than to simply look for details within a text. Questions, rethinking, and refined understandings result when students discuss their understandings of themes or concepts that appear in a text (Langer, 1993). Questioning is a vital element in the processes of reading that also include the ability to predict, summarize, clarify, and build knowledge. Formats for supporting students in using questioning as an effective reading strategy include the following:

- *Question–answer relationships (QARs)* (Raphael, 1986): Readers are given clues to help them find information in the text and in their heads. Because of its specificity, Thompson and colleagues (1996) suggest this format for culturally diverse students.

- *Reciprocal teaching* (Palincsar & Brown, 1984): Students take turns in pairs asking questions about and summarizing pieces of text. Gradually, they work independently from the teacher. This strategy improves engagement, comprehension, and cognitive processing.

- *Questioning the author (QtA)* (Beck, McKeown, Hamilton, & Kucan, 1997): Teachers and students engage in a process of questioning before, during, and after reading to support the construction of meaning from texts. QtA involves students in collaborative discussion where everyone talks together to construct meaning. Teachers are able to demonstrate and model strategies for meaning making within this structure.

Fluency. Successful readers are *fluent* readers; that is, they are able to rapidly and smoothly process text in what appears to be an effortless construction of meaning. Clearly, then, fluent reading is a critical component of reading development (Allington, 1983; Chomsky, 1976; Dowhower, 1991; Kuhn & Stahl, 2000; NICHD, 2000; Snow et al., 1998).

Although some believe that *automaticity*, that is, the ability to quickly decode words, is the critical aspect of fluency (Samuels, 1994), others believe fluency to be the complex interrelationship of processes that allows the reader to flexibly, rapidly, and often without conscious attention access information and simultaneously gain meaning from the text (Clay, 1991a). Becoming a fluent reader may have as much to do with meaning construction as it has to do with attending to the words on a page (Pinnell et al., 1995). Fluency varies with the type and difficulty of a text; those readers who are fluent also know how to change the rate of reading to meet the needs of the transaction between the text and themselves. It is thus impossible to become consistently fluent with every kind of text.

Recognizing that the ultimate goal of reading is the construction of meaning, Dowhower (1991) suggests that the role fluency plays in a reader's comprehension needs to be determined. She offers two aspects of this role: (1) the contribution of automatic word recognition to comprehension and (2) prosody, the ability to read with appropriate expression.

Rasinski (2004) is concerned with the current emphasis on speed and accuracy over meaning. He views this emphasis as a corruption of the concept of reading fluency: If speed is emphasized at the expense of prosodic and meaningful reading, students will become fast readers who understand little of what they have read.

One imperative goal, then, is for students to gain an increasingly wider range of reading situations in which they are fluent. In addition to the fluency studies previously discussed, research on reading fluency has produced the following noteworthy findings:

- Oral reading fluency has a significant relationship with reading comprehension during early stages of reading development. The results of the National Assessment of Educational Progress Integrated Reading Performance Record Assessment suggest reading fluency may have as much to do with gaining meaning from text as it does with being highly accurate with words (Pinnell et al., 1995). In comparison, the relationship between accuracy and overall fluency appears to be much weaker.

- Oral reading fluency appears to be related to the access to and interaction with a wide variety of literacy experiences, including the use of libraries and other activities outside of school (Pinnell et al., 1995). Fluent reading may be, in part, a result of frequent practice in reading (Anderson, Wilson, & Fielding, 1988; Watkins & Edwards, 1992).

- Accuracy, rate, and fluency are interrelated in some ways. Pinnell and colleagues (1995) found that highly accurate performance did not necessarily guarantee highly fluent reading; this is also true to some extent for reading rate.

- Fluency appears to be more than simply a sum of its parts (Pinnell et al., 1995). Reading accurately, while important, is not sufficient for supporting fluent reading. Fluent readers must be able to use an awareness of syntax, phrasing, and expression that undoubtedly goes beyond simply being able to read words.

- A lack of fluency in reading could be situated in several interrelated sources including the student's perception that reading is the correct recognition of words, the student's fear of taking risks in the process of reading, and the student's store of knowledge about reading as language (Harste & Burke, 1980).

- Miscue research demonstrates that often no difference exists in the use of graphophonics by proficient and nonproficient readers; rather, the difference is found in their use of syntax and semantics in conjunction with graphophonics (Cambourne & Rousch, 1982; Goodman, Watson, & Burke, 1987; Pflaum & Bryan, 1982). Nonproficient readers' limited store of information about reading can also limit their fluency.

- Students' perceptions about reading affect their reading performance (Harste & Burke, 1980). Helping students to understand their own perceptions of what reading is and what good readers do is a critical step in moving them toward more fluent reading.

Word Identification. Readers use a variety of cues through which to gain access to texts (Clay, 1991a). These include visual (symbolic) cues, structural (syntactic) cues, and semantic (meaning) cues. Word identification takes place using information from any or all of these cues; however, one of the main goals of beginning reading instruction is to help young children become efficient and strategic at putting this information to work.

Word identification occurs through decoding strategies, often employing knowledge of patterns and structures of language, through recognition of familiar sight vocabulary, and through the use of context clues to validate word recognition. (See Core Understanding 9 for further discussion.)

Teaching Strategies for Effective Reading Instruction

As teachers devise ways to effectively meet the needs of all students, they should provide a variety of opportunities for students to interact with text. Depending on the purpose and amount of guidance, an individual child will work with texts at various levels of difficulty. Using strategies before, during, and after reading supports fluency and comprehension.

In his study of effective teaching and learning activities in literacy instruction, Cambourne (2001) found that these activities meet three criteria: (1) They engage learners in the activity; (2) they allow students to internalize and transfer knowledge, skill, and strategy; and (3) they promote collaborative, independent, and interdependent learning. He describes such teaching and learning activities as follows:

- Explicitly linked to other parts of classroom content. Literacy instruction is not a stand-alone experience. Deliberate links are explicit to both teachers and students.

- Frequently introduced by language that explicitly states the teacher's learning purposes for the activity.

- Providing opportunities for students to engage in social interaction and cognitive collaboration employing discussion and reflection.

- Structured so that learners were encouraged to use more than one mode of language.
- Structured so that learners were encouraged to draw on more than one sub-system of language.
- Structured so that learners were frequently encouraged to transfer meaning across or within different semiotic systems.
- Structured so that learners were able to offer a range of acceptable responses.
- Cost-efficient and developmentally appropriate.

Particular kinds of teaching models and demonstrations have been documented as important to include in effective reading programs. These models and demonstrations will be discussed in the sections that follow.

Shared Reading. Holdaway (1979) built this model on his observations of the scaffolding opportunities found in lap-reading sessions with young children. He found adult readers incorporating many strategies to support emergent readers in the knowledge, skill, and strategy they were learning, including asking questions and encouraging children to participate in various ways in the reading. This strategy traditionally involves the use of an enlarged text (e.g., a Big Book), allowing readers to work collaboratively with a teacher and peers to read the text.

Usually designed for use in a whole-group setting, shared reading provides many models and demonstrations within the context of real text. The teacher provides an introduction to a particular reading concept, strategy, or skill often using the enlarged text. Fountas and Pinnell (1996) found that a shared reading experience explicitly demonstrates early strategies such as word-by-word matching; builds a sense of story and ability to predict; demonstrates processes of reading extended text; like reading aloud, involves students in an enjoyable and purposeful way; provides social support from the group; provides an opportunity to participate and behave like a reader; and creates a body of known texts that students can use for independent reading and as resources for writing and word study (Holdaway, 1979; Martinez & Roser, 1985; Pappas & Brown, 1987; Rowe, 1987; Snow, 1983; Sulzby, 1985; Teale & Sulzby, 1986). Eldredge, Reutzel, and Hollingsworth (1996) found that shared reading experiences were superior to round robin reading in measures of decoding accuracy, fluency, vocabulary, and comprehension for all levels of readers.

Fountas and Pinnell (2001) describe shared reading for upper elementary and adolescent readers as a process of sharing cognitive processes for reading a shared text. All students have the same text, either a personal copy or a projected copy to be viewed. Students may choral read or simply follow along as the teacher talks about features and strategies pertaining to the text. Fountas and Pinnell suggest that this style of shared reading supports the development of fluency.

Allen (2003) describes shared reading experiences for upper elementary and adolescents including choral reading, collaborative reading, and Readers Theatre. Allen views these experiences as opportunities for incidental word study where students have the opportunity to see and hear words at the same time.

Reading Aloud. With the publication of *Becoming a Nation of Readers* (Anderson, Hiebert, Scott, & Wilkinson, 1985), the practice of reading aloud children's and young adult literature has been endorsed as one of the most important things educators can do to enhance students' achievement and pleasure reading. Elley (1992) found that frequent story reading aloud by teachers was a factor consistently differentiating countries with high reading scores. Much research supports this strategy of continually modeling reading practices and allowing children to "experience and contemplate literary work they cannot yet read" (Fountas & Pinnell, 1996, p. 1). Reading aloud involves students in reading for enjoyment; demonstrates reading for a purpose; provides for an adult demonstration of phrased, fluent reading; develops a sense of story; develops knowledge of written language syntax; develops knowledge of how texts are structured; increases vocabulary; expands linguistic repertoire; supports intertextual ties; creates a community of readers through enjoyment and shared knowledge; makes complex ideas available to students; promotes oral language development; and establishes known texts to use as a basis for writing and other activities through rereading (Adams, 1990; Beck & McKeown, 2001; Clark, 1976; Cochran-Smith, 1984; Cohen, 1968; Durkin, 1966; Goodman, 1984; Green & Harker, 1982; Hiebert, 1983; Ninio, 1980; Pappas & Brown, 1987; Schickedanz, 1978; Wells, 1986).

Duchein and Mealey (1993) found that teachers who read aloud to upper elementary, middle, and high school students made significant, positive, and long-lasting impressions on their students. Richardson (2000) provides support for reading aloud to adolescents in middle and high schools. She suggests that secondary teachers who read aloud are exposing students to important messages about reading, including the following:

- Teachers like to read a wide variety of materials.

- Teachers enjoy their students and want to share this reading with them.

- Teachers see connections between content topics and pleasure reading.

- Teachers show students how to be expressive readers. (pp. 3–4)

Duke (2000) and Pressley and colleagues (2001) found that incorporating children's and young adult literature via read-alouds into content area lessons provided significant models of nonfiction texts as well as models of appropriate strategies for successfully reading informational texts.

Fisher, Flood, Lapp, and Frey (2004) studied teachers as they implemented interactive read-alouds with their students and determined a set of essential components of an interactive read-aloud:

- *Text selection*: Texts are selected based on the interests and needs of the students. Teachers were consistently observed selecting high-quality children's and young adult literature, often including award-winning books such as Newbery or Caldecott Medal and Honor winners.

- *Previewed and practiced*: Teachers practiced reading aloud before reading in front of students, working on where they would model and point out particular aspects of the text.

- *Clear purpose established*: Teachers established a clear purpose for the read-aloud. Students know what they are to be focusing on while they are listening or as they respond to the text.

- *Fluent reading modeled*: Teachers practice so they are modeling fluent reading. There are few errors.

- *Animation and expression*: Students were engrossed in books in part because of the way their teachers read them—with animation and expression.

- *Discussing the text*: Expert teachers constantly demonstrated the strategic use of book discussions. These teachers use a balance of efferent and aesthetic questions during their read-alouds.

- *Independent reading and writing*: Expert teachers were able to connect their read-alouds to independent reading and writing that were occurring over the day.

Oral Reading. In traditional methodology, round robin reading, in which each child takes a turn reading the same text, is still a commonly observed practice. However, many researchers have been critical of such practices (Taubenheim & Christensen, 1978; Taylor & Connor, 1982; True, 1979). Several reasons are cited regarding why group oral reading is often not the best choice, including the lack of provision for opportunities for a great deal of reading of complete text (Allington, 1980; Hoffman, 1981) and lack of the development of effective, efficient, and independent reading strategies. Also, round robin reading often interferes with comprehension development because of the focus on correctly pronouncing the words; this is particularly true for poor readers (Hoffman, 1981; Winkeljohann & Gallant, 1979). Despite its pervasive use in elementary reading instruction throughout most of the 20th century, round robin reading has never been widely advocated or endorsed by scholars of reading (Beach, 1993).

Currently, oral reading still holds a purpose in reading instruction. Rasinski and Hoffman (2003) suggest four strands that support the potential role for oral reading in instruction: (1) oral reading fluency, (2) teacher responses to oral reading miscues, (3) self-monitoring and miscue analysis, and (4) guided reading and strategy development. In their view, oral reading is a strategy to practice fluency and to monitor and assess accuracy and comprehension.

Teachers can provide a variety of oral reading opportunities for students to enhance their reading development:

- *Repeated readings* (Dahl, 1979; Dowhower, 1989, 1994; Samuels, 1979): Students repeatedly read selected passages until a predetermined level of fluency is reached. Freeland, Skinner, Jackson, McDaniel, and Smith (2000) find this strategy particularly helpful for adolescent readers.

- *Assisted readings* (Knapp & Winsor, 1998; Topping 1987, 1989, 1995): Students read a text aloud while listening to a fluent rendering of the same text by a reading partner, a group reading chorally, or a recording. Kuhn and Stahl (2000) and the National Reading Panel (NICHD, 2000) agree that oral reading with assistance holds significant promise for helping developing fluency and overall reading achievement among elementary grade students and students at all ages experiencing difficulties in reading (Rasinski & Hoffman, 2003).

- *Fluency instruction routines*: These routines may include shared book experiences (Holdaway, 1979), oral recitation lessons (Hoffman, 1987), and fluency development lessons (Rasinski, Padak, Linek, & Sturtevant, 1994).

- *Embedded fluency instruction*: Rasinski and Hoffman (2003) suggest that fluency instruction may play an important and integral role in more elaborate instructional routines. Including intentional instruction focusing on fluency in combination with other learning outcomes provides learners with opportunities to orchestrate a range of strategies and skills.

- *Indirect approaches to fluency instruction*: Rasinksi and Hoffman (2003) suggest that natural ways of integrating oral reading practice throughout the curriculum is essential to supporting fluency development. Integrating performance opportunities is one way to provide students with authentic experiences. One approach is Readers Theatre (Worthy & Prater, 2002), appropriate across all grade levels (Ivey & Broaddus, 2001; Martinez, Roser, & Strecker, 1999; Rinehart, 1999; Worthy & Broaddus, 2002).

Explicit Strategy Instruction. Alexander, Graham, and Harris (1998) identified six attributes of strategies: They are (1) procedural, (2) purposeful, (3) effortful, (4) willful, (5) essential, and (6) facilitative. They differentiate skills from strategies: Skills are essential academic habits—routinized, automatic procedures we employ in any nontrivial tasks. Skills become strategies when readers become cognizant of their performance limitations, intentionally weigh their options, and willfully execute compensatory procedures (Alexander & Jetton, 2000). Readers must be able to determine which strategies to use depending on the content and difficulty of the text (Alexander & Jetton, 2000; Bransford, Brown, & Cocking, 1999; Paris & Jacobs, 1984). Explicit instruction in such strategies, where teachers continually model and demonstrate as well as talk about what they are doing, is critical to students gaining the necessary metacognitive awareness (Greenleaf, Schoenbach, Cziko, & Mueller, 2001; Paris, Wasik, & Turner, 1991; Pressley, 1998). Dowhower (1999) calls for explicit instruction of strategies to enhance comprehension.

Explicit Word Study. Word study can encompass a variety of aspects of words—from the letter–sound level, to the word level, to the meaning level. Cunningham and Allington (2003; cf. Cunningham, 2000) talk about activities that help students build basic understandings about words and letter–sound patterns, that ensure students develop an instant and automatic ability to read and write high-frequency words, that focus on the important skill of cross-checking meaning with letter–sound knowledge, and that establish learning patterns for decoding and spelling. Vocabulary development also fits into this category of explicit word study.

Focus on understanding word structures and patterns. Patterns and structures of words are important focuses for instruction. Beginning readers will spend more time focusing at the word level (see Core Understanding 9). Upper elementary and adolescent readers will focus more on cross-checking meaning with letter–sound knowledge and working with multisyllabic words. Cunningham and Allington (2003; cf. Cunningham, 2000) suggest a wide range of activities to support students in their acquisition of word knowledge across grade levels, including the following:

- *Beginning readers*: Counting words (understanding a duration of a word, ability to count words said); clapping syllables (pulling apart aspects of a word); playing blending and segmenting games; reading rhyming books (use rhyming books to point out patterns in words); saying tongue twisters (highlighting beginning sounds).

- *Elementary school readers*: Using word walls (Cunningham, 2000); cross-checking through activities such as guess-the-covered-word; making words (Cunningham, 2000).

- *Adolescent readers*: Studying patterns and structures of more complex words (Fountas & Pinnell, 2001).

Focus on vocabulary acquisition. Blachowicz and Fisher (2000, 2003) describe the guidelines for effective vocabulary instruction that applies across most situations. Such instruction accomplishes the following:

- Builds a word-rich environment in which students are immersed in words for both incidental and intentional learning and the development of *word awareness*.

- Helps students develop as independent word learners; that is, they are active in developing their understanding of words and ways to learn them.

- Uses instructional strategies that not only teach vocabulary but also model good word-learning behaviors; students should be able to personalize their word learning.

- Provides explicit instruction for important content and concept vocabulary drawing from multiple sources of meaning through repeated exposure.

- Uses assessment that matches the goal of instruction.

Rich vocabulary can be modeled in classrooms in a variety of ways: By providing an environment rich in oral language opportunities, immersing students in a "flood of words" (Cunningham & Stanovich, 1998; Hart & Risley, 1995); reading aloud to students (Elley, 1988; Snow et al., 1998); providing opportunities for active listening to storybooks (Dickinson & Smith, 1994; Stahl, Richek, & Vandevier, 1991); providing opportunities for wide reading (Herman, Anderson, Pearson, & Nagy, 1987; Nagy, Herman, & Anderson, 1985); engaging students in discussion (Stahl & Vancil, 1986; Snow, 1991); and modeling pleasurable word learning and participation in word games (Blachowicz & Fisher, 2003). Bos and Anders (1989, 1990, 1992) found that interactive techniques for teaching and learning vocabulary were much more effective than traditional definitional instruction. Specific strategies include the following:

- *Word play*: Blachowicz and Fisher (2000, 2003) suggest that playing with words is one way to incorporate explicit attention to word aspects. The ability to play with words shows an ability to reflect on, manipulate, combine, and recombine the components of words and helps to develop metalinguistic reflection on words as objects to be manipulated intelligently and for humor (Nagy & Scott, 2000; Tunmer, Herriman, & Nesdale, 1988).

- *Semantic mapping* (Pittelman, Levin, & Johnson, 1985). Finesilver (1994) highlights the successful use of semantic mapping as a strategy for adolescent readers.

- *Concept of definition maps* (MacKinnon, 1993; Schwartz & Raphael, 1985). Similar to semantic mapping, this strategy focuses on helping learners define a concept and determine the essential aspects of the concept.

Guided Reading. Usually designed for use with small groups of students, guided reading provides a setting where teachers can focus on reading strategies for particular students as they evolve into independent readers. This teaching strategy provides the opportunity for students to read a wide variety of texts; to problem solve while reading for meaning; to use strategies on complete, extended text; and to attend to words in text. In addition, guided reading requires that teacher selection of text, guidance, demonstration, and explanation be made explicit to the reader (Clay, 1991a, 1991b; Holdaway, 1979; Lyons, Pinnell, & DeFord, 1993; McKenzie, 1986; Meek, 1988; Routman, 1991; Wong, Groth, & O'Flavahan, 1994). Guided reading offers teachers specific opportunities to model and show readers particular aspects of the reading process. It gives students the opportunity to develop as individual readers while participating in a socially supported activity and gives teachers ongoing opportunities to observe individuals as they process new texts (cf. Clay, 1991a; Fountas & Pinnell, 1996). Biddulph (2002) highlights that the teacher's role in guided reading is to actively enhance students' understanding, enabling teachers to become aware of and cater effectively to the diversity of understanding that students bring to their readings. She suggests that guided reading is essentially a carefully managed "social occurrence."

For upper elementary and middle school students, a similar framework for instruction can be found in the directed reading–thinking activity (Wilkerson, 1999). For middle and high school students, content area strategies can also be developed through concept-oriented reading instruction (see Core Understandings 7 and 10).

Individual (Independent) Reading. Individual reading can take several forms. A more structured format focuses on particular kinds of reading to support practice in specific teacher-modeled strategies, often in conjunction with guided reading (Fountas & Pinnell, 1996, 2001). A less structured format focuses on giving readers opportunities to make independent choices of interesting texts to read for enjoyment and information. Both formats can provide opportunities to apply reading strategies independently; provide time for sustained reading behavior; challenge readers to work on their own and to use strategies on a variety of texts; challenge readers to solve words independently while reading texts well within their own control; promote fluency through rereading; build confidence through sustained, successful reading; and provide the opportunity for students to support one another while reading (Clay, 1991a; Holdaway, 1979; McKenzie, 1986; Meek, 1988; Taylor, 1983). Taylor and colleagues (1999) found that approximately 30 minutes a day of independent reading was a hallmark of successful elementary school classrooms.

Sustained silent reading (SSR) is the most familiar structure found in schools K–12. Yoon (2002) found in a meta-analysis of studies on SSR that this experience showed significant reading attitude gains (cf. Mathewson, 1994; McKenna, 1994). Smith and Joyner (1990; cf. Block & Mangieri, 2002) found that students who engaged in ongoing recreational literacy activities during school hours read books out of school more frequently and significantly increased their independent reading levels on informal reading inventories. Gallik (1999) found that the amount of time that students spend in recreational reading is a predictor of students' academic success. Schoenbach and colleagues (1999) describe a way of creating an accountability system for students to document their independent reading. Students write in response to their reading in daily reading logs, often referring to their responses to make connections and support reading and writing tasks within the curriculum.

Writing. As highlighted in Core Understanding 4, writing processes are parallel to, and thus in support of, reading processes. Students who write in response to reading use reading models to support their writing projects, and through such practice they continue to develop the abilities to think, read, and write.

Successful teachers of reading and language arts integrate writing throughout the daily curriculum (Allington & Johnston, 2000, 2002; Langer, 2002; Pressley et al., 2001; Taylor et al., 1999). They provide students with a variety of opportunities for scaffolded instruction in learning how to write, while students are participating in authentic and meaningful writing tasks.

Strategies for Struggling Readers

In their studies of effective first-grade, fourth-grade, and secondary English teachers, Pressley and colleagues (2001), Allington and Johnston (2000, 2002), and Langer (2002), respectively, found that effective teachers tended not to treat struggling readers differently in their philosophy, approach, instructional design, and high expectation. However, struggling readers were given more intense time and focus during instruction. Taylor and colleagues (1999) also found that high-poverty schools beating the odds of success had a majority of teachers who provided this type of instruction to help struggling students become successful readers. Baker and Allington (2003) believe that students who find learning to read and write more difficult are best served not by identifying or labeling them, but by designing and delivering sufficient and appropriate instruction and substantial opportunities to actually engage in real reading and writing activities.

Cunningham and Allington (2003) agree, suggesting that teachers can provide support for students who find learning to read a challenge by incorporating instruction in which students develop thoughtful literacy across the curriculum. This type of literacy instruction includes the following:

- Lots of reading and writing activities that are meaningful and connect to the real world.

- Activities designed to produce fluent decoders and spellers, even of big words.

- Comprehension lessons in which students learn to think about, compare, and evaluate what they read.

- Writing lessons in which students learn to write thoughtful responses to what they are learning and reading about.

- Multilevel instruction that has a variety of things to be learned and allows everyone to experience success.

- An emphasis on applying reading and writing strategies to learn content area knowledge, particularly in science and social studies. (p. 193)

Much of the research around successful interventions for struggling readers also emphasizes explicit, direct instruction incorporating continued models and demonstrations for important reading strategies, consistent and constant informal assessment to guide instruction and track progress, and the use of collaborative work with peers as an effective scaffold (cf. Allington & Johnston, 2000, 2002; Baker & Allington, 2003; Cunningham & Allington, 2003; Guthrie & Davis, 2003; Langer, 2002; Pressley, 1998; Pressley et al., 2001; Snow et al., 1998; Taylor et al., 1999). (See initial discussion of struggling readers in chapter 3.)

Beginning Readers. Snow and colleagues (1998) review intervention strategies for beginning readers who show signs of struggling. These strategies often focus on small-group and one-on-one tutoring experiences for learners that provide more intensive and focused instruction on reading knowledge, skill, and strategy. Snow and others highlight the need for continual assessment and documentation of students' progress in gaining developmentally appropriate reading ability. However, they agree that most students who struggle to read do not require instruction that is substantially different from their more successful peers; rather, they require a greater intensity of high-quality instruction (cf. Klenk & Kibby, 2000).

Elementary-Grade Readers. Baker and Allington (2003) suggest that exemplary classroom teachers are critical to the continued support of students who are at risk for struggling with literacy tasks. They also suggest that the roles of special program personnel are to work with classroom teachers to enhance the quality of literacy instruction offered as part of the general education experience in a variety of ways and to provide additional direct instruction to students who find learning to read difficult, extending classroom lessons and offering more intensive and personalized attention.

Adolescent Readers. Guthrie and Davis (2003) define struggling adolescent readers as students who are disengaged from any or all aspects of literacy (social, emotional, cognitive, pragmatic); in particular, they are disengaged from reading activities that are related to schooling. These students possess lower cognitive competence and lower intrinsic motivation and self-efficacy; they are socially marginalized as well. Guthrie and Davis suggest that teachers create classrooms that include literacy activities as previously described by Cunningham and Allington (2003), including constructing rich knowledge goals as the basis of reading instruction, using real-world interactions to connect reading to student experiences, providing students with an abundance of interesting books and materials, offering some choice among materials to read, providing direct instruction for important reading strategies, and encouraging collaboration in many aspects of learning. Ivey and Baker (2004) agree, highlighting that most often these readers need this kind of support rather than continued, repeated emphasis on phonics instruction.

One successful intervention found in the literature matches struggling high school readers with elementary school students as reading buddies (Brozo & Hargis, 2003). The most potent benefit of this type of program is that it imbues struggling readers with a sense of responsibility and purpose for improving their own abilities (Avery & Avery, 2001; Wilhelm, Baker, & Dube, 2001).

English-Language Learners. Miller and Endo (2004) suggest ways in which classroom teachers can help create a more inclusive learning environment for immigrant students:

- *Reduce the cognitive load*: Choose activities and assignments that allow students to draw from their prior knowledge and life experience.

- *Evaluate teaching strategies and approaches*: Reflect on classroom management styles: Do they support cultural expectations of immigrant students?

Provide structures and routines that outline clear directions and allow for a variety of acceptable responses (oral, written, with a partner, in groups).

- *Reduce the cultural load*: Show respect for students' homes and communities, their primary languages, and cultures; accept different ways of speaking English (Alidou, 2000).

- *Reduce the language load*: Rewrite difficult texts using simpler terms; break up complex sentences into smaller sentences; provide instruction for unfamiliar vocabulary; offer a variety of texts around subject area topics.

- *Native language versus English*: Some studies show benefits to students holding on to their native language whether it is used in the classroom or at home. Students who continue to speak their native language have greater success in learning English; bilingual speakers have been found to have a lower dropout rate than those who speak only English (Rong & Preissle, 1997). Teachers can support the use of native languages in the classroom while also being sensitive to the students' need to learn English (Igoa, 1995).

- *Parents and teachers as a team*: Wong Fillmore (2000) suggests four steps parents and teachers need to take to support immigrant students: (1) see the need for the student to learn the native language in addition to English, (2) be aware of potentially traumatic emotional experiences that immigrant students may face, (3) watch for negative experiences in the immigrant student's life, and (4) encourage involvement in community events that help promote ethnic languages and cultures.

Walqui (2003) sees scaffolding instruction for ELLs as critical. She suggests the following strategies:

- *Modeling*: Give students clear examples of what is requested of them so they can try it on their own. One suggestion is to provide a bookmark with explicit clarifying strategies on it for students to try.

- *Bridging*: Build on previous knowledge, understanding, and experience. It is important for ELLs to see that their background knowledge is valued in the classroom. A common example is to activate students' prior knowledge.

- *Contextualization*: Provide students with a sensory context—such as using manipulatives, pictures, a few minutes of film without sound, and other types of realia—to make expository language accessible.

- *Schema building*: Provide students with ways to preview a text, building on background knowledge, or provide an advance organizer that helps students see the important information.

- *Text re-presentation*: Use a variety of texts around a particular topic area. For example, to flesh out the deeper meanings of a journalistic article, the teacher may re-present the text through a play or other format. The students will need to reread the original article to add meaning to the re-presented text, and they will need to write, practice, and perform the language.

As is true for all students, metacognitive development is crucial for ELLs' success. Those strategies described in Core Understanding 10, including reciprocal teaching and think-alouds, also support the development of ELLs' speaking, reading, and writing abilities.

Clearly, the research literature on effective literacy instruction strongly supports the critical role of well-informed teachers who can make essential instructional decisions to meet the varying needs of their students.

TEACHER RESOURCES

Allen, J. (1999). *Words, words, words: Teaching vocabulary in grades 4–12*. York, ME: Stenhouse.

Burke, J. (2000). *Reading reminders: Tools, tips, and techniques*. Portsmouth, NH: Boynton/Cook.

Cunningham, P.M., & Allington, R.L. (2003). *Classrooms that work: They can ALL read and write* (3rd ed.). Boston: Allyn & Bacon.

Fountas, I.C., & Pinnell, G.S. (1996). *Guided reading: Good first teaching for all children*. Portsmouth, NH: Heinemann.

Fountas, I.C., & Pinnell, G.S. (2001). *Guiding readers and writers, grades 3–6: Teaching comprehension, genre, and content literacy*. Portsmouth, NH: Heinemann.

Harvey, S., & Goudvis, A. (2000). *Strategies that work: Teaching comprehension to enhance understanding*. York, ME: Stenhouse.

Marzano, R.J. (2004). *Building background knowledge for academic achievement: Research on what works in schools*. Alexandria, VA: Association for Supervision and Curriculum Development.

Robb, L. (2000). *Teaching reading in middle school*. New York: Scholastic.

Routman, R. (2000). *Conversations: Strategies for teaching, learning, and evaluating*. Portsmouth, NH: Heinemann.

Stephens, D. (Ed.). (1990). *What matters? A primer for teaching reading*. Portsmouth, NH: Heinemann.

Wilhelm, J.D., Baker, T.N., & Dube, J. (2001). *Strategic reading: Guiding students to lifelong literacy 6–12*. Portsmouth, NH: Boynton/Cook.

Yatvin, J. (2004). *A room with a differentiated view: How to serve all children as individual learners*. Portsmouth, NH: Heinemann.

Students need many opportunities to read, read, read.

CORE UNDERSTANDING 12

Access, time, modeling, choice, multiple readings, difficulty: All of these are factors in providing students with many opportunities to read (Allington, 1977, 1980;

Allington & Cunningham, 1996; Cunningham & Allington, 2003; Stanovich, 1986). What is critical is that students do read—lots, for sustained periods, for meaning, and for real and authentic purposes. Pearson (1993) observes, "One is tempted to conclude that some of the best 'practice' for enhancing reading skill occurs when children are given greater opportunity to read everyday materials" (pp. 507–508).

Opportunity to read has an effect on various measures of reading skill or achievement, as described in the following findings:

- "Just plain reading" improves students' comprehension (Anderson, Wilson, & Fielding, 1988), vocabulary knowledge (Herman, Anderson, Pearson, & Nagy, 1987), ability to monitor their own reading for sense (Pinnell, 1989), disposition to read independently (Ingham, 1982), English grammar skills (Elley & Mangubhai, 1983), and writing style into more sophisticated forms (Block, 2001; Gallik, 1999).

- A consistently positive relationship occurs between the amount of voluntary reading completed at home or at school and gains on standardized reading achievement tests (Pearson & Fielding, 1991; Taylor, Pearson, Clark, & Walpole, 1999).

- Fifteen minutes a day of independent, recreational reading significantly increases students' reading abilities. Average and below-average readers experience the greatest gains (Collins, 1980; Smith & Joyner, 1990; Taylor, Frye, & Maruyama, 1990; Wiesendanger & Bader, 1989).

- When adolescents increase their pleasure reading, performance also increases in academic work (Baumann & Duffy, 1997).

- Middle school students want to read on their own in order to make an otherwise difficult text interesting and comprehensible (Ivey & Broaddus, 2001).

One focus of reading instruction is to develop the lifelong habit of reading. Holdaway (1979), however, points out that schools spend a great deal of time teaching literacy skills, then leave little room for students to practice those skills by really reading. Why is the success of most reading programs gauged by the "successful" scores on standardized reading tests rather than by the personal reading habits of their students (Irving, 1980; Speigel, 1981)? If instructional programs do not provide ample opportunities for students to read for enjoyment in school, desire and motivation to do so may not develop (Lamme, 1976; Speigel, 1981). Successful school experiences help to motivate students to read voluntarily. Allington and McGill-Franzen (2003) suggest that effective instruction must ensure that all students engage in extensive, high-success reading activities throughout the school day and must reliably enhance the volume of voluntary reading students do outside of the school day. When students are held accountable for a wide variety of reading experiences (e.g., compiling reading logs, participating in sustained silent reading [SSR], documenting reading-at-home experiences), positive attitudes toward reading will develop.

Making the Choice to Read

The notion of *recreational reading* has long been a goal of reading instruction, that is, when readers choose to read on their own, motivated by their own interests, inquiries, and purposes. Programs to encourage recreational reading beyond the classroom are varied; they are often, although not always, incentive based.

Many adolescents read less than did their peers of 30 years ago (Brozo & Hargis, 2003; Glenn, 1994; Libsch & Breslow, 1996) or choose not to read at all (Beers, 1996; Schumm, Vaughn, & Saumell, 1994). Poor readers often lack the self-confidence and self-efficacy to choose to read on their own (Beers, 2003). They also lack the understanding of purposes for reading that might otherwise motivate them to read.

Neuman and Celano (2002, 2004) found that students who feel confident in reading will read more challenging materials and for higher level purposes. Less efficacious readers will do just the opposite. In particular, they found in the case of increased computer access in libraries, students from middle-income families were more likely to spend computer time on applications with more print; students from lower income families tended to spend more time playing computer games that contained little print (2004).

Access to Quality Reading Materials

Neuman and Celano (2001) note the prevailing assumption seems to be that books and other literacy-related resources are easily and equally accessible for all students and their families (cf. Allington & McGill-Franzen, 2003). However, recent studies have found this is not the case. Neuman and Celano state,

> If access to print is highly differentiated in our culture, it may result in differential opportunities for certain types of learning and thinking that are related to literacy development. Differences in access could influence the degree of familiarity with book language and the cognitive behaviors associated with reading, helping to explain the substantial educational differences among low- and middle-income students in beginning formal instruction. (p. 11)

Neuman and Celano (2001) found that low-income students had consistently less access to quality reading materials than did middle-income students. This includes access to places selling children's and young adult reading resources, signage, and public spaces for reading (coffee shops and restaurants, local preschools, school libraries, and public libraries). Duke (2000) studied very low and very high socioeconomic status first graders and found similar results, suggesting that social reproduction through schooling may begin quite early in the schooling process as students from different socioeconomic backgrounds were offered qualitatively different print environments and experiences.

Advocates of secondary school reform (Alvermann et al., 2002; Langer, 2001; Moore, Bean, Birdyshaw, & Rycik, 1999) concur that students need multiple opportunities for engaged, sustained print encounters in the classroom every day. The easier the access is to interesting print materials, the more frequently adolescents read (McQuillan & Au, 2001).

The Summer Lag. Allington and McGill-Franzen (2003) argue that summer reading setback is a key element in closing the achievement gap between low-income and more advantaged students. Hayes and Grether (1983) showed that students in both high-poverty and low-poverty schools made substantially similar gains when school was in session. However, the effects of summer vacation (spring to fall comparisons) on reading achievement looked very different; they calculate that the differential progress made during the four summers between second and sixth grade accounts for upward of 80% of the achievement difference between the two groups.

Borman and D'Agostino (1996) found the effects of remedial reading instruction during the school year were diminished when the summer vacation period was included in the estimates of achievement growth. Allington and McGill-Franzen (2003) suggest that a critical support for low-income learners is easy—literally fingertip access to books that provide engaging, successful reading experiences throughout the calendar year if we want them to read in volume.

Libraries. Krashen (1993, 1996) has found a critical relationship between access to books via public and school libraries and reading achievement. Indicators of school library quality and public library use were found to be significant predictors of reading comprehension scores. Allington and Cunningham (1996; cf. Cunningham & Allington, 2003) also emphasize this relationship. The U.S. trend of shrinking library funding is particularly hard on low-income areas; schools enrolling many poor students have 50% fewer books than do schools enrolling primarily more advantaged students (Guice & Allington, 1994). Some suggest that very broad national differences in literacy are related to the per-capita amount of print available to the average adult (Guthrie & Greaney, 1991; cf. Pearson, 1993; Pearson & Fielding, 1991).

To best support students, books need to be available through both classroom collections and schoolwide libraries. Classroom libraries give students immediate access, a factor likely to increase the amount of voluntary reading students do in and out of school (Allington & McGill-Franzen, 2003; Fractor, Woodruff, Martinez, & Teale, 1993; Neuman & Celano, 2001). Students in classrooms without literature collections read 50% less than do students in classrooms with such collections (Morrow, 1998).

Neuman and Celano (2001) found wide discrepancies between low-income and middle-income communities in both school and public library collections (cf. Smith, Constantino, & Krashen, 1997). They note that students most likely to benefit most from school libraries were offered the poorest services and resources and the least access. Schools serving many at-risk students need particularly good collections in both classrooms and libraries because these students typically have much less access out of school; public libraries need increased resources and programming to support students and families throughout the calendar year (Allington & McGill-Franzen, 2003; Neuman & Celano, 2001; Smith et al., 1997).

Neuman and Celano (2002, 2004) remind us that even as libraries struggle to survive in difficult economic times, libraries and librarians are vital to the development of literacy skills of children and young adults. Their study of the transformation of library services in Philadelphia, Pennsylvania, focused on creating a model urban library that offered a wide range of access, programs, and services for all community members. Libraries serving low-income families are just as busy as those serving middle-income families; Neuman and Celano observed that low-income libraries were often more crowded. It is interesting to note, however, several critical differences: Low-income families do not check out as many books (for fear of loss, overdue fines, damage), and low-income students tend to read at or below their grade level, in contrast to middle-income students who read at or above their grade level when choosing library materials. Their study also found that excellent librarians are critical to the transformation of access in low-income neighborhoods. These librarians pushed students to reach beyond their current abilities, often helping to close the gap caused by poor literacy environments.

International studies confirm the importance of high-quality libraries and librarians as critical factors in effective reading instruction and overall literacy acquisition ("Libraries called key," 2004; "New study supports," 2004). Recognizing the urgent need to provide students with materials to read, Allington and Cunningham (1996; cf. Allington & McGill-Franzen, 2003; Neuman & Celano, 2004) recommend the expansion of library collections and services.

Time and Opportunity

Clearly, providing time and opportunity for learners to read is a critical aspect in successful reading instruction. As Krashen (1996) notes, access means having not only the availability of books but also time for reading them (cf. International Reading Association, 1999).

Elley and Mangubhai (1983) found that increasing access to books for students with limited access to books increased their literacy achievement, particularly for second-language learners. Elley (1992) found key factors that consistently differentiated between countries with high reading achievement scores and low reading achievement scores focused on access and availability of books: large school libraries, large classroom libraries, regular book borrowing, frequent silent reading in class, and frequent story reading aloud by teachers. The highest scoring countries typically provide students with greater access to books in the home, in nearby community libraries and bookstores, and in the school.

Neuman (1999) found that increasing 3- and 4-year-old children's access to books in child-care centers serving economically disadvantaged students, as well as training child-care providers to use the books effectively to promote early literacy development, significantly increased the students' emergent literacy development.

Block and Mangieri (2002), in a survey of teachers about recreational reading practices, found that response to legislative mandates at both the federal and state levels has decreased the time teachers allow for independent, recreational reading. Both parents and teachers reported that today's students spend less time in leisure reading activities at home and school than these adults did when they were students (cf. Mahiri & Godley, 1998).

The following list describes several ways that teachers can provide children with wide opportunities for extensive reading:

- Schedule at least one block of structured sustained silent reading for students each day (e.g., SSR, Drop Everything And Read [DEAR]). Model your own reading pleasure in various ways in your classroom. Regularly read aloud from the texts you are reading for pleasure, particularly those relevant to content areas. Display the books; give brief book talks about them; connect them to everyday classroom activities.

- Provide a varied collection of print material in your classroom: library books, personal books, student-written books; newspapers (community, city, regional); magazines (for students, community-based); brochures and pamphlets of interest to the students in your class; menus, and other such environmental print. Content area classrooms need to have available a wide range of texts—fiction and nonfiction, as well as journals, magazines, and newspapers—on particular topics and events relevant to topic study.

- Provide an opportunity for all students to acquire a library card. Many public libraries have programs that work closely with public schools to make their services accessible to all students.

- Provide a wide variety of content area texts linked to the curriculum. Topical literature is especially important as students move into middle and high school.

- Create ways to consistently interact with and support families accessing appropriate, high-quality reading materials for learners.

- Create book bag programs for young students to take home classroom or school materials to read with families. These programs usually include opportunities for families and students to respond to the reading in some fashion and to document the reading time spent.

The research literature highlights the importance of both access and opportunity to appropriate materials and reading experiences to support successful reading development and growth.

TEACHER RESOURCES

Allington, R.L. (2002). You can't learn much from books you can't read. *Educational Leadership, 60*(3), 16–19.

Allington, R.L., & McGill-Franzen, A. (2003). The impact of summer setback on the reading achievement gap. *Phi Delta Kappan, 85*(1), 68–75.

Day, R.R., & Bamford, J. (1998). *Extensive reading in the second language classroom*. New York: Cambridge University Press.

Krashen, S.D. (2004). *The power of reading: Insights from the research* (2nd ed.). Westport, CT: Libraries Unlimited.

Lesesne, T.S. (2003). *Making the match: The right book for the right reader at the right time, grades 4–12*. Portland, ME: Stenhouse.

Marshall, J.C. (2002). *Are they really reading? Expanding SSR in the middle grades*. Portland, ME: Stenhouse.

Pilgreen, J. (2000). *The SSR handbook: How to organize and manage a sustained silent reading program*. Portsmouth, NH: Boynton/Cook.

Pilgreen, J. (2003). Questions teachers are asking about sustained silent reading. *California Reader, 37*(1), 42–53.

Monitoring the development of reading processes is vital to student success.

CORE UNDERSTANDING 13

Monitoring learners' progress calls for a variety of assessment and evaluation strategies. Assessment and instruction are integral processes, each informing the other to meet the individual needs of students. *Authentic assessment* describes a fusion of instruction and assessment; that is, activities that involve real reading and real writing provide assessment information on literacy (Cooper & Kiger, 2005). Teachers must constantly use keen observation of student growth and development to inform instruction. Also, students must learn to become critically aware of their own reading processes, that is, to become metacognitive, to support their development as competent, engaged, and effective readers. We might see assessment as an ongoing process of gathering information about what students can and cannot do. Evaluation, the next step, takes into account all assessments and observations in order to make a judgment about an individual student. In general, the purpose for assessment is to inform instruction, ultimately to support learning. Purposes for evaluation may include grading and placement.

Current Emphasis on Accountability

A central tenet of the No Child Left Behind (NCLB) Act of 2001 (2002) is that all students make adequate yearly progress as defined by each state and as measured on the adopted standardized test. Virtually all the states now have state standards in reading and have developed or adopted assessments aligned with them, although alignment is not a uniform concept across the states (Wixon, Fisk, Dutro, & McDaniel, 2002). Since the publication of *Standards for the English Language Arts* by the International Reading Association (IRA) and National Council of Teachers of English (NCTE) in 1996, literacy standards and assessments to measure students' attainment of them have proliferated. Complicating the problem of alignment, that is, whether the assessments actually measure the valued reading behaviors set forth in the standards, is the current emphasis on number of students tested. At the present time, the NCLB requirement to test nearly 100% of students in a school appears to be causing some confusion between ends and means. Is the goal universal testing, or is the test a means to an end: assessing the impact of instruction and monitoring student progress in literacy?

Many eminent educational researchers and assessment experts have voiced their concern that students, teachers, and schools are being judged successful or deficient on the basis of a single standardized assessment (American Educational Research Association [AERA], 2000; Cooper & Kiger, 2005; IRA, 1999; Meisels & Piker, 2001; RAND Reading Study Group, 2002). They further note that no one test can serve the needs of instruction and accountability. Ironically, the national focus on accountability in the United States may leave little room for assessment linked to instruction that could actually improve literacy outcomes for students who are being left behind.

> *Ironically, the national focus on accountability in the United States may leave little room for assessment linked to instruction that could actually improve literacy outcomes for students who are being left behind.*

In addition, despite research that clearly shows more negative than positive consequences of retaining a student in a grade, many school districts (Chicago and New York City among them) are holding students back on the basis of their scores on a single test. Recently, a number of cities and states have been forced to relax this requirement in the face of high numbers of students so identified and objections to the rule by student advocates and parents (Goldberg, 2004). These tests have become high stakes indeed, prompting calls for change from such groups as IRA (1999) and AERA (2000). In its position statement *High-Stakes Assessments in Reading*, IRA (1999) calls for the use of assessment to "improve instruction and benefit students rather than compare and pigeonhole them" (n.p.). The statement goes on to recommend positive assessment actions for teachers, parents, child-advocacy groups, and policymakers.

In the current climate of test-driven accountability, some see a return to an outdated manufacturing model of productivity that no longer fits with our education goals. Indeed, the practices of standardization, ranking, and top-down control, evident in high-stakes testing, have historically been associated with the process of sorting students for the work force (Gallagher, 2004). As Darling-Hammond (1997) notes, education reform driven by high-stakes tests focuses on designing controls rather than developing capacity. Instead of labeling students, teachers, and schools as failing to meet standards, how might school communities improve instruction and academic outcomes for students who are not meeting the standards?

Traditional modes of monitoring development are standardized and norm-referenced instruments and criterion-referenced tests. Although these measures show where an individual falls within a peer group, they do not necessarily show in detail what an individual can do as a reader. Some drawbacks of traditional modes include the following:

- They are largely unreliable bases for making any judgments about an individual's reading development.
- They rarely have much demonstrated validity as they assess only a narrow range of literacy activity.
- They are given infrequently and at odd times of the year so the results, even if reliable and valid, are not of much use in planning and instruction.
- They tend to narrow the curriculum as teachers feel the need to "teach the test"; some see this as working to discourage teacher–learner collaborative evaluation of literacy learning.
- They can play a role in discouraging those children whose performance on the tests suggests that their reading development lags behind that of their peers. (Allington & Walmsley, 1995, pp. 78–79; cf. Darling-Hammond, 1991; Stallman & Pearson, 1990)

In addition, the traditional tests' content and format tend to focus instruction on coverage and right answers (Meier, 2003) rather than on substantive learning. A heightened concern with raising scores also drives the curriculum to become test preparation rather than a coherent, in-depth learning experience (Goldberg, 2004). And regarding the comprehension tests available for assessing reading, the RAND Reading Study Group (2002) asserts that they "sort children on a single dimension using a single method" (p. 53) and lack a clear or viable theory of comprehension. As part of the research agenda on comprehension they set forth, the RAND group calls for improvements in comprehension assessment that will accurately reflect the dynamic, developmental nature of comprehension and the interactions among reader, activity, text, and context.

Despite such criticisms, standardized tests will likely remain an important aspect of school literacy programs. However, many standardized tests are being revised to incorporate current definitions of reading. Many strategies for monitoring and assessing reading development incorporate the research developments of the past 25 years, including comprehension monitoring (cognitive development), response to texts beyond a literal level (cognitive development, response theory), errors as ways of indicating knowledge (language acquisition, emergent literacy), strategy use, and attitude. Many reform efforts highlight the need for *performance* assessments to determine whether learners are able to translate and apply skills and strategies in new, authentic tasks. They focus on the question, What do learners do? The impact of research can be seen in both informal classroom-level assessments and more formal standardized types of assessments.

The most current National Assessment of Educational Progress (NAEP) reading assessment (Grigg, Daane, Jin, & Campbell, 2003) illustrates this trend toward performance-based assessments grounded in current theories of reading. The framework, on which the assessment is based, has been in place since 1992 and reflects a long-held consensus about the nature of reading and proficient reading behaviors. The test is informed by a definition of reading as an interactive and constructive process that involves the reader, the text, and the context of the reading experience. Reading involves moving from a general understanding of text to thinking about text in different ways and reading differently depending on one's purpose, strongly affected by the context. Assessment of reading in the NAEP is done in three contexts: (1) reading for literary experience, (2) reading to gain information, and (3) reading to perform a task. Within each of these contexts, the assessment also looks at valued reading processes, including forming an understanding, developing interpretation, making reader–text and text–text connections, and examining content and structure.

The landscape of high-stakes testing serves as a backdrop for our discussion of assessment in reading that serves the teaching–learning enterprise. Ironically, the focus on large-scale testing threatens to discourage teachers from using classroom assessments, feeling that students are overburdened with tests. However, as the remainder of this section will explain, assessment is an essential part of literacy instruction. Teachers should reclaim this as part of their professional domain.

Assessment to Serve Teaching and Learning in Reading

Current understandings of how children learn to read and readers continue to develop suggest the following assessment recommendations: Assess authentic reading and writing in texts that make all cue systems available to students; assess reading in a variety of contexts and situations; assess products as well as processes; use multiple sources of data to find patterns in student growth and development; bring all involved with the student into the assessment process (students, parents, school personnel); and make assessment an ongoing part of everyday reading and writing tasks (Rhodes & Dudley-Marling, 1996). Assessment experts emphasize the importance of systematic assessments that are tied to the curriculum and have the strong buy-in of teachers. Research shows a statistically significant relationship between such assessment and students' growth in reading fluency and retelling performance (Taylor, Pearson, Clark, & Walpole, 1999). Research also shows that improved formative assessment helps lower performing students by providing feedback they can use to improve their achievement (Black & Wiliam, 1998). Cooper and Kiger (2005) suggest three principles for literacy instruction that is assessment based:

1. All teachers work from shared understandings of stages of literacy development in planning instruction appropriate to their students.

2. Assessment of literacy development focuses on student strengths in relation to these stages.

3. Assessment is an ongoing process based on results of instruction for literacy development. (p. 14)

Aspects of Reading Development to Monitor

Personal Perceptions, Attitudes, and Interests. Students' personal perceptions are affected by their attitudes, beliefs about reading, and interests. Social and historical values and expectations, both known and unknown, also influence their comprehension of texts. These perceptions help teachers to understand how individuals socially situate the act of reading and whether they have an identity as a reader: How is time spent with reading? Who is involved in conversations about reading? The importance of reading and the sense of one's ability to read will affect the choices students make in regard to reading, including types and time of reading.

Ways that teachers can document students' personal perceptions, attitudes, and interests include the following:

- *Interviews* to provide insight into individual perceptions. Teachers can construct their own interviews or use Burke's Reading Interview (Goodman, Watson, & Burke, 1987), which focuses on perceptions of what reading is and what good readers do. Rhodes and Dudley-Marling (1996) also emphasize the particular importance for at-risk readers to gain insight into their own beliefs and perceptions of the reading process and their interactions with this process. The Learning Record (Barr & Syverson, 1999) includes an interview with the student's parent as well as with the student to build a beginning picture of the student's literacy interests and practices.

- *Surveys and personal reading histories* to document experiences in and attitudes toward reading, reading material preferences, and literacy behaviors. For older students, administering pre- and post-surveys helps track important changes over time, for example, in amount of reading, repertoire of strategies, and attitude toward reading. (For examples, see Atwell, 1998; Schoenbach, Greenleaf, Cziko & Hurwitz, 1999.)

- *Inventories* to help teachers to find out about students' interests and connections to reading in and out of school. This might include inventories of the number of books read and owned at home as well as reading logs of what is read at school.

- *Observation* of how students act in a variety of situations that require reading. How does this individual interact with others in regard to reading and books? What choices do individuals make for reading, for example, during sustained silent reading or when allowed to select a book for literature study? Checklists are helpful for organizing observations in this and other areas of interest in reading development.

Comprehension. The meaning made by readers is at the heart of the reading process. How is background knowledge used in constructing meaning? What kind of sense is made of the texts read? What comprehension strategies (e.g. predicting, questioning, skimming, rereading) are used in order to construct meaning? Is the reader activating schema appropriate to understanding the text? What background knowledge might need to be developed for text comprehension? Is the appropriate literary knowledge in place to apply in understanding this text (e.g., story structures, formats, literary elements, genres, and particular authors)?

Ways that teachers can document students' comprehension include the following:

- *Response*: Responding to texts in a variety of ways helps learners to demonstrate a synthesis of what they have gained from interaction with the text. How does it apply to their own lives? What sense can they make of the text? How does this compare with other texts they have read? This response may happen through writing in literature logs, more formal written responses to the text, a dramatic presentation, discussing the book in a literature discussion group with peers, or book talks as a way to convince others to read the book.

- *Retelling*: Brown and Cambourne (1990) and Goodman and colleagues (1987) encourage teachers to use oral and written forms of retelling to get at what students understand about a text as well as what processes they are using to construct that understanding. Retellings enhance the learner's encounter with the text and actually mirror the reading process because the student constructs the retelling. Retellings are an excellent example of good literacy instruction that also serves as an assessment (Braunger, 1996).

- *Individually administered inventories*: The Informal Reading Inventory (IRI) and the Qualitative Reading Inventory (QRI-3) provide normed assessments that focus on a reader's comprehension of text. An IRI can be locally constructed or obtained from a variety of publishers. The QRI-3, in particular, incorporates elements of miscue analysis and retelling in its procedures and includes expository as well as narrative passages (Leslie & Caldwell, 2001).

- *Interviews*: Teachers can use interviews to find out what students have gained through their reading of a text.

- *Work samples*: The actual work produced by students as part of their process of reading or responding to a text provides important information about their comprehension and their reading process (e.g., the strategies they are using to understand the text) (McDonald, 2001). Reading logs, including metacognitive logs, and written records of interaction with text are examples (Schoenbach et al., 1999).

- *Conferences*: Short (5–10 minute) conferences with individual students about their response to a book allow the teacher a window into students' reading processes and a chance to provide necessary help to support comprehension.

- *Observations*: Teachers can watch as students read, asking questions and keeping anecdotal records.

- *Teacher anecdotal records or student self-evaluations of contributions to a discussion of text*: While a literature study group meets, for example, or a small group discusses its understanding of a passage in a history text, the teacher can make note of individual students' understandings and reading strategies in evidence. Students can assess their comprehension in a specific reading task, for example, applying a comprehension rubric to their performance with a specific text (for an example, see the Learning Record in Barr & Syverson, 1999) or they can assess their performance as a contributor to the literature study discussion (for an example, see Daniels, 2002).

Processing Words and Other Text Features. How students process words and other text features is integrally related to their comprehension and understanding of a text. Probably the most debate centers about how to view instruction at the word level and, thus, how best to assess and monitor the development of students' abilities in this area.

At one level, students must understand the concepts of letters, words, and sentences. Clay's (1985, 1991, 1993) work with children at the emergent stage of literacy development highlights the importance of monitoring the development of concepts about print. Clay stresses that teachers should present these tasks in ways as authentic and meaningful as possible.

Ways that teachers can document students' processing of words and text features include the following:

- *Concepts of print*: Children are interviewed, with a book, about directionality (Where is the front of this book? Where do I begin to read? Where do I go from here?) and about their concepts of letters and words (Show me one letter; show me two letters; show me a word; show me a sentence). Clay's (1985) Sand and Stones texts provide a structured format from which to assess these concepts.

- *Identification of letter names and sounds*: Children point to and tell letter names and sounds they know. At emergent levels, this identification focuses on single letter names and sounds but can move to more sophisticated groupings of letters (blends and digraphs) as they are introduced and taught to children.

- *Word knowledge*: Children are asked to read familiar words (usually high-frequency words with which they have had some interaction).

- *Writing*: Children are asked to write whatever they would like. Teachers observe how children go about this task: How do they perceive writing? What types of symbols do they choose to use? What does their attempt say about their knowledge of phonemic awareness and phonic knowledge?

- *Hearing and recording sounds in words*: Children write a dictated sentence. Teachers analyze their responses by counting the representation of sounds by letters.

Some educators believe it is important to continue to document children's phonemic awareness; that is, how able they are to discriminate and segment letter sounds in speech (e.g., c-a-t). Often, this can be observed in the context of daily classroom experiences by clapping syllables, observing the growth of invented spelling, and work with rhyming words.

What kinds of errors (miscues) do readers make? How do these miscues seem to affect comprehension? What do the miscues reveal about the strategies and cues they use to process text? Do students use other text features to comprehend text?

Ways teachers can use students' miscues and interpretations of text features to assess their comprehension include the following:

- *Error analysis, miscue analysis, retrospective miscue analysis*: Research in miscue analysis (Goodman et al., 1987) and running records (Clay, 1985, 1991, 2002) provides teachers with important insights into how children read and with valuable tools for documenting their reading behaviors. For older readers, retrospective miscue analysis allows teacher and student to recognize current strategies and plan for developing additional ones to improve reading competence (Goodman & Marek, 1996; Moore & Aspegren, 2001). All readers make miscues, depending on the text and task; it is through analysis of these miscues that intent and strategy can be determined. Oral reading of a text is an important avenue through which teachers can observe reading behaviors (Pinnell et al., 1995). Clay (1991) highlights the importance of a reader's use of language patterns and text structures in successful reading; error analysis can help teachers to understand the thought processes and problem-solving strategies readers use and do not use. There are many formats to follow for this assessment (Clay, 2002; Goodman et al., 1987; Rhodes, 1993). In general, students read an unfamiliar text and provide a retelling when they have finished. Teachers record their miscues, then analyze them to discover the strategies used and the ability of the reader to make sense of the text.

- *Anecdotal records and observation*: Teachers must carefully watch what readers are doing and continue to record these observations for analysis over time.

- *Student self-assessment*: Within a structure and set of expectations provided by the teacher, students reflect on their abilities (What am I able to do well? What have I learned to do?) and set new personal goals (What is an appropriate next step for me?).

Fluency. According to Chall (1996), the stage at which young readers are accurately decoding allows them to "unglue from print" (p. 18), that is, confirm what they already know to develop fluency. Fluency, as described by the National Reading Panel (NRP) is the ability to read aloud words of connected text smoothly and accurately (National Institute of Child Health and Human Development [NICHD], 2000). Put another way, fluency is a well-paced, accurate, coherent, and expressive reading of text. But the relevance of fluency to reading comprehension is what matters: Automaticity in word recognition is important because it frees up the reader's attention to the meaning of what is being read (Kuhn & Stahl, 2000; LaBerge & Samuels, 1974; Perfetti, 1985; Pressley, 2002; Stanovich, 1980). The less energy readers need to expend on decoding the text, the more they have to spend on making meaning with the text. In fact, current definitions of fluency include comprehension processes as well as word recognition (Samuels, 2002). (See Core Understanding 11 for a fuller discussion of fluency.)

For very young readers, oral reading is the best way to get at fluency. But we should caution that oral reading fluency is not a reliable indicator of either silent fluency or comprehension. Automatic word processing does not guarantee comprehension any more than lack of oral fluency signals a lack of comprehension. And a student who gives a halting oral reading of a text may produce a strong summary or retelling after reading. For readers past the period of formal reading instruction, the goal is to increase silent fluency. To this end, it is important that readers have many opportunities to read engaging materials at their independent level (Allington, 1977; Allington & McGill-Franzen, 2003). Samuels (2002) concurs and notes that the lack of endorsement of extensive reading or independent silent reading by the NRP (NICHD, 2000) was not for lack of evidence that it has positive effects, especially on building reading fluency. Rather, the NRP decided to look only at experimental studies, and while many studies (Krashen, 2001) point to the strong relationship between extensive reading and reading improvement—including fluency—the studies were correlational. Ways that teachers can document students' fluency include the following:

- *Repeated readings*: Students return to a familiar text to practice increasing their fluency.

- *Listening and oral reading with two texts*: The teacher reads aloud to the student a text and then asks the student some questions to ascertain comprehension. The purpose is to determine the student's ability to comprehend when decoding is not an issue. For the second text, the student is asked to read it aloud and then to retell or tell what he or she remembers after completing the reading. As the student reads, the teacher keeps track of oral word recognition errors, word-per-minute rate, oral reading expression, and indications of the student's comprehension. Features recorded are similar to those in a running record or miscue analysis.

- *Timed readings of short texts*: With older readers whose lack of fluency interferes with their comprehension, teachers can provide short texts that are graduated in difficulty for silent timed reading by students. Students and teacher keep track of their increased reading speed as part of monitoring their reading growth. Where fluency practice seems warranted, for example, because a student has difficulty moving beyond the word level in processing text, instructional techniques such as repeated oral reading and echo reading may help free the reader to process larger chunks of text.

Metacognition and Reading Strategies. Students who are able to think and talk about the strategies they use are better able to draw from their own resources to problem solve as they encounter difficulties in their reading, "thinking about their thinking" as they go about a task. Students need to be able to understand when, how, and why they are applying particular reading strategies and skills and what might be important to help them progress in their development.

Ways teachers can document students' metacognition and knowledge of reading strategies include the following:

- *Think-alouds*: Thinking aloud as a text is read gives insight into the strategies readers are using. Teachers can gauge why comprehension is or is not occurring as they listen to what strategy choices the reader is making (Brown & Lytle, 1988; Schoenbach et al., 1999).

- *Metacognitive logs*: Students keep a metacognitive log on their reading in self-chosen or sustained silent reading books. Periodically, they reflect on their reading process, responding to prompts as appropriate, such as "I was confused by...," "I started to think about...," "I figured out that...," and "I stopped because...." They use the logs to keep track of their own reading process, and as part of classroom conversation about metacognition and reading strategies, they expand their strategic repertoire (Schoenbach et al., 1999; Schoenbach, Braunger, Greenleaf, & Litman, 2003).

- *Metacognitive inventories*: For older students, a metacognitive inventory completed at the beginning of the year can reveal the strategies they currently are aware of using as they read. With data from the inventory, teacher and students can set goals for new strategies to learn and control in the process of strengthening their reading competence. A student who already rereads to solve comprehension problems may also learn to pose questions to focus and guide his or her reading of challenging texts. Readministering the metacognitive inventory at the end of the year provides useful information on strategy acquisition and metacognitive development. For a sample inventory, see the description of the Metacognitive Awareness of Reading Strategies Inventory (Bennett, 2003; Mokhtari & Reichard, 2002).

- *Student self-assessment*: Given a set of expectations, students reflect on their ability to use metacognitive strategies and set new goals as appropriate.

- *Interviews*: Teachers interview students concerning what they do as they read. An interview often occurs as students are reading a text.

- *Anecdotal records and observation*: Teachers observe and record what they see students doing as they read.

Environment and Instruction. Reading is a transaction between the reader, the text, and the environment within which they rest. It is appropriate to move assessment beyond what is perceived to be "in" a student. Home, school, and community environments all contribute to literacy development. Ways teachers can document the relationship between the reader, the text, and the environment include the following:

- *Teacher self-assessment and reflection*: Teachers must reflect on the matches necessary among the classroom environment, instructional decisions, and the needs of individual students. When students do not appear to be succeeding, teachers consider why this is so from as many perspectives as possible. What factors might be an obstacle for students? What alternatives might be employed?

- *Student self-assessment and reflection*: As students reflect on their own learning, insights into obstacles and issues can provide new options for instruction.

During the past 10 years, portfolios as a means of gathering and monitoring reading development have gained favor. Portfolios work well with performance-based assessments. They allow a collection of work samples assessed by a classroom-based rubric to document students' movement along a literacy continuum. Accompanying reflections by the student and teacher at evaluation points make the portfolio a living document of the student's literacy growth. The Learning Record is an example of a literacy portfolio system for K–12 use (Barr & Syverson, 1999).

Recommendations in this section focus on assessment as a tool to serve teaching and learning. With authentic assessments of students' reading, teachers have important information to use in designing instruction for the whole class and meeting individual students' needs. Students' self-assessment is important for reflection on current progress and for goal setting. Classroom-based literacy assessment is an essential part of accountability.

TEACHER RESOURCES

Calkins, L.M., Montgomery, K., & Santman, D. (1998). *A teacher's guide to standardized reading tests*. Portsmouth, NH: Heinemann.

Clay, M.M. (2002). *An observation survey: Of early literacy achievement* (2nd ed.). Portsmouth, NH: Heinemann.

Crowley, P. (1995). Listening to what readers tell us. *Voices From the Middle, 2*(2), 3–12.

Farr, B.P., & Trumbull, E. (1996). *Assessment alternatives for diverse classrooms*. Norwood, MA: Christopher-Gordon.

Harp, B. (2000). *The handbook of literacy assessment and evaluation* (2nd ed.). Norwood, MA: Christopher-Gordon.

Moore, R.A., & Aspegren, C.M. (2001). Reflective conversations between two learners: Retrospective miscue analysis. *Journal of Adolescent & Adult Literacy, 44*(6), 492–503.

Wilde, S. (2000). *Miscue analysis made easy: Building on student strengths*. Portsmouth, NH: Heinemann.

Wilde, S. (2002). *Testing and standards: A brief encyclopedia*. Portsmouth, NH: Heinemann.

Conclusion

There are, in the end, only two main ways human beings learn, by observing others (directly or vicariously) and by trying things out for themselves. Novices learn from experts or experience. That's all there is to it. Everything else is in the details.
—Deborah Meier (1995, p. 181)

What Helps Readers Develop?

Location, location, location: the "three" factors to consider in buying a house. Can we reduce the complex body of research knowledge presented here, even our 13 core understandings about learning to read, to a single, powerful mantra? We think we can:

Learning to read and growing as a reader are about access.

Access Is Key

In both oral language acquisition and learning to read, access is the critical component. Children with access to rich and responsive language interactions about their experiences in the first three years of life develop power over language even as they learn to talk. Their orientation to the world around them is one of agency and curiosity. They acquire ever-larger vocabularies as they notice, talk about, and receive adult feedback on experiences. These children come to school ready to continue that quest for knowledge and to make their own the words that name it.

In the same way, young people learning to read and becoming more skillful readers need access to meaningful and personally interesting texts. This opens another way of learning about the world to them. And because background knowledge and experience are so important to reading comprehension, the more students are reading, the more they increase the grounding they bring to the next text...and the next. They increase their *world knowledge* even as they are acquiring *word knowledge* (Allington & Cunningham, 1996). The motivation to read builds as the learner finds meaning in texts and then follows a trajectory similar to that experienced in learning to talk: Increased engagement in the process fuels learning, positive disposition, and control of skills and strategies. Juel (1992) found the differences in achievement between poor and good first-grade readers are remarkably consistent, even though all the children were making gains. She believes that the critical factor was the amount of reading children actually did—their access to real encounters with books. First graders who were good readers read approximately twice as many words during the year as did poor readers. This pattern held fast through fourth grade. Reading frequently and widely is essential for reading achievement. For struggling readers more time for real reading is imperative if we are ever to narrow this gap. The critical role of extensive reading also has been confirmed in more recent studies for students across the educational spectrum and particularly for underperforming students and students from low-income households (Krashen, 2004; McQuillan, 2001; Neuman & Celano, 2001). To say that children learn to read by reading is not to deny the need to provide explicit instruction and many demonstrations in the classroom. The point to be made is that the amount of extended text reading that children do is directly related to their reading achievement. Without real engagement with meaningful texts, students will not become readers. Thus, a focus on early instruction in isolated skills is potentially damaging for young readers, especially those who struggle to learn to read.

Specifically, readers at all stages of development need access to the following:

- Time for reading and learning.

- Texts of all kinds and rich resources for reading.

- Knowledgeable and supportive teachers.

- Appropriate instruction in skills and strategies.

- Demonstrations of how readers, writers, and texts work.

- Other readers, both novice and expert.

- Their own reading processes.

Allington (2002) provides a shorthand for these in his six common features, or "the six T's of effective elementary literacy instruction" (p. 742): time, texts, teaching, talk, tasks, and testing.

Providing Access to Critical Components in the Classroom

Time. Learners need to have sustained periods of engagement with texts (blocks of time in the school day with plenty of time for guided reading, independent reading in texts of their own choice, working with words, talking about books, and reading curriculum-linked texts). Students need time to grow to love reading and to choose it for both learning and pleasure.

Texts and Resources. Classrooms and schools need richly stocked libraries that offer readers information and enjoyment, representing the many cultures and perspectives of our diverse society. Included in the school's resources must be books of all sorts as well as electronic texts and literacy applications, including computers with high-quality reading software, integrated media technology, and the Internet (Sharp, Bransford, Goldman, Kinzer, & Soraci, 1992). As children are learning to read, they "need to read lots of easy stuff" (Allington & Cunningham, 1996, p. 53). And students at all levels need "enormous quantities of successful reading to become independent, proficient readers" (Allington, 2002, p. 743). Trained librarians work closely with teachers to keep the media center collection current and are available to put just the right resource in a child's hands. Children's access to quality school library media centers, staffed by professionals, has a direct correlation with reading achievement and with positive attitudes about reading (Routman, 1996).

Knowledgeable and Supportive Teachers. Teachers must thoroughly understand current theories of language, literacy, and learning. This understanding must be demonstrated in and enhanced by their classroom practice. It is vitally important that teachers see themselves as lifelong learners, always updating their practitioner knowledge, and for this reason institutional structures to nurture teachers' professional development are essential. Schools need to be seen as places where teachers learn, too. But knowledge is not enough for teachers of reading.

In addition, teachers must communicate both high expectations for children's learning and the assurance of their support for each learner to succeed. The desire to learn to read and write is powerfully affected by teacher expectations, the patience and caring of the teacher, and the quality of communication that motivates and engages students in the learning process (Rosenholtz, 1989). Yatvin (1992), former superintendent of a rural district in Oregon, writes:

> In order to learn, a child must believe: I am a learner; I can do this work; craftsmanship and effort will pay off for me; this is a community of friends, and I belong to it. Because such beliefs often are not the inherent property of children who come from splintered families and dangerous neighborhoods, teachers today must work as hard on them as they have always worked on the intellectual side of learning. (p. 7)

Appropriate Instruction. This component of providing access is also the responsibility of the teacher. Excellent teachers of reading establish regular literacy routines that provide opportunities for learners to work independently, in small groups, and as a whole class (see Core Understanding 11). It should be noted, though, that a reliance on whole-class instruction for reading is not good because it distances teachers from children's development as readers (Allington & McGill-Franzen, 1997). Teachers need to know how individual children are progressing and what understandings of literacy they are developing. Teachers need to work closely with children to know what a child needs at the present moment to support the child's next steps as a reader. Classrooms should be organized to provide children access to the teacher, time, one another, books, and other components that they need to be successful in learning to read.

In becoming readers, all children must develop the same understandings, that is, the ability to use all four of the cueing systems to construct meaning with text (see Core Understanding 5 for discussion of the four cueing systems). But children will not all need the same amount or kind of instruction in all the systems. Providing instruction that is responsive to the learner's needs is key. Beginning or developing readers who require more explicit instruction in any aspect of reading will understandably need more time. One way teachers meet this need is the use of flexible groups as part of their literacy routines. The best resources for skill and strategy instruction in such groups are real texts, for example, trade books (fiction and nonfiction) and students' own writing.

Baumann (1997) recommends that although literacy instruction activities should be enjoyable, it is also important to acknowledge to children that learning to read is hard work. Children need to be taught how to read words and puzzle out texts. Furthermore, children need to experience the power of strenuous effort as they grapple with sometimes-difficult material (Carnegie Task Force, 1996). For older students, especially those who have disengaged from reading and may be struggling with academic texts, teachers need to help them build their stamina as readers and successfully read increasingly challenging texts (Schoenbach, Greenleaf, Cziko, & Hurwitz, 1999).

Demonstrations of How Readers, Writers, and Texts Work. Learners need to see lots of examples of how readers and writers work and of how reading and writing are used for various purposes. Reading aloud to students is a powerful way to demonstrate not only how books work but also to model a love for reading. One important use of reading is as a learning tool; young readers need to see how it works this way. As students are involved in whole-class, small-group, paired, and individual literacy activities, these demonstrations are provided and used by readers of varying degrees of expertise.

Furthermore, classroom experiences and instruction that integrate reading, writing, speaking, and listening support literacy development because they keep the language picture whole. Talking and writing in response to reading, listening to stories, writing original stories all feed "the linguistic data pool" described in chapter 2 (Brown & Cambourne, 1990; Harste, Burke, & Woodward, 1982). Basically, reading, writing, listening, and speaking are streams that flow into the same pool; they are constantly refreshing one another, if our classrooms take advantage of their complementarity. Across the wealth of beating-the-odds studies, the findings are consistent: Students at all grade levels benefit from integrated literacy experiences in a coherent, meaning-based curriculum with many opportunities for small-group interaction (Allington, 2002; Langer, 2001; Morrow, Tracey, Woo, & Pressley, 1999; Taylor et al., 1999).

Other Readers. Some students are surrounded by readers in their home and community, adults who share books with them from their earliest years. As Cullinan notes, "Children who sit beside a reader and follow the print from an early age learn to read quite 'naturally.' We know that the modeling has a lasting effect; children do what they see others do" (as cited in Putnam, 1994, p. 363). But children who come to school without rich reading experiences at home need access not only to books but also to skilled readers who will envelop them in the language and experience of books. Sometimes the reader will be the teacher, sometimes another adult from the school or the community, or sometimes an older student. The important thing is that children experience the support of a skilled reader to help them bond with books.

As students move through the grades and encounter more demanding content area texts, they need access to other readers to help them master the ways of reading and thinking in the disciplines. Teachers can create supportive classroom communities in which the invisible processes of reading in the disciplines are made visible and accessible to students (Schoenbach, Braunger, Greenleaf, & Litman, 2003).

Readers also need to talk with one another about what they are reading. They learn about books they would like to read, sharpen their own understandings of a text by listening to others' responses, and become a community of readers. The powerful role of authentic classroom discussion in increasing student learning has been well documented (Applebee, Langer, Nystrand, & Gamoran, 2003) and talk should be an essential component of classroom life.

Students' Own Reading Processes. Students' awareness of what they know and can do as readers is essential to their literacy growth. The goal of the Reading Recovery program, for beginning readers, is to foster a "self-extending system of literacy expertise" (Clay, 1991, p. 317), developed as the child reads more and consciously acquires and applies an ever-widening repertoire of reading strategies. As with all of Reading Recovery's interventions for struggling readers, this goal is derived from careful observation of what good readers do. The title of one of Clay's books (1991) says it all—*Becoming Literate: The Construction of Inner Control.* (See chapter 3 for more discussion of the Reading Recovery program.)

Across the developmental continuum, readers need to be aware of their reading process, know how to repair comprehension when it breaks down, and understand how to vary their reading process to suit reading in different genres and for various purposes. Research on learning to high levels of literacy points out important cognitive strategies that readers must develop and consciously implement, including (a) problem-solving, or fix-up, strategies; (b) self-regulatory procedures; (c) executive structures, or goals and purposes for reading; and (d) intentional learning procedures (Dreher & Slater, 1992). Ongoing instruction and assessment should involve students in setting such goals and monitoring progress toward them.

What Can Hinder Readers in Their Development?

Classroom practices that isolate skills from meaningful reading make learning to read difficult. They do not help children develop inner control and strategic functioning as readers. Smith (1983) made the point in a widely circulated essay titled "Twelve Easy Ways to Make Learning to Read Difficult." Smith's 12 ways were all variations on the theme of distancing children from their attempts to read for meaning. However well intentioned, these instructional approaches denied children access to reading as a meaning-making process. In contrast, the simple but elegant prescription for how to make learning to read easy was to "respond to what the child is trying to do" (p. 24). Recently, Smith (2003) reprised that advice, saying that reading—like learning to talk or walk—is a marvel but not a mystery. He goes on to say that when teachers make it into a mystery by isolating component skills in the process, then making sense of print becomes elusive, even confusing, for learners.

Consensus is considerable among literacy researchers to support Smith's overall point and especially the core understandings contained in this book (Flippo, 1998, 2001). The practices that researchers agree are helpful are all incorporated in the foregoing discussion. The practices that they agree would hinder effective reading development are

- emphasizing only phonics,
- drilling on isolated letters or sounds,
- teaching letters and words one at a time,
- insisting on correctness,
- expecting students to spell correctly all the words they can read,
- making perfect oral reading the goal of reading instruction,
- focusing on skills rather than interpretation and comprehension,
- constant use of workbooks and worksheets,
- fixed ability grouping, and
- blind adherence to a basal program.

The phrasing of some of the practices suggests why agreement across the spectrum was possible, for example, "emphasizing only," "drilling," "focusing on," and "blind adherence." Nevertheless, the pressure from some quarters today to make explicit, systematic phonics the core of reading instruction in the primary grades and to focus on similar basic skill instruction for older readers who struggle could lead to valuable classroom time being used for the very practices soundly rejected by these reading experts. Students could lose access to the rich resources and interactions that prompt engagements with reading, as outlined in the 13 core understandings.

Roles and Responsibilities: Supporting All Students to Reach High Levels of Literacy

Our challenge, to bring all students to Myers's (1996) "critical/translation" level of literacy, as defined in chapter 1, is daunting. At the same time that our standards for literacy are rising, some learners in U.S. schools struggle to acquire basic skills in reading, and U.S. school populations are more diverse than ever before. How can we meet the varied needs of individuals and help them all develop a firm command of basic skills and strategies, the ability to construct and negotiate meanings with text, and the knowledge and the disposition to be critical, lifelong readers? As policymakers, educators, parents, or other adults involved in children's education, we all have significant roles to play.

Allington (2002) observes, "Good teachers, effective teachers, matter much more than particular curriculum materials, pedagogical approaches, or 'proven programs'" (p. 740). The usefulness of all professionals in the school—administrators, specialists (Title I, special education, talented and gifted), librarians, social workers, English as a second language/bilingual teachers, school psychologists—should be judged by the impact they have on enhancing the quality of classroom instruction. For children who experience difficulty learning to read, the focus on delivering high-quality, consistent classroom instruction is especially important. They cannot afford a fragmented or confused message about reading.

Ensuring excellent classroom instruction will take collaboration among professional staff, initially to agree on goals for the literacy program and then to develop shared understandings of effective literacy practices. This effort may mean that staff members undertake a program of learning for themselves, possibly in a reading and study group or through action research on some aspect of their literacy program.

Because we know that students' reading achievement is directly related to the amount of reading they do, building support with parents for reading at home is very important. And although independent reading is a goal, reading with children and talking about books is also necessary. Not only does talking about books motivate children to read, it enhances their development of important cognitive strategies. Classroom studies have shown that social interaction and strategy instruction are strongly related to the amount and breadth of students' reading (Applebee et al., 2003; Guthrie, Schafer, Wang, & Afflerbach, 1995).

Finally, the importance of a supportive, united community of adults across the literacy-learning continuum cannot be underestimated. The school can take the leadership in welcoming parents and community members into the schools, building bridges between home and school literacy, providing access to rich literacy materials, and offering appropriate training or strategy information for parents and volunteers. Children learning to read and older students developing as readers need adults who support them to be on the same page: understanding that reading is a construction of meaning.

References

Preface

Berliner, D.C. (2002). Educational research: The hardest science of all. *Educational Researcher, 31*(8), 18–20.

Braunger, J., & Lewis, J.P. (1997). *Building a knowledge base in reading*. Portland, OR: Northwest Regional Educational Laboratory; Urbana, IL: National Council of Teachers of English; Newark, DE: International Reading Association.

Donahue, P.L., Finnegan, R.J., Lutkus, A.D., Allen, N.L., & Campbell, J.R. (2001). *The nation's report card: Fourth-grade reading 2000* (NCES Report No. 2001-499). Washington, DC: U.S. Department of Education, National Center for Education Statistics.

Edmondson, J. (2004). Reading policies: Ideologies and strategies for political engagement. *The Reading Teacher, 57*(5), 418–428.

Eisenhart, M., & Towne, L. (2003). Contestation and change in national policy on "scientifically based" education research. *Educational Researcher, 32*(7), 31–38.

Gambrell, L.B., Morrow, L.M., Neuman, S.B., & Pressley, M. (Eds.). (1999). *Best practices in literacy instruction*. New York: Guilford.

Grigg, W.S., Daane, M.C., Jin, Y., & Campbell, J.R. (2003). *The nation's report card: Reading 2002* (NCES Report No. 2003-521). Washington, DC: U.S. Department of Education, National Center for Education Statistics.

International Reading Association (IRA). (2002). *What is evidence-based reading instruction?* (Position statement). Newark, DE: Author. Retrieved June 7, 2005, from http://www.reading.org/resources/issues/positions_evidence_based.html

Maxwell, J.A. (2004). Causal explanation, qualitative research, and scientific inquiry in education. *Educational Researcher, 33*(2), 3–11.

National Institute of Child Health and Human Development (NICHD). (2000). *Report of the National Reading Panel. Teaching children to read: An evidence-based assessment of the scientific research literature on reading and its implications for reading instruction* (NIH Publication No. 00-4769). Washington, DC: U.S. Government Printing Office.

No Child Left Behind Act of 2001, Pub. L. No. 107-110, 115 Stat. 1425 (2002).

Olson, D.R. (2004). The triumph of hope over experience in the search for "what works": A response to Slavin. *Educational Researcher, 33*(1), 24–26.

Pressley, M. (2003). A few things reading educators should know about instructional experiments. *The Reading Teacher, 57*(1), 64–71.

RAND Reading Study Group. (2002). *Reading for understanding: Toward an R&D program in reading comprehension*. Santa Monica, CA: RAND.

Snow, C.E., Burns, M.S., & Griffin, P. (Eds.). (1998). *Preventing reading difficulties in young children*. Washington, DC: National Academy Press.

Chapter 1

Adams, M.J. (1990). *Beginning to read: Thinking and learning about print*. Cambridge, MA: MIT Press.

Allington, R.L. (2002a). What I've learned about effective reading instruction from a decade of studying exemplary elementary classroom teachers. *Phi Delta Kappan, 83*(10), 740–747.

Allington, R.L. (2002b). *Big brother and the national reading curriculum: How ideology trumped evidence*. Portsmouth, NH: Heinemann.

Allington, R.L. (2005). Ideology is still trumping evidence. *Phi Delta Kappan, 86*(6), 462–468.

Allington, R.L., & Cunningham, P.M. (1996). *Schools that work: Where all children read and write*. New York: HarperCollins.

American Educational Research Association. (2003). *Resolution on the essential elements of scientifically-based research*. Retrieved August 18, 2005, from http://35.8.171.42/aera/meeting/councilresolution03.htm

Atwell, N. (1987). *In the middle: Writing, reading, and learning with adolescents*. Portsmouth, NH: Boynton/Cook.

Berliner, D.C. (2002). Educational research: The hardest science of all. *Educational Researcher, 31*(8), 18–20.

Bond, G.L., & Dykstra, R. (1997). The cooperative research program in first-grade reading instruction. *Reading Research Quarterly, 32*(4), 348–427. (Original work published 1967)

Boyer, E.L. (1995). *The basic school: A community for learning*. Princeton, NJ: Carnegie Foundation for the Advancement of Teaching.

Bullock, M. (2004). What is evidence and what is the problem? *APA Online Psychological Science Agenda, 18*(3). Retrieved May 21, 2005, from http://www.apa.org/science/psa/mar4edcolumn.html

Campbell, J.R., Voelkl, K.E., & Donahue, P.L. (1997). *NAEP 1996 trends in academic progress* (NCES Publication No. 97-985). Washington, DC: U.S. Department of Education, National Center for Education Statistics.

Carnegie Task Force. (1994, April). *Starting points: Meeting the needs of our youngest children* (Report of the Carnegie Task Force on Meeting the Needs of Young Children). New York: Carnegie Corporation.

Center for the Improvement of Early Reading Achievement (CIERA). (2001). *Put reading first: The research building blocks for teaching children to read*. Washington, DC: U.S. Department of Education, Partnership for Reading.

Clay, M.M. (1991). *Becoming literate: The construction of inner control*. Portsmouth, NH: Heinemann.

Coles, G. (2003). *Reading the naked truth: Literacy, legislation, and lies*. Portsmouth, NH: Heinemann.

Collier, V.P. (1995). Acquiring a second language for school. *Directions in Language and Education, 1*(4), 3–14.

Darling-Hammond, L. (2000). How teacher education matters. *Journal of Teacher Education, 51*(3), 166–173.

Edmondson, J. (2004). Reading policies: Ideologies and strategies for political engagement. *The Reading Teacher, 57*(5), 418–428.

Eisenhart, M., & Towne, L. (2003). Contestation and change in national policy on "scientifically based" education research. *Educational Researcher, 32*(7), 31–38.

Freire, P. (1970). *Pedagogy of the oppressed* (M.B. Ramos, Trans.). New York: Continuum.

Freire, P., & Macedo, D. (1987). *Literacy: Reading the word and the world*. South Hadley, MA: Bergin & Garvey.

Garan, E.M. (2002). *Resisting reading mandates: How to triumph with the truth*. Portsmouth, NH: Heinemann.

Gee, J.P. (1996). *Social linguistics and literacies: Ideology in discourse* (2nd ed.). London; Bristol, PA: Taylor & Francis.

Glesne, C., & Peshkin, A. (1992). *Becoming qualitative researchers: An introduction*. White Plains, NY: Longman.

Goodman, K.S. (1965). A linguistic study of cues and miscues in reading. *Elementary English, 42*(6), 639–643.

Goodman, Y.M. (1976). Strategies for comprehension. In P.D. Allen & D.J. Watson (Eds.), *Findings of research in miscue analysis: Classroom implications* (pp. 94–102). Urbana, IL: ERIC Clearinghouse on Reading and Communication Skills; National Council of Teachers of English.

Goodman, Y.M., & Marek, A.M. (1996). *Retrospective miscue analysis: Revaluing readers and reading*. Katonah, NY: Richard C. Owen.

Graves, D.H. (1982). *A case study observing the development of primary children's composing, spelling, and motor behaviors during the writing process* (Final report, September 1, 1978–August 31, 1981). Durham, NH: University of New Hampshire. (ERIC Document Reproduction Service No. ED218653)

Graves, M.F., van den Broek, P., & Taylor, B.M. (Eds.). (1996). *The first R: Every child's right to read*. New York: Teachers College Press; Newark, DE: International Reading Association.

Green, J., & Dixon, C. (1996). Language of literacy dialogues: Facing the future or reproducing the past. *Journal of Literacy Research, 28*(2), 290–301.

Grigg, W.S., Daane, M.C., Jin, Y., & Campbell, J.R. (2003). *The nation's report card: Reading 2002* (NCES Report No. 2003-521). Washington, DC: U.S. Department of Education, National Center for Education Statistics.

Guthrie, J.T., & Anderson, R.E. (1999). Engagement in reading: Processes of motivated, strategic, knowledgeable, social readers. In J.T. Guthrie & D.E. Alvermann (Eds.), *Engaged reading: Processes, practices, and policy implications* (pp. 17–45). New York: Teachers College Press.

Guthrie, J.T., & Wigfield, A. (2000). Engagement and motivation in reading. In M.L. Kamil, P.B. Mosenthal, P.D. Pearson, & R. Barr (Eds.), *Handbook of reading research* (Vol. 3, pp. 403–422). Mahwah, NJ: Erlbaum.

Hart, B., & Risley, T.R. (1995). *Meaningful differences in the everyday experience of young American children*. Baltimore: Paul H. Brookes.

Haycock, K. (2001). Closing the achievement gap. *Educational Leadership, 58*(6), 6–11.

Healy, J.M. (1990). *Endangered minds: Why our children don't think*. New York: Simon & Schuster.

Heath, S.B. (1983). *Ways with words: Language, life, and work in communities and classrooms*. Cambridge, England: Cambridge University Press.

International Reading Association (IRA). (2002). *What is evidence-based reading instruction?* (Position statement). Newark, DE: Author. Retrieved June 7, 2005, from http://www.reading.org/resources/issues/positions_evidence_based.html

International Reading Association (IRA) & National Council of Teachers of English (NCTE). (1996). *Standards for the English language arts*. Newark, DE; Urbana, IL: Authors.

International Reading Association (IRA) & National Middle School Association (NMSA). (2001). *Supporting young adolescents' literacy learning* (Position statement). Newark, DE; Westerville, OH: Authors. Retrieved June 7, 2005, from http://www.reading.org/resources/issues/positions_young_adolescents.html

Kamil, M.L. (2003). *Adolescents and literacy: Reading for the 21st century*. Washington, DC: Alliance for Excellent Education.

Kamil, M.L., Mosenthal, P.B., Pearson, P.D., & Barr, R. (Eds.). (2000). *Handbook of reading research* (Vol. 3). Mahwah, NJ: Erlbaum.

Krashen, S.D. (2005). Is in-school free reading good for children? Why the National Reading Panel report is (still) wrong. *Phi Delta Kappan, 86*(6), 444–447.

Land, R., & Moustafa, M. (2005). Scripted reading instruction: Help or hindrance? In B. Altwerger (Ed.), *Reading for profit: How the bottom line leaves kids behind* (pp. 63–77). Portsmouth, NH: Heinemann.

Lytle, S.L., & Cochran-Smith, M. (1992). Teacher research as a way of knowing. *Harvard Educational Review, 62*(4), 447–474.

Maxwell, J.A. (2004). Causal explanation, qualitative research, and scientific inquiry in education. *Educational Researcher, 33*(2), 3–11.

McCracken, N.M. (2004). Surviving shock and awe: NCLB vs. colleges of education. *English Education, 36*(2), 104–118.

McDaniel, J.E., & Miskel, C.G. (2002). *The effect of groups and individuals on national decisionmaking* (CIERA Report No. 3-025). Ann Arbor: Center for the Improvement of Early Reading Achievement, University of Michigan.

Moje, E.B., Young, J.P., Readence, J.E., & Moore, D.W. (2000). Reinventing adolescent literacy for new times: Perennial and millennial issues. *Journal of Adolescent & Adult Literacy, 43*(5), 400–410.

Moll, L.C., Amanti, C., Neff, D., & Gonzalez, N. (1992). Funds of knowledge for teaching: Using a qualitative approach to connect homes and classrooms. *Theory Into Practice, 31*(1), 132–141.

Moore, D.W., Bean, T.W., Birdyshaw, D., & Rycik, J.A. (1999). *Adolescent literacy: A position statement for the Commission on Adolescent Literacy of the International Reading Association*. Newark, DE: International Reading Association. Retrieved June 7, 2005, from http://www.reading.org/downloads/positions/ps1036_adolescent.pdf

Morrow, L.M. (1996). *Motivating reading and writing in diverse classrooms: Social and physical contexts in a literature-based program* (Research Report No. 28). Urbana, IL: National Council of Teachers of English.

Moustafa, M., & Land, R.E. (2002). The reading achievement of economically disadvantaged children in urban schools using Open Court vs. comparably disadvantaged children in urban schools using nonscripted reading programs. In *Urban Learning, Teaching, and Research* (2002 yearbook, pp. 44–53). Washington, DC: American Educational Research Association. Retrieved May 21, 2005, from http://instructional1.calstatela.edu/mmousta/The_Reading_Achievement_of_Economically_Disadvantaged_Children_in_Urban_Schools_Using_Open_Court.pdf

Myers, M. (1996). *Changing our minds: Negotiating English and literacy*. Urbana, IL: National Council of Teachers of English.

National Council of Teachers of English (NCTE). (2004). *On reading, learning to read,* and effective reading instruction: An overview of what we know and how we know it (NCTE guideline by the Commission on Reading). Urbana, IL: Author. Retrieved March 18, 2005, from http://www.ncte.org/about/over/positions/category/read/118620.htm

National Institute of Child Health and Human Development (NICHD). (2000). *Report of the National Reading Panel. Teaching children to read: An evidence-based assessment of the scientific research literature on reading and its implications for reading instruction* (NIH Publication No. 00-4769). Washington, DC: U.S. Government Printing Office.

National Research Council (NRC). (2002). *Scientific research in education* (Report of the Committee on Scientific Principles for Education Research). Washington, DC: National Academy Press.

No Child Left Behind Act of 2001, Pub. L. No. 107-110, 115 Stat. 1425 (2002).

Obidah, J.E. (1998). Black-mystory: Literate currency in everyday schooling. In D. Alvermann, K. Hinchman, D. Moore, S. Phelps, & D. Waff (Eds.), *Reconceptualizing the literacies in adolescents' lives* (pp. 51–71). Mahwah, NJ: Erlbaum.

Olson, D.R. (2004). The triumph of hope over experience in the search for "what works": A response to Slavin. *Educational Researcher, 33*(1), 24–26.

Orange, C., & Horowitz, R. (1999). An academic standoff: Literacy task preferences of African American and Mexican American male adolescents versus teacher-expected preference. *Journal of Adolescent & Adult Literacy, 43*(1), 28–39.

Paratore, J.R. (2002). Home and school together: Helping beginning readers succeed. In A.E. Farstrup & S.J. Samuels (Eds.), *What research has to say about reading instruction* (3rd ed., pp. 48–68). Newark, DE: International Reading Association.

Patterson, L., & Shannon, P. (1993). Reflection, inquiry, action. In L. Patterson, C.M. Santa, K.G. Short, & K. Smith (Eds.), *Teachers are researchers: Reflection and action* (pp. 7–11). Newark, DE: International Reading Association.

Pearson, P.D. (1996). Six ideas in search of a champion: What policymakers should know about the teaching and learning of literacy in our schools. *Journal of Literacy Research, 28*(4), 302–309.

Pearson, P.D., & Stephens, D. (1994). Learning about literacy: A 30-year journey. In R.B. Ruddell, M.R. Ruddell, & H. Singer (Eds.), *Theoretical models and processes of reading* (4th ed., pp. 22–42). Newark, DE: International Reading Association.

Pressley, M. (2003). A few things reading educators should know about instructional experiments. *The Reading Teacher, 57*(1), 64–71.

Purcell-Gates, V. (1995). *Other people's words: The cycle of low literacy*. Cambridge, MA: Harvard University Press.

Purcell-Gates, V. (1997). The future of research in language arts. *Language Arts, 74*(4), 280–283.

RAND Reading Study Group. (2002). *Reading for understanding: Toward an R&D program in reading comprehension*. Santa Monica, CA: RAND.

Robinson, D. (2004). An interview with Gene V. Glass. *Educational Researcher, 33*(3), 26–30.

Shanahan, T., & Neuman, S.B. (1997). Conversations: Literacy research that makes a difference. *Reading Research Quarterly, 32*(2), 202–210.

Siegel, M., & Fernandez, S.L. (2000). Critical approaches. In M.L. Kamil, P.B. Mosenthal, P.D. Pearson, & R. Barr (Eds.), *Handbook of Reading Research* (Vol. 3, pp. 141–151). Mahwah, NJ: Erlbaum.

Snow, C.E., & Biancarosa, G. (2003). *Adolescent literacy and the achievement gap: What do we know and where do we go from here?* (Adolescent Literacy Funders Meeting Report). New York: Carnegie Corporation.

Snow, C.E., Burns, M.S., & Griffin, P. (Eds.). (1998). *Preventing reading difficulties in young children*. Washington, DC: National Academy Press.

Sticht, T.G., Caylor, J.S., Kern, R.P., & Fox, L.C. (1972). Project REALISTIC: Determination of adult functional literacy skill levels. *Reading Research Quarterly, 7*(3), 424–465.

Taylor, D. (1993). *From the child's point of view*. Portsmouth, NH: Heinemann.

Walqui, A. (2002). *Quality teaching for English learners*. San Francisco: WestEd.

Wenglinsky, H. (2004). Facts or critical thinking skills? What NAEP results say. *Educational Leadership, 62*(1), 32–35.

Wilhelm, J.D., Baker, T.N., & Dube, J. (2001). *Strategic reading: Guiding students to lifelong literacy*. Portsmouth, NH: Boynton/Cook.

Yatvin, J. (2002). Babes in the woods: The wanderings of the National Reading Panel. *Phi Delta Kappan, 83*(5), 364–369.

Yatvin, J., Weaver, C., & Garan, E. (2003). Reading First: Cautions and recommendations. *Language Arts, 81*(1), 28–33.

Chapter 2

Alexander, P.A., & Fox, E. (2004). A historical perspective on reading research and practice. In R.B. Ruddell & N.J. Unrau (Eds.), *Theoretical models and processes of reading* (5th ed., pp. 33–68). Newark, DE: International Reading Association.

Anderson, R.C. (1977). The notion of schemata and the educational enterprise. In R.C. Anderson, R.J. Spiro, & W.E. Montague (Eds.), *Schooling and the acquisition of knowledge* (pp. 415–431). Hillsdale, NJ: Erlbaum.

Anderson, R.C., & Nagy, W.E. (1992). The vocabulary conundrum. *American Educator, 16*(4), 14–18, 44–47.

Anderson, R.C., & Pearson, P.D. (1984). A schema-theoretic view of basic processes in reading comprehension. In P.D. Pearson, R. Barr, M.L. Kamil, & P.B. Mosenthal (Eds.), *Handbook of reading research* (pp. 255–292). New York: Longman.

Applebee, A.N. (1996). *Curriculum as conversation: Transforming traditions of teaching and learning*. Chicago: University of Chicago Press.

Applebee, A.N., & Langer, J.A. (1983). Instructional scaffolding: Reading and writing as natural activities. *Language Arts, 60*(2), 168–175.

Applebee, A.N, Langer, J.A., Nystrand, M., & Gamoran, A. (2003). Discussion-based approaches to developing understanding: Classroom instruction and student performance in middle and high school English. *American Educational Research Journal, 40*(3), 685–730.

Auerbach, E.R. (1989). Toward a socio-contextual approach to family literacy. *Harvard Educational Review, 59*, 165–187.

Bakhtin, M.M. (1981). *The dialogic imagination* (C. Emerson & M. Holquist, Trans.). Austin: University of Texas Press.

Bakhtin, M.M. (1990). *Art and answerability* (V. Liapurnov, Trans.). Austin: University of Texas Press.

Bevans, B., Furnish, B., Ramsey, A., & Talsma, S. (2001). *Effective strategies for home-school partnerships in reading*. Unpublished master's thesis, Saint Xavier University, Chicago.

Bissex, G. (1980). *GNYS AT WRK: A child learns to write and read*. Cambridge, MA: Harvard University Press.

Bloom, B.S. (Ed.). (1985). *Developing talent in young people*. New York: Ballantine.

Bodrova, E., & Leong, D. (1996). *Tools of the mind: The Vygotskian approach to early childhood education*. Englewood Cliffs, NJ: Merrill.

Brown, H., & Cambourne, B. (1990). *Read and retell: A strategy for the whole-language/natural learning classroom*. Portsmouth, NH: Heinemann.

Brown, R. (1973). *A first language: The early stages*. Cambridge, MA: Harvard University Press.

Bruner, J.S. (1975). The ontogenesis of speech acts. *Journal of Child Language, 2*(1), 1–19.

Bruner, J.S. (1990). *Acts of meaning*. Cambridge, MA: Harvard University Press.

Bus, A.G., van IJzendoorn, M.H., & Pelligrini, A.D. (1995). Joint book reading makes for success in learning to read: A meta-analysis on intergenerational transmission of literacy. *Review of Educational Research, 65*(1), 1–21.

Caine, R.N., & Caine, G. (1991). *Making connections: Teaching and the human brain*. Alexandria, VA: Association for Supervision and Curriculum Development.

Caine, R.N., & Caine, G. (1997). *Education on the edge of possiblity*. Alexandria, VA: Association for Supervision and Curriculum Development.

Calkins, L.M. (1983). *Lessons from a child*. Exeter, NH: Heinemann.

Calkins, L.M. (1986). *The art of teaching writing*. Portsmouth, NH: Heinemann.

Calkins, L.M. (1994). *The art of teaching writing* (New ed.). Portsmouth, NH: Heinemann.

Cambourne, B. (1988). *The whole story: Natural learning and the acquisition of literacy in the classroom*. Auckland, New Zealand: Ashton Scholastic.

Carnegie Task Force. (1994, April). *Starting points: Meeting the needs of our youngest children* (Report of the Carnegie Task Force on Meeting the Needs of Young Children). New York: Carnegie Corporation.

Carr, M., Saifer, S., & Novick, R. (2002). *Inquiring minds: Learning and literacy in early adolescence*. Portland, OR: Northwest Regional Educational Laboratory.

Cazden, C.B. (1988). *Classroom discourse: The language of teaching and learning*. Portsmouth, NH: Heinemann.

Chafe, W., & Danielwicz, J. (1987). *Properties of spoken and written language*. Berkeley, CA: Berkeley Center for the Study of Writing.

Chomsky, N. (1959). A review of B.F. Skinner's Verbal Behavior. *Language, 35*(1), 26–58.

Chomsky, N. (1965). *Aspects of the theory of syntax*. Cambridge, MA: MIT Press.

Christie, J.F. (1991). Psychological research on play: Connections with early literacy development. In J.F. Christie (Ed.), *Play and early literacy development* (pp. 27–43). Albany: State University of New York Press.

Clark, R. (1983). *Family life and school achievement: Why poor black children succeed or fail*. Chicago: University of Chicago Press.

Clay, M.M. (1966). *Emergent reading behavior*. Unpublished doctoral dissertation, University of Auckland, New Zealand.

Clay, M.M. (1975). *What did I write?* Exeter, NH: Heinemann.

Clay, M.M. (1985). *The early detection of reading difficulties: A diagnostic survey with recovery procedures* (3rd ed.). Auckland, New Zealand: Heinemann.

Cochran-Smith, M. (1984). *The making of a reader*. Norwood, NJ: Ablex.

Csikszentmihalyi, M. (1990). *Flow: The psychology of optimal experience*. New York: Harper & Row.

Dahl, K.L., & Farnan, N. (1998). *Children's writing: Perspectives from research*. Newark, DE: International Reading Association; Chicago: National Reading Conference.

Dahl, K.L., & Freppon, P.A. (1995). The comparison of inner-city children's interpretations of reading and writing instruction in the early grades in skills-based and whole language classrooms. *Reading Research Quarterly, 30*(1), 50–74.

Edwards, P.A. (1989). Supporting lower SES mothers' attempts to provide scaffolding for book reading. In J. Allen & J.M. Mason (Eds.), *Risk makers, risk takers, risk breakers: Reducing the risks for young literacy learners* (pp. 199–213). Portsmouth, NH: Heinemann.

Edwards, P.A. (1991). Fostering early literacy through parent coaching. In E. Hiebert (Ed.), *Literacy for a diverse society: Perspectives, practices, and policies* (pp. 199–213). New York: Teachers College Press.

Ferreiro, E., & Teberosky, A. (1982). *Literacy before schooling*. Exeter, NH: Heinemann.

Flood, J., & Menyuk, P. (1981). *Detection of ambiguity and production of paraphrase in written language*. Washington, DC: National Institute of Education.

Gadsen, V.L. (2000). Intergenerational literacy within families. In M.L. Kamil, P.B. Mosenthal, P.D. Pearson, & R. Barr (Eds.), *Handbook of reading research* (Vol. 3, pp. 871–888). Mahwah, NJ: Erlbaum.

Garner, R. (1994). Metacognition and executive control. In R.B. Ruddell, M.R. Ruddell, & H. Singer (Eds.), *Theoretical models and processes of reading* (4th ed., pp. 715–732).

Newark, DE: International Reading Association.

Gee, J.P. (1996). *Social linguistics and literacies: Ideology in discourse* (2nd ed.). London; Bristol, PA: Taylor & Francis.

Gee, J.P. (2000). Discourse and sociocultural studies in reading. In M.L. Kamil, P.B. Mosenthal, P.D. Pearson, & R. Barr (Eds.), *Handbook of reading research* (Vol. 3, pp. 195–207). Mahwah, NJ: Erlbaum.

Gillet, J.W., & Temple, C. (1996). *Language and literacy: A lively approach*. New York: HarperCollins.

Goodman, Y.M. (1984). The development of initial literacy. In H. Goelman, A. Oberg, & F. Smith (Eds.), *Awakening to literacy* (pp. 102–109). Exeter, NH: Heinemann.

Graves, D.H. (1983). *Writing: Children and teachers at work*. Exeter, NH: Heinemann.

Graves, D.H. (1994). *A fresh look at writing*. Portsmouth, NH: Heinemann.

Graves, M.F. (1986). Vocabulary learning and instruction. In E.Z. Rothkopf & L.C. Ehri (Eds.), *Review of research in education* (Vol. 13, pp. 49–89). Washington, DC: American Educational Research Association.

Guthrie, J.T., & Davis, M.H. (2003). Motivating struggling readers in middle school through an engagement model of classroom practice. *Reading and Writing Quarterly, 19*(1), 59–85.

Guthrie, J.T., & Wigfield, A. (2000). Engagement and motivation in reading. In M.L. Kamil, P.B. Mosenthal, P.D. Pearson, & R. Barr (Eds.), *Handbook of reading research* (Vol. 3, pp. 403–422). Mahwah, NJ: Erlbaum.

Halliday, M.A.K. (1973). *Explorations in the functions of language*. London: Edward Arnold.

Halliday, M.A.K. (1975). *Learning how to mean: Exploration in the development of language*. London: Edward Arnold.

Hansen, J. (1987). *When writers read*. Portsmouth, NH: Heinemann.

Harste, J.C., Burke, C.L., & Woodward, V.A. (1982). Children's language and world: Initial encounters with print. In J.A. Langer & M.T. Smith-Burke (Eds.), *Reader meets author: Bridging the gap* (pp. 105–131). Newark, DE: International Reading Association.

Harste, J.C., Woodward, V.A., & Burke, C.L. (1984). *Language stories and literacy lessons*. Exeter, NH: Heinemann.

Hart, B., & Risley, T.R. (1995). *Meaningful differences in the everyday experience of young American children*. Baltimore: Paul H. Brookes.

Heath, S.B. (1982). What no bedtime story means. *Language in Society, 11*(1), 49–76.

Heath, S.B. (1983). *Ways with words: Language, life, and work in communities and classrooms.* Cambridge, England: Cambridge University Press.

Holdaway, D. (1979). *The foundations of literacy.* Sydney, NSW, Australia: Ashton Scholastic; Portsmouth, NH: Heinemann.

International Reading Association (IRA). (2002). *Family–school partnerships: Essential elements of literacy instruction in the United States* (Position statement). Newark, DE: Author. Retrieved June 7, 2005, from http://www.reading.org/resources/issues/positions_family_school.html

Ivey, G. (1999). A multicase study in the middle school: Complexities among young adolescent readers. *Reading Research Quarterly, 34*(2), 172–192.

Jackson, A.W., & Davis, G.A. (2000). *Turning points 2000: Educating adolescents in the 21st century* (Report of the Carnegie Corporation of New York). New York: Teachers College Press.

Kamil, M.L. (2003). *Adolescents and literacy: Reading for the 21st century.* Washington, DC: Alliance for Excellent Education.

Kucer, S. (2005). *Dimensions of literacy: A conceptual base for teaching reading and writing in school settings* (2nd ed.). Mahwah, NJ: Erlbaum.

Langer, J.A. (1985). A sociocognitive approach to language learning. *Research in the Teaching of English, 19*(4), 235–237.

Langer, J.A. (2000). *Teaching middle and high school students to read and write well: Six features of effective instruction.* Albany: National Research Center on English Learning and Achievement, State University of New York.

Langer, J.A. (2001). Beating the odds: Teaching middle and high school students to read and write well. *American Educational Research Journal, 38*(4), 837–880.

Langer, J.A. (2002). *Effective literacy instruction: Building successful reading and writing programs.* Urbana, IL: National Council of Teachers of English.

Leichter, H.J. (1984). Families as environments for literacy. In H. Goelman, A. Oberg, & F. Smith (Eds.), *Awakening to literacy* (pp. 38–50). Exeter, NH: Heinemann.

Loban, W. (1963). *Language development: Kindergarten through grade 12.* Urbana, IL: National Council of Teachers of English.

Mason, J.M. (1980). When do children begin to read? An exploration of four-year-old children's letter and word reading competencies. *Reading Research Quarterly, 15*(2), 203–227.

Mason, J.M. (1992). Reading stories to preliterate children: A proposed connection to reading. In P.B. Gough, L.C. Ehri, & R. Treiman (Eds.), *Reading acquisition* (pp. 215–224). Hillsdale, NJ: Erlbaum.

Moje, E.B., & Sutherland, L.M. (2003). The future of middle school literacy education. *English Education, 35*(2), 149–164.

Moje, E.B., Young, J.P., Readence, J.E., & Moore, D.W. (2000). Reinventing adolescent literacy for new times: Perennial and millennial issues. *Journal of Adolescent & Adult Literacy, 43*(5), 400–410.

Moore, D.W., Bean, T.W., Birdyshaw, D., & Rycik, J.A. (1999). *Adolescent literacy: A position statement for the Commission on Adolescent Literacy of the International Reading Association.* Newark, DE: International Reading Association. Retrieved June 7, 2005, from http://www.reading.org/downloads/positions/ps1036_adolescent.pdf

Morrow, L.M. (1978). Analysis of syntax in the language of six-, seven-, and eight-year-old children. *Research in the Teaching of English, 12*(2), 149–153.

Morrow, L.M. (1996). *Motivating reading and writing in diverse classrooms: Social and physical contexts in a literature-based program* (Research Report No. 28). Urbana, IL: National Council of Teachers of English.

Morrow, L.M. (1997). *Literacy development in the early years: Helping children read and write* (3rd ed.). Boston: Allyn & Bacon.

Morrow, L.M., O'Connor, E.M., & Smith, J. (1990). Effects of a story reading program on the literacy development of at-risk kindergarten children. *Journal of Reading Behavior, 22*(3), 255–275.

Morrow, L.M., & Young, J. (1997). A collaborative family literacy program: The effects on children's motivation and literacy achievement. *Early Child Development and Care, 127–128,* 13–25.

Moustafa, M. (1997). *Beyond traditional phonics: Research discoveries and reading instruction.* Portsmouth, NH: Heinemann.

Myers, M., & Paris, S.G. (1978). Children's metacognitive knowledge about reading. *Journal of Educational Psychology, 70*(5), 680–690.

Nagy, W.E., & Anderson, R.C. (1984). How many words are there in printed school English? *Reading Research Quarterly, 19*(3), 304–330.

Nagy, W.E., & Scott, J.A. (2000). Vocabulary processes. In M.L. Kamil, P.B. Mosenthal,

P.D. Pearson, & R. Barr (Eds.), *Handbook of reading research* (Vol. 3, pp. 269–284). Mahwah, NJ: Erlbaum.

National Council of Teachers of English (NCTE). (2004). *A call to action: What we know about adolescent literacy and ways to support teachers in meeting students' needs* (NCTE guideline by the Commission on Reading). Urbana, IL: Author. Retrieved May 21, 2005, from http://www.ncte.org/about/over/positions/category/read/118622.htm

Neuman, S.B., & Roskos, K. (1992). Literary objects as cultural tools: Effects on children's literacy behaviors in play. *Reading Research Quarterly, 27*(3), 202–225.

Ninio, A. (1980). Picture-book reading in mother-infant dyads belonging to two subgroups in Israel. *Child Development, 51*(2), 587–590.

Ninio, A., & Bruner, J. (1978). The achievement and antecedents of labeling. *Journal of Child Language, 5*(1), 1–15.

Nystrand, M. (1997). *Opening dialogue: Understanding the dynamics of language and learning in the English classroom.* New York: Teachers College Press.

Olson, D.R. (1977). From utterance to text: The bias of language in speech and writing. *Harvard Educational Review, 47*(3), 257–281.

Pace, G. (1993). *Making decisions about grouping in language arts.* Portland, OR: Northwest Regional Educational Laboratory.

Palincsar, A.S., & Brown, A.L. (1984). Reciprocal teaching of comprehension-fostering and comprehension-monitoring activities. *Cognition & Instruction, 1*(2), 117–175.

Pappas, C.C. (1991). Young children's strategies in learning the "book language" of information books. *Discourse Processes, 14*(2), 203–225.

Paratore, J.R. (1993). Influence of an intergenerational approach to literacy on the practice of literacy of parents and their children. In C.K. Kinzer & D.J. Leu (Eds.), *Examining central issues in literacy research, theory, and practice* (42nd yearbook of the National Reading Conference, pp. 83–91). Chicago: National Reading Conference.

Paratore, J.R., Melzi, G., & Krol-Sinclair, B. (1999). *What should we expect of family literacy? Experiences of Latino children whose parents participate in an intergenerational literacy project.* Newark, DE: International Reading Association; Chicago: National Reading Conference.

Paris, S.G. (1988). Models and metaphors of learning strategies. In C.E. Weinstein, E.T. Goetz, & P.A. Alexander (Eds.), *Learning and study strategies: Issues in assessment, instruction, and evaluation* (pp. 299–321). San Diego, CA: Academic.

Paris, S.G., Lipson, M.Y., & Wixon, K.K. (1983). Becoming a strategic reader. *Contemporary Educational Psychology, 8*(3), 293–316.

Paris, S.G., & Winograd, P. (1990). How metacognition can promote academic learning and instruction. In B.F. Jones & L. Idol (Eds.), *Dimensions of thinking and cognitive instruction* (pp. 15–51). Hillsdale, NJ: Erlbaum.

Pearson, P.D., & Stephens, D. (1994). Learning about literacy: A 30-year journey. In R.B. Ruddell, M.R. Ruddell, & H. Singer (Eds.), *Theoretical models and processes of reading* (4th ed., pp. 22–42). Newark, DE: International Reading Association.

Pelligrini, A.D., & Galda, L. (1991). Longitudinal relations among preschoolers' symbolic play, metalinguistic verbs, and emergent literacy. In J.F. Christie (Ed.), *Play and early literacy development* (pp. 47–67). Albany: State University of New York Press.

Pelligrini, A.D., & Galda, L. (1993). Ten years after: A reexamination of symbolic play and literacy research. *Reading Research Quarterly, 28,* 162–175.

Piaget, J., & Inhelder, B. (1969). *The psychology of the child* (H. Weaver, Trans.). New York: Basic Books.

Pikulski, J.J. (1991). The transition years: Middle school. In J. Flood, J.M. Jensen, D. Lapp, & J.R. Squire (Eds.), *Handbook of research on teaching the English language arts* (pp. 303–319). New York: MacMillan.

Pinnell, G.S. (1985). Ways to look at the functions of children's language. In A. Jaggar & M.T. Smith-Burke (Eds.), *Observing the language learner* (pp. 57–72). Newark, DE: International Reading Association.

Purcell-Gates, V. (1988). Lexical and syntactic knowledge of written narrative held by well-read-to kindergartners and second graders. *Research in the Teaching of English, 22*(2), 128–160.

Purcell-Gates, V. (1995). *Other people's words: The cycle of low literacy.* Cambridge, MA: Harvard University Press.

Purcell-Gates, V. (1996). Stories, coupons, and the *TV Guide*: Relationships between home literacy experiences and emergent literacy knowledge. *Reading Research Quarterly, 31*(4), 406–428.

Purcell-Gates, V. (2000). Family literacy. In M.L. Kamil, P.B. Mosenthal, P.D. Pearson, & R. Barr (Eds.), *Handbook of reading research* (Vol. 3, pp. 853–870). Mahwah, NJ: Erlbaum.

Purcell-Gates, V., McIntyre, E., & Freppon, P. (1995). Learning written storybook language in school: A comparison of low-SES children in skills-based and whole language classrooms. *American Educational Research Journal, 32*(3), 659–685.

Read, C. (1975). *Children's categorization of speech sounds in English* (Research Report No. 17). Urbana, IL: National Council of Teachers of English.

Roller, C.M. (2001). How will we develop the concept of comprehensive reading instruction across the grade levels? In C.M. Roller (Ed.), *Comprehensive reading instruction across the grade levels: A collection of papers from the Reading Research 2001 Conference* (pp. 1–9). Newark, DE: International Reading Association.

Rubin, A.D. (1978). *A theoretical taxonomy of the differences between oral and written language* (Technical Report No. 35). Urbana: Center for the Study of Reading, University of Illinois.

Rumelhart, D.E. (1980). Schemata: The building blocks of cognition. In R.J. Spiro, B.C. Bruce, & W.F. Brewer (Eds.), *Theoretical issues in reading comprehension: Perspectives from cognitive psychology, linguistics, artificial intelligence, and education* (pp. 38–58). Hillsdale, NJ: Erlbaum.

Rumelhart, D.E., & Ortony, A. (1977). The representation of knowledge in memory. In R.C. Anderson, R.J. Spiro, & W.E. Montague (Eds.), *Schooling and the acquisition of knowledge* (pp. 99–135). Hillsdale, NJ: Erlbaum.

Schallert, D.L., & Martin, D.B. (2003). A psychological analysis of what teachers and students do in the language arts classroom. In J. Flood, D. Lapp, J.R. Squire, & J.M. Jensen (Eds.), *Handbook of research on teaching the English language arts* (2nd ed., pp. 31–45). Mahwah, NJ: Erlbaum.

Schank, R.C., & Abelson, R.P. (1977). *Scripts, plans, goals, and understanding: An inquiry into human knowledge structures.* Hillsdale, NJ: Erlbaum.

Schoenbach, R., Greenleaf, C., Cziko, C., & Hurwitz, L. (1999). *Reading for understanding: A guide to improving reading in middle and high school classrooms.* San Francisco: Jossey-Bass.

Shanklin, N.J. (2000). Adolescent literacy: Encouraging the development of adolescent readers. In *NCTE reading initiative handbook* (pp. 3–7). Urbana, IL: National Council of Teachers of English.

Simmons, J., & Carroll, P.S. (2003). Today's middle grades: Different structures, students, and classrooms. In J. Flood, D. Lapp, J.R. Squire, & J.M. Jensen (Eds.), *Handbook of research on teaching the English language arts* (2nd ed., pp. 357–392). Mahwah, NJ: Erlbaum.

Skinner, B.F. (1974). *About behaviorism.* New York: Knopf.

Smith, F. (1971). *Understanding reading: A psycholinguistic analysis of reading and learning to read.* New York: Holt, Rinehart and Winston.

Strickland, D.S, & Feeley, J.T. (2003). Development in the elementary school years. In J. Flood, D. Lapp, J.R. Squire, & J.M. Jensen (Eds.), *Handbook of research on teaching the English language arts* (2nd ed., pp. 339–391). Mahwah, NJ: Erlbaum.

Sulzby, E. (1985). Children's emergent reading of favorite storybooks: A developmental study. *Reading Research Quarterly, 20*(4), 458–481.

Tannen, D. (1982). *Spoken and written language: Exploring orality and literacy: Vol. 9. Advances in discourse processes.* Norwood, NJ: Ablex.

Taylor, D. (1983). *Family literacy: Young children learning to read and write.* Exeter, NH: Heinemann.

Taylor, D., & Strickland, D.S. (1986). *Family storybook reading.* Portsmouth, NH: Heinemann.

Taylor, R.G., Chatters, L.M., Tucker, M.B., & Lewis, E. (1990). Developments in research on black families: A decade review. *Journal of Marriage & the Family, 52*(4), 993–1014.

Teale, W.H. (1978). Positive environments for learning to read: What studies of early readers tell us. *Language Arts, 55*(8), 922–932.

Teale, W.H. (1982). Toward a theory of how children learn to read and write naturally. *Language Arts, 59*(6), 555–570.

Teale, W.H. (1986). The beginning of reading and writing: Written language development during the preschool and kindergarten years. In M.R. Sampson (Ed.), *The pursuit of literacy: Early reading and writing* (pp. 1–29). Dubuque, IA: Kendall/Hunt.

Teale, W.H. (1987). Emergent literacy: Reading and writing development in early childhood. In J. Readence & R.S. Baldwin (Eds.), *Research in literacy: Merging perspectives* (36th yearbook of the National Reading Conference, pp. 45–74). Rochester, NY: National Reading Conference.

Thorndike, E.L. (1971). Reading as reasoning: A study of mistakes in paragraph reading. *Reading Research Quarterly, 6*(4), 425–434.

Trumbull, E., & Farr, B. (2005). *Language and learning: What teachers need to know.* Norwood, MA: Christopher-Gordon.

Tunmer, W.E., Herriman, M., & Nesdale, A. (1988). Metalinguistic abilities and beginning reading. *Reading Research Quarterly, 23*(2), 134–158.

Vygotsky, L.S. (1978). *Mind in society: The development of higher psychological processes* (M. Cole, V. John-Steiner, S. Scribner, & E. Souberman, Eds. & Trans.). Cambridge, MA: Harvard University Press. (Original work published 1934)

Walqui, A. (2003). *Conceptual framework: Scaffolding instruction for English learners.* San Francisco: WestEd.

Wells, C.G. (1986). *The meaning makers: Children learning language and using language to learn.* Portsmouth, NH: Heinemann.

Wells, C.G. (1999). *Dialogic inquiry: Towards a sociocultural practice and theory of education.* New York: Cambridge University Press.

Wertsch, J.A. (1991). A sociocultural approach to socially shared cognition. In L.B. Resnick, J.M. Levine, & S.D. Teasley (Eds.), *Perspectives on socially shared cognition* (pp. 85–100). Washington, DC: American Psychological Association.

Wiggins, G., & McTighe, S. (1998). *Understanding by design.* Alexandria, VA: Association for Supervision and Curriculum Development.

Wood, D. (1988). *How children think and learn.* Oxford, England; New York: Blackwell.

Woolfolk, A. (2001). *Educational psychology* (8th ed.). Boston: Allyn & Bacon.

Yaden, D.B., Rowe, D.W., & MacGillivray, L. (2000). Emergent literacy: A matter (polyphony) of perspectives. In M.L. Kamil, P.B. Mosenthal, P.D. Pearson, & R. Barr (Eds.), *Handbook of reading research* (Vol. 3, pp. 425–454). Mahwah, NJ: Erlbaum.

Chapter 3

Ada, A.F. (n.d.). *No one learns twice: The transferability of reading skills.* Unpublished manuscript.

Adams, M.J. (1990). *Beginning to read: Thinking and learning about print.* Cambridge, MA: MIT Press.

Allington, R.L. (1977). If they don't read much, how they ever gonna get good? *Journal of Reading, 21*(1), 57–61.

Allington, R.L. (1980). Poor readers don't get to read much in reading groups. *Language Arts, 5*(8), 873–875.

Allington, R.L. (1983). The reading instruction provided readers of differing abilities. *The Elementary School Journal, 83*(5), 548–559.

Allington, R.L. (1991). Effective literacy instruction for at-risk children. In M.S. Knapp & P.M. Shields (Eds.), *Better schooling for the children of poverty: Alternatives to conventional wisdom* (pp. 9–30). Berkeley, CA: McCutchan.

Allington, R.L. (1994a). The schools we have, the schools we need. *The Reading Teacher, 48*(1), 14–29.

Allington, R.L. (1994b). What's special about special programs for children who find learning to read difficult? *Journal of Reading Behavior, 26*(1), 95–115.

Allington, R.L. (2002). Research on reading/learning disability interventions. In A.E. Farstrup & S.J. Samuels (Eds.), *What research has to say about reading instruction* (3rd ed., pp. 261–290). Newark, DE: International Reading Association.

Allington, R.L. (2004a). Continuing the discussion: Reply to G. Reid Lyon and colleagues. *Educational Leadership, 61*(6), 86–87.

Allington, R.L. (2004b). Setting the record straight. *Educational Leadership, 61*(6), 22–25.

Allington, R.L., & Cunningham, P.M. (1996). *Schools that work: Where all children read and write.* New York: HarperCollins.

Allington, R.L., & Johnston, P.H. (2002). *Reading to learn: Lessons from exemplary fourth-grade classrooms.* New York: Guilford.

Allington, R.L., & McGill-Franzen, A. (1989). School response to reading failure: Instruction for Chapter 1 and special education students in grades 2, 4, and 8. *The Elementary School Journal, 89*(5), 529–542.

Allington, R.L., & McGill-Franzen, A. (2003). The impact of summer setback on the reading achievement gap. *Phi Delta Kappan, 85*(1), 68–75.

Allington, R.L., & Walmsley, S.A. (Eds.). (1995). *No quick fix: Rethinking literacy programs in America's elementary schools.* Newark, DE: International Reading Association.

Artiles, A.J., & Trent, S.C. (1994). Overrepresentation of minority students in special education: A continuing debate. *Journal of Special Education, 27*(4), 410–437.

Artiles, A.J., Trent, S.C., & Palmer, J.D. (2004). Culturally diverse students in special education: Legacies and prospects. In J.A. Banks & C.A.M. Banks (Eds.), *Handbook of research on multicultural education* (2nd ed., pp. 716–735). San Francisco: Jossey-Bass.

Au, K.H., & Mason, J.M. (1981). Social organization factors in learning to read: The balance of rights hypothesis. *Reading Research Quarterly, 17*(1), 115–152.

Au, K.H., & Mason, J.M. (1983). Cultural congruence in classroom participation structures: Achieving a balance of rights. *Discourse Processes, 6*(2), 145–167.

August, D., & Hakuta, K. (Eds.). (1997). *Improving schooling for language-minority children: A research agenda*. Washington, DC: National Academy Press.

Barton, P.E. (2003). *Parsing the achievement gap: Baselines for tracking progress*. (Policy Information Report). Princeton, NJ: Educational Testing Service.

Beers, K. (2003). *When kids can't read: What teachers can do: A guide for teachers 6–12*. Portsmouth, NH: Heinemann.

Berko Gleason, J. (1993). *The development of language* (3rd ed.). New York: Macmillan.

Bialystock, E. (Ed.). (1991). *Language processing in bilingual children*. Cambridge, England: Cambridge University Press.

Bialystock, E. (1997). Effects of bilingualism and biliteracy on children's emerging concepts of print. *Developmental Psychology, 33*(3), 429–440.

Bond, G.L., & Dykstra, R. (1997). The cooperative research program in first grade reading instruction. *Reading Research Quarterly, 32*(4), 348–427. (Original work published 1967)

Bryk, A.S., Lee, V.E., & Holland, P.B. (1993). *Catholic schools and the common good*. Cambridge, MA: Harvard University Press.

Camilli, G., Vargas, S., & Yurecko, M. (2003). Teaching children to read: The fragile link between science and federal education policy. *Education Policy Analysis Archives, 11*(15). Retrieved May 10, 2003, from http://epaa.asu.edu/epaa/v11n15

Camilli, G., & Wolfe, P. (2004). Research on reading: A cautionary tale. *Educational Leadership, 61*(6), 26–29.

Cardenas, J., Robledo, M., & Waggoner, D. (1988). *The undereducation of American youth*. San Antonio, TX: Intercultural Development Research Association. (ERIC Document Reproduction Service No. ED309201)

Carnegie Task Force. (1996, September). *Years of promise: A comprehensive learning strategy for America's children* (Report of the Carnegie Task Force on Learning in the Primary Grades). New York: Carnegie Corporation.

Center for Research on Education, Diversity and Excellence. (2000). *The sociocultural context of Hawaiian language revival and learning* (Project 1.6 executive summary). Retrieved May 3, 2004, from http://www.crede.org/research/llaa/1.6es.html

Chavkin, N. (1989). Debunking the myth about minority parents. *Educational Horizons, 67*(4), 199–123.

Chubb, J.E., & Moe, T.M. (1990). *Politics, markets, and America's schools*. Washington, DC: Brookings Institution.

Clay, M.M. (1979). *The early detection of reading difficulties: A diagnostic survey with recovery procedures*. Exeter, NH: Heinemann.

Clay, M.M. (1993). *An observation survey: Of early literacy achievement*. Portsmouth, NH: Heinemann.

Cole, M. (1990). Cognitive development and formal schooling: The evidence from cross-cultural research. In L.C. Moll (Ed.), *Vygotsky and education: Instructional implications and applications of sociohistorical psychology* (pp. 89–110). Cambridge, England: Cambridge University Press.

Coles, G. (2001). Reading taught to the tune of the "scientific" hickory stick. *Phi Delta Kappan, 83*(3), 204–212.

Coles, G. (2003). *Reading the naked truth: Literacy, legislation, and lies*. Portsmouth, NH: Heinemann.

Collier, V.P. (1989). How long? A synthesis of research on academic achievement in a second language. *TESOL Quarterly, 23*(3), 509–531.

Collier, V.P. (1992). A synthesis of studies examining long-term language minority student data on academic achievement. *Bilingual Research Journal, 16*(1–2), 187–212.

Collier, V.P. (1995). Acquiring a second language for school. *Directions in Language & Education, 1*(4), 3–14.

Comer, J. (1986). Parent participation in the schools. *Phi Delta Kappan, 67*(6), 442–446.

Corson, D. (1992). Bilingual education policy and social justice. *Journal of Education Policy, 7*(1), 45–69.

Cuevas, J.A. (1997). *Educating limited-English proficient students: A review of the research on school programs and classroom practices*. San Francisco: WestEd.

Cummins, J. (1984). The role of primary language development in promoting educational success for language minority students. In *Schooling and language minority students: A theoretical framework* (pp. 16–62). Los Angeles: California State University Evaluation Dissemination, and Assessment Center. (ERIC Document Reproduction Service No. ED249773)

Cunningham, J.W. (2001). Essay book review: The National Reading Panel report. *Reading Research Quarterly, 36*(3), 326–335.

Cunningham, P., & Allington, R.L. (2003). *Classrooms that work: They can all read and write* (3rd ed.). New York: Longman.

Deford, D., Lyons, C., & Pinnell, G. (Eds.). (1991). *Bridges to learning: Learning from Reading Recovery*. Portsmouth, NH: Heinemann.

Delpit, L.D. (1986). Skills and other dilemmas of a progressive black educator. *Harvard Educational Review, 56*(4), 379–385.

Delpit, L.D. (1988). The silenced dialogue: Power and pedagogy in educating other people's children. *Harvard Educational Review, 58*(3), 280–287.

Diaz, S., Moll, L., & Mehan, H. (1986). Sociocultural resources in instruction: A context-specific approach. In California State Department of Education, *Beyond language: Social and cultural factors in schooling language minority students* (pp. 187–230). Los Angeles: California State University Evaluation, Dissemination, and Assessment Center.

Donovan, M.S., & Cross, C.T. (Eds.). (2002). *Minority students in special and gifted education*. Washington, DC: National Academy Press.

Durkin, D. (1978). What classroom observations reveal about reading comprehension. *Reading Research Quarterly, 14*(4), 481–533.

Dyson, A.H. (with Bennett, A., Brooks, W., Garcia, J., Howard-McBride, C., Malekzadeh, J., et al.). (1997). *What difference does difference make? Teacher reflections on diversity, literacy, and the urban primary school*. Urbana, IL: National Council of Teachers of English.

Edwards, P.A. (1989). Supporting lower SES mothers' attempts to provide scaffolding for book reading. In J. Allen & J.M. Mason (Eds.), *Risk makers, risk takers, risk breakers: Reducing the risks for young literacy learners* (pp. 199–213). Portsmouth, NH: Heinemann.

Edwards, P.A. (1991). Fostering early literacy through parent coaching. In E. Hiebert (Ed.), *Literacy for a diverse society: Perspectives, practices, and policies* (pp. 199–213). New York: Teachers College Press.

Edwards, P.A., Danridge, J.C., & Pleasants, H.M. (2000). *Exploring urban teachers' and administrators' conceptions of at-riskness* (CIERA Report No. 2-010). Ann Arbor: Center for the Improvement of Early Reading Achievement, University of Michigan.

Ellis, R. (1985). *Understanding second language acquisition*. Oxford, England: Oxford University Press.

Entwisle, D.R., Alexander, K.L., & Olson, L.S. (1997). *Children, schools, and inequality*. Boulder, CO: Westview.

Erickson, F. (1993). Transformation and school success: The politics and culture of educational achievement. In E. Jacob & C. Jordan (Eds.), *Minority education: Anthropological perspectives*. Norwood, NJ: Ablex.

Erickson, F., & Mohatt, G. (1982). Cultural organization of participation structures in two classrooms of Indian students. In G. Spindler (Ed.), *Doing the ethnography of schooling: Educational anthropology in action* (pp. 132–175). New York: Holt, Rinehart and Winston.

Fu, D. (1995). *"My trouble is my English."* Portsmouth, NH: Boynton/Cook.

Gallimore, R., Boggs, J., & Jordan, C. (1974). *Culture, behavior, and education: A study of Hawaiian-Americans*. Beverly Hills, CA: Sage.

Gallimore, R., & Goldenberg, C. (1989). *Action research to increase Hispanic students' exposure to meaningful text: A focus on reading and content area instruction* (Final Report to the Presidential Grants for School Improvement Committee, University of California). Berkeley: University of California.

Garan, E.M. (2002). *Resisting reading mandates: How to triumph with the truth*. Portsmouth, NH: Heinemann.

Garcia, E. (1994). *Understanding and meeting the challenge of student cultural diversity*. Boston: Houghton Mifflin.

Garcia, O. (1999). Educating Latino high school students with little formal schooling. In C.J. Faltis & P.M. Wolfe (Eds.), *So much to say: Adolescents, bilingualism, and ESL in the secondary school* (pp. 267–272). New York: Teachers College Press.

Garcia, P., & Keresztes-Nagy, S.K. (1993). *Curriculum guide: English as a second language for the workplace: Worker education program*. Chicago: Amalgamated Clothing & Textile Workers Union; Chicago: Northeastern Illinois University Chicago Teachers' Center.

Gay, G. (1988). Designing relevant curricula for diverse learners. *Education & Urban Society, 20*(4), 327–340.

Gee, J.P. (1996). *Social linguistics and literacies: Ideology in discourse* (2nd ed.). London; Bristol, PA: Taylor & Francis.

Gee, J.P. (1999). *An introduction to discourse analysis: Theory and method*. New York: Routledge.

Genesee, F. (1987). *Learning through two languages: Studies of immersion and bilingual education*. Cambridge, MA: Newbury House.

Genesee, F. (1994). *Educating second language children: The whole child, the whole curriculum, the whole community*. Cambridge, England: Cambridge University Press.

Goldenberg, C.N. (1987). Low-income Hispanic parents' contributions to their first-grade children's word-recognition skills. *Anthropology & Education Quarterly, 18*(3), 149–179.

Goldenberg, C.N., & Gallimore, R. (1991). Local knowledge, research knowledge, and educational change: A case study of early Spanish reading improvement. *Educational Researcher, 20*(8), 2–14.

Goldenberg, C.N., & Sullivan, J. (1994). *Making change happen in a language-minority school: A search for coherence* (Educational Practice Report No. 13). Washington, DC: Center for Applied Linguistics.

Goodman, K., Goodman, Y.M., & Flores, B. (1979). *Reading in the bilingual classroom: Literacy and biliteracy*. Rosslyn, VA: National Clearinghouse for Bilingual Education.

Greenleaf, C.L., Schoenbach, R., Cziko, C., & Mueller, F.L. (2001). Apprenticing adolescents to academic literacy. *Harvard Educational Review, 71*(1), 79–129.

Hakuta, K. (1986). *Mirror of language: The debate on bilingualism*. New York: Basic Books.

Hall, N. (1987). *The emergence of literacy*. Portsmouth, NH: Heinemann.

Harklau, L. (1999). The ESL learning environment in secondary school. In C.J. Faltis & P.M. Wolfe (Eds.), *So much to say: Adolescents, bilingualism, and ESL in the secondary school* (pp. 267–272). New York: Teachers College Press.

Hayes, D.P., & Grether, J. (1983). The school year and vacations: When do students learn? *Cornell Journal of Social Relations, 17*(1), 56–71.

Haynes, M.C., & Jenkins, J.R. (1986). Reading instruction in special education resource rooms. *American Educational Research Journal, 23*(2), 162–190.

Heath, S.B. (1983). *Ways with words: Language, life, and work in communities and classrooms*. Cambridge, England: Cambridge University Press.

Herman, R. (1999). *An educator's guide to schoolwide reform*. Arlington, VA: Educational Research Service.

Hiebert, E.H. (1983). An examination of ability grouping for reading instruction. *Reading Research Quarterly, 18*(2), 231–255.

Hudelson, S. (1987). The role of native language literacy in the education of language minority children. *Language Arts, 64*(8), 827–841.

Hudelson, S., Poyner, L., & Wolfe, P. (2003). Teaching bilingual and ESL children and adolescents. In J. Flood, D. Lapp, J.R. Squire, & J.M. Jensen (Eds.), *Handbook of research on teaching the English language arts* (2nd ed., pp. 421–434). Mahwah, NJ: Erlbaum.

Huerta-Macias, A., & Gonzalez, M.L. (1997). Beyond ESL instruction: Creating structures that promote achievement for all secondary students. *TESOL Journal, 6*(4), 16–19.

International Reading Association (IRA). (2001). *Second-language literacy instruction* (Position statement). Newark, DE: Author. Retrieved June 7, 2005, from http://www.reading.org/resources/issues/positions_second_language.html

International Reading Association (IRA). (2003). *The role of reading instruction in addressing the overrepresentation of minority children in special education in the United States* (Position statement). Newark, DE: Author. Retrieved June 7, 2005, from http://www.reading.org/resources/issues/positions_minorities.html

Janopoulos, M. (1986). The relationship of pleasure reading and second language writing proficiency. *TESOL Quarterly, 20*(4), 763–768.

Jenkins, J., & O'Connor, R. (2002). Early identification and intervention for young children with reading/learning disabilities. In R. Bradley, L. Danielson, & D.P. Hallahan (Eds.), *Identification of learning disabilities: Research in practice* (pp. 99–150). Mawah, NJ: Erlbaum.

Jordan, C. (1984). Cultural compatibility and the education of Hawaiian children: Implications for mainland educators. *Educational Research Quarterly, 8*(4), 59–71.

Jordan, C. (1992). The role of culture in minority school achievement. *The Kamehameha Journal of Education, 3*(2), 53–67.

Jordan, C. (1995). Creating cultures of schooling: Historical and conceptual background of the KEEP/Rough Rock Collaboration. *Bilingual Research Journal, 19*(1), 83–100.

Klenk, L., & Kibby, M.W. (2000). Remediating reading difficulties: Appraising the past, reconciling the present, constructing the future. In M.L. Kamil, P.B. Mosenthal, P.D. Pearson, & R. Barr (Eds.), *Handbook of reading research* (Vol. 3, pp. 667–690). Mahwah, NJ: Erlbaum.

Kozol, J. (1991). *Savage inequalities: Children in America's schools*. New York: Crown.

Krashen, S.D. (1981). *Second language acquisition and second language learning*. Oxford, England: Pergamon.

Krashen, S.D. (1982). *Principles and practice in second language acquisition*. New York: Pergamon.

Krashen, S.D. (2004). False claims about literacy development. *Educational Leadership, 61*(6), 18–21.

Krashen, S.D., & Terrell, T.D. (1983). *The natural approach: Language acquisition in the classroom*. New York: Pergamon.

Labov, W. (2001). Applying our knowledge of African American English to the problem of raising reading levels in inner-city schools. In S.L. Lanehart (Ed.), *Sociocultural and historical contexts of African American English* (pp. 299–317). Philadelphia: Benjamins.

Labov, W. (2003). When ordinary children fail to read. *Reading Research Quarterly, 38*(1), 128–131.

Labov, W., Baker, B., Bullock, S., Ross, L., & Brown, M. (1998). *A graphemic-phonemic analysis of the reading errors of inner city children*. Retrieved March 10, 2004, from http://www.ling.upenn.edu/~labov/Papers/GAREC/GAREC.html

Langer, J.A. (2001). Beating the odds: Teaching middle and high school students to read and write well. *American Educational Research Journal, 38*(4), 837–880.

Langer, J.A. (2002). *Effective literacy instruction: Building successful reading and writing programs*. Urbana, IL: National Council of Teachers of English.

Larrivee, B. (1985). *Effective teaching for successful mainstreaming*. New York: Longman.

Lindfors, J. (1987). *Children's language and learning* (2nd ed.). Englewood Cliffs, NJ: Prentice Hall.

Lindholm-Leary, K. (2000). *Biliteracy for a global society: An idea book on dual language education*. Washington, DC: National Clearinghouse for Bilingual Education.

Losen, D.J., & Orfield, G. (Eds.). (2002). *Racial inequality in special education*. Cambridge, MA: Harvard Education Press.

Lucas, T., Henze, R., & Donato, R. (1990). Promoting the success of Latino language-minority students: An exploratory study of six high schools. *Harvard Educational Review, 60*(3), 315–340.

Lyon, G.R. (2004, May). *Evidence-based reading instruction: The critical role of scientific research in teaching children, empowering teachers, and moving beyond the either-or box*. Keynote address presented at the International Reading Association Annual Conference, Reno, NV.

Lyon, G.R., & Chhabra, V. (2004). The science of reading research. *Educational Leadership, 61*(6), 12–17.

Lyon, G.R., Fletcher, J.M., Torgeson, J.K., Shaywitz, S., & Chhabra, V. (2004). Continuing the debate: Preventing and remediating reading failure: Response to Allington. *Educational Leadership, 61*(6), 86–89.

Lyons, C.A. (1989). Reading Recovery: An effective early intervention program that can prevent mislabeling children as learning disabled. *ERS Spectrum, 7*, 3–9.

Mace-Matluck, B.J. (1982). *Literacy instruction in bilingual settings: A synthesis of current research* (Professional Papers M-1). Los Alamitos, CA: National Center for Bilingual Research. (ERIC Document Reproduction Service No. ED222079)

McCormick, C., & Mason, J.M. (1986). *Use of little books at home: A minimal intervention strategy that fosters early reading* (Technical Report No. 388). Urbana: Illinois University Center for the Study of Reading. (ERIC Document Reproduction Service No. ED314742)

McDermott, R.P. (1987). The explanation of minority school failure, again. *Anthropology & Education Quarterly, 18*(4), 361–364.

McGill-Franzen, A. (1987). Failure to learn to read: Formulating a policy problem. *Reading Research Quarterly, 22*(4), 475–490.

Michaels, S. (1981). Sharing time: Children's narrative style and differential access to literacy. *Language in Society*, *10*, 423–442.

Moje, E.B., Ciechanowski, K.M., Kramer, K., Ellis, L., Carrillo, R., & Collazo, T. (2004). Working toward third space in content area literacy: An examination of everyday funds of knowledge and discourse. *Reading Research Quarterly*, *39*(1), 38–70.

Moll, L.C. (1988). Key issues in teaching Latino students. *Language Arts*, *65*(5), 465–472.

Moll, L.C (1991). Social and instructional issues in literacy instruction for "disadvantaged" students. In M.S. Knapp & P.M. Shields (Eds.), *Better schooling for the children of poverty: Alternatives to conventional wisdom* (pp. 61–84). Berkeley, CA: McCutchan.

Moll, L.C. (1992). Bilingual classroom studies and community analysis: Some recent trends. *Educational Researcher*, *21*(2), 20–24.

Moll, L.C., Amanti, C., Neff, D., & Gonzalez, N. (1992). Funds of knowledge for teaching: Using a qualitative approach to connect homes and classrooms. *Theory Into Practice*, *31*(1), 132–141.

Moll, L.C., & Diaz, S. (1987). Change as the goal of educational research. *Anthropology & Educational Quarterly*, *18*(4), 300–311.

Moore, D.W., Bean, T.W., Birdyshaw, D., & Rycik, J.A. (1999). *Adolescent literacy: A position statement for the Commission on Adolescent Literacy of the International Reading Association*. Newark, DE: International Reading Association. Retrieved June 7, 2005, from http://www.reading.org/downloads/positions/ps1036_adolescent.pdf

Morrow, L.M. (1996). *Motivating reading and writing in diverse classrooms: Social and physical contexts in a literature-based program* (Research Report No. 28). Urbana, IL: National Council of Teachers of English.

Moss, M., & Puma, M. (1995). *Prospects: The congressionally mandated study of educational growth and opportunity* (First year report on language minority and limited English proficiency students). Washington, DC: National Clearinghouse for Bilingual Education. (ERIC Document Reproduction Service No. ED394334)

National Institute of Child Health and Human Development (NICHD). (2000). *Report of the National Reading Panel. Teaching children to read: An evidence-based assessment of the scientific research literature on reading and its implications for reading instruction* (NIH Publication No. 00-4769). Washington, DC: U.S. Government Printing Office.

Neuman, S.B., & Celano, D. (2001). Access to print in low-income and middle-income communities: An ecological study of four neighborhoods. *Reading Research Quarterly*, *36*(1), 8–26.

No Child Left Behind Act of 2001, Pub. L. No. 107-110, 115 Stat. 1425 (2002).

Ogbu, J. (1981). School ethnography: A multilevel approach. *Anthropology & Education Quarterly*, *12*(1), 3–29.

Ogbu, J. (1990). Minority status and literacy in comparative perspective. *Daedalus*, *119*(2), 141–168.

Ogbu, J. (1993). Variability in minority school performance: A problem in search of an explanation. In E. Jacob & C. Jordan (Eds.), *Minority education: Anthropological perspectives* (pp. 83–111). Norwood, NJ: Ablex.

Orange, C., & Horowitz, R. (1999). An academic standoff: Literacy task preferences of African American and Mexican American male adolescents versus teacher-expected preferences. *Journal of Adolescent & Adult Literacy*, *43*(1), 28–39.

Oswald, D.P., Coutinho, M.J., Best, A.M., & Singh, N.N. (1999). Ethnic representation in special education: The influence of school-related economic and demographic variables. *Journal of Special Education*, *32*(4), 194–206.

Paratore, J.R. (2002). Home and school together: Helping beginning readers succeed. In A.E. Farstrup & S.J. Samuels (Eds.), *What research has to say about reading instruction* (3rd ed., pp. 48–68). Newark, DE: International Reading Association.

Parrish, T. (2002). Racial disparities in the identification, funding, and provision of special education. In D.J. Losen & G. Orfield (Eds.), *Racial inequity in special education* (pp. 15–37). Cambridge, MA: Harvard Education Press.

Philips, S.U. (1983). *The invisible culture: Communication in classroom and community on the Warm Springs Indian Reservation*. New York: Longman.

Pressley, M., Allington, R.L., Wharton-McDonald, R., Block, C.C., & Morrow, L.M. (2001). *Learning to read: Lessons from exemplary first-grade classrooms*. New York: Guilford.

Primeaux, J. (2000). Shifting perspectives on struggling readers. *Language Arts*, *77*(6), 537–542.

Purcell-Gates, V., McIntyre, E., & Freppon, P. (1995). Learning written storybook language in school: A comparison of low-SES children in skills-based and whole language classrooms. *American Educational Research Journal, 32*(3), 659–685.

Rhodes, L.K., & Dudley-Marling, C. (1996). *Readers and writers with a difference: A holistic approach to teaching struggling readers and writers* (2nd ed.). Portsmouth, NH: Heinemann.

Roberts, C.A. (1994). Transferring literacy skills from L1 to L2: From theory to practice. *Journal of Educational Issues of Language Minority Students, 13*, 209–221.

Rogers, R. (2002). Between contexts: A critical discourse analysis of family literacy, discursive practices, and literate subjectivities. *Reading Research Quarterly, 37*(3), 248–277.

Roller, C.M. (1996). *Variability not disability: Struggling readers in a workshop classroom.* Newark, DE: International Reading Association.

Shaywitz, S.E., & Shaywitz, B.A. (2004). Reading disability and the brain. *Educational Leadership, 61*(6), 6–11.

Singham, M. (2003). The achievement gap: Myths and reality. *Phi Delta Kappan, 84*(8), 586–591.

Snow, C.E. (1992). Perspectives on second-language development: Implications for bilingual education. *Educational Researcher, 21*(2), 16–19.

Snow, C.E., Barnes, W., Chandler, J., Goodman, J., & Hemphill, L. (1991). *Unfulfilled expectations: Home and school influences on literacy.* Cambridge, MA: Harvard University Press.

Snow, C.E., Burns, M.S., & Griffin, P. (Eds.). (1998). *Preventing reading difficulties in young children.* Washington, DC: National Academy Press.

Spear-Swerling, L. (2004). A road map for understanding reading disability and other reading problems: Origins, prevention, and intervention. In R.B. Ruddell & N.J. Unrau (Eds.), *Theoretical models and processes of reading* (5th ed., pp. 517–573). Newark, DE: International Reading Association.

Spear-Swerling, L., & Sternberg, R. (1996). *Off track: When poor readers become "learning disabled".* New York: Westview.

Stanovich, K.E. (1986). Matthew effects in reading: Some consequences of individual differences in the acquisition of literacy. *Reading Research Quarterly, 21*(4), 360–407.

Street, B.V. (1995). *Social literacies: Critical approaches to literacy in development, ethnography, and education* (Real Language Series). New York: Longman.

Taylor, B.M., Pearson, P.D., Clark, K.F., & Walpole, S. (1999). *Beating the odds in teaching all children to read* (CIERA Report No. 2-006). Ann Arbor: Center for the Improvement of Early Reading Achievement, University of Michigan.

Taylor, D. (1983). *Family literacy: Young children learning to read and write.* Exeter, NH: Heinemann.

Taylor, D., & Dorsey-Gaines, C. (1988). *Growing up literate: Learning from inner-city families.* Portsmouth, NH: Heinemann.

Teale, W.H. (1981). Parents reading to their children: What we know and what we need to know. *Language Arts, 58*(8), 902–912.

Teale, W.H. (1987). Emergent literacy: Reading and writing development in early childhood. In J.E. Readence & R.S. Baldwin (Eds.), *Research in literacy: Merging perspectives* (36th yearbook of the National Reading Conference, pp. 45–74). Rochester, NY: National Reading Conference.

Tharp, R.G., & Gallimore, R. (1988). *Rousing minds to life.* Cambridge, England: Cambridge University Press.

Thomas, W.P., & Collier, V.P. (1997). *School effectiveness for language minority students* (NCBE Resource Collection Series, No. 9). Washington, DC: National Clearinghouse for Bilingual Education. Retrieved February 20, 2004, from www.ncela.gwu.edu/pubs/resource/effectiveness/index.htm

Thomas, W.P., & Collier, V.P. (2002). *A national study of school effectiveness for language minority students' long-term academic achievement.* Santa Cruz: Center for Research on Education, Diversity, and Excellence, University of California-Santa Cruz. Retrieved March 1, 2004, from http://www.crede.ucsc.edu/research/llaa/1.1_final.html

Valdes, G. (1996). *Con respeto: Bridging the distances between culturally diverse families and schools: An ethnographic portrait.* New York: Teachers College Press.

Valdes, G. (1999). Incipient bilingualism and the development of English language writing abilities in the secondary school. In C.J. Faltis & P.M. Wolfe (Eds.), *So much to say: Adolescents, bilingualism, and ESL in the secondary school* (pp. 138–175). New York: Teachers College Press.

Vanecko, J., Ames, N., & Archambault, F.X. (1980). *Who benefits from federal education dollars?* Cambridge, MA: ABT Books.

Van Sluys, K. (2004). Engaging in critical literacy practices in a multiliteracies classroom. In C.M. Fairbanks, J. Worthy, B. Maloch, J.V. Hoffman, & D.L. Schallert (Eds.), *53rd yearbook of the National Reading*

Conference (pp. 400–416). Oak Creek, WI: National Reading Conference.

Vygotsky, L.S. (1978). *Mind in society: The development of higher psychological processes* (M. Cole, V. John-Steiner, S. Scribner, & E. Souberman, Eds. & Trans.). Cambridge, MA: Harvard University Press. (Original work published 1934)

Waggoner, D. (1999). Who are the secondary newcomer and linguistically different youth? In C.J. Faltis & P.M. Wolfe (Eds.), *So much to say: Adolescents, bilingualism, and ESL in the secondary school* (pp. 13–41). New York: Teachers College Press.

Wells, C.G. (1986). *The meaning makers: Children learning language and using language to learn*. Portsmouth, NH: Heinemann.

WestEd. (2004). A framework for teaching English learners. *R&D Alert, 6*(3), 1, 8–9. Retrieved June 7, 2005, from http://www.wested.org/online_pubs/rd-06-03.pdf

Wilhelm, J.D., & Smith, M.W. (2002). *"Reading don't fix no Chevys": Literacy in the lives of young men*. Portsmouth, NH: Heinemann.

Yatvin, J., Weaver, C., & Garan, E. (2003). Reading First: Cautions and recommendations. *Language Arts, 81*(1), 28–33.

Zhang, D., & Katsiyannis, A. (2002). Minority representation in special education: A persistent challenge. *Remedial & Special Education, 23*(3), 180–187.

Chapter 4

Allington, R.L., & Cunningham, P.M. (1996). *Schools that work: Where all children read and write*. New York: HarperCollins.

Core Understanding 1

Cambourne, B. (2002). Holistic, integrated approaches to reading and language arts instruction: The constructivist framework of an instructional theory. In A.E. Farstrup & S.J. Samuels (Eds.), *What research has to say about reading instruction* (3rd ed., pp. 25–47). Newark, DE: International Reading Association.

Duke, N.K., & Pearson, P.D. (2002). Effective practices for developing reading comprehension. In A.E. Farstrup & S.J. Samuels (Eds.), *What research has to say about reading instruction* (3rd ed., pp. 205–242). Newark, DE: International Reading Association.

Gee, J.P. (1996). *Social linguistics and literacies: Ideology in discourse* (2nd ed.). London; Bristol, PA: Taylor & Francis.

Goodman, K.S. (1996). *On reading*. Portsmouth, NH: Heinemann.

Halliday, M.A.K. (1973). *Explorations in the functions of language*. London: Edward Arnold.

Halliday, M.A.K. (1975). *Learning how to mean: Exploration in the development of language*. London: Edward Arnold.

Kucer, S.B., & Tuten, J. (2003). Revisiting and rethinking the reading process. *Language Arts, 80*(4), 284–290.

Pearson, P.D., Roehler, L.R., Dole, J.A., & Duffy, G.G. (1990). *Developing expertise in reading comprehension: What should be taught? How should it be taught?* (Technical Report No. 512). Champaign, IL: Center for the Study of Reading.

RAND Reading Study Group. (2002). *Reading for understanding: Toward an R&D program in reading comprehension*. Santa Monica, CA: RAND.

Rosenblatt, L.M. (1978). *The reader, the text, the poem: The transactional theory of literary work*. Carbondale: Southern Illinois University Press.

Rosenblatt, L.M. (1995). *Literature as exploration* (5th ed.). New York: Modern Language Association. (Original work published 1938)

Smith, F. (2004). *Understanding reading: A psycholinguistic analysis of reading and learning to read* (6th ed.). Mahwah, NJ: Erlbaum.

Core Understanding 2

Allington, R.L., & Cunningham, P.M. (1996). *Schools that work: Where all children read and write*. New York: HarperCollins.

Anderson, R.C., & Nagy, W. (1992). The vocabulary conundrum. *American Educator, 16*(4), 14–18, 44–47.

Anderson, R.C., & Pearson, P.D. (1984). A schema-theoretic view of basic processes in reading comprehension. In P.D. Pearson, R. Barr, M.L. Kamil, & P.B. Mosenthal (Eds.), *Handbook of reading research* (pp. 255–292). New York: Longman.

Beck, I.L., Omanson, R.C., & McKeown, M.G. (1982). An instructional redesign of reading lessons: Effects on comprehension. *Reading Research Quarterly, 17*(4), 462–481.

Clay, M.M. (1985). *The early detection of reading difficulties: A diagnostic survey with recovery procedures* (3rd ed.). Auckland, New Zealand: Heinemann.

Cunningham, A.E., & Stanovich, K.E. (1998). What reading does for the mind. *American Educator, 22*(1–2), 8–15.

Goldenberg, C. (1991). *Instructional conversations and their classroom application* (Educational Practice Report No. 2). Santa Cruz, CA: National Center for Research on Cultural Diversity and Second Language Learning.

Kucer, S. (2005). *Dimensions of literacy: A conceptual base for teaching reading and writing in school settings* (2nd ed.). Mahwah, NJ: Erlbaum.

Lee, C.D. (1995). A culturally based cognitive apprenticeship: Teaching African American high school students skills in literary interpretation. *Reading Research Quarterly, 30*(4), 608–630.

McKeown, M.G., Beck, I.L., Omanson, R.D., & Pople, M.T. (1985). Some effects of the nature and frequency of vocabulary instruction on the knowledge and use of words. *Reading Research Quarterly, 20*(5), 522–535.

Moje, E.B., Ciechanowski, K.M., Kramer, K., Ellis, L., Carrillo, R., & Collazo, T. (2004). Working toward third space in content area literacy: An examination of everyday funds of knowledge and discourse. *Reading Research Quarterly, 39*(1), 38–70.

Moll, L., Amanti, C., Neff, D., & Gonzalez, N. (1992). Funds of knowledge for teaching: Using a qualitative approach to connect homes and classrooms. *Theory Into Practice, 31*(1), 132–141.

Moustafa, M. (1997). *Beyond traditional phonics: Research discoveries and reading instruction*. Portsmouth, NH: Heinemann.

Nagy, W.E., Anderson, R.C., & Herman, P.A. (1987). Learning word meanings from context during normal reading. *American Educational Research Journal, 24*(2), 237–270.

Roberts, C.A. (1994). Transferring literacy skills from L1 to L2: From theory to practice. *Journal of Educational Issues of Language Minority Students, 13*, 209–221.

Rumelhart, D.E. (1980). Schemata: The building blocks of cognition. In R.J. Spiro, B.C. Bruce, & W.F. Brewer (Eds.), *Theoretical issues in reading comprehension: Perspectives from cognitive psychology, linguistics, artificial intelligence, and education* (pp. 38–58). Hillsdale, NJ: Erlbaum.

Schoenbach, R., Greenleaf, C., Cziko, C., & Hurwitz, L. (1999). *Reading for understanding: A guide to improving reading in middle and high school classrooms*. San Francisco: Jossey-Bass.

Snow, C.E., & Biancarosa, G. (2003). *Adolescent literacy and the achievement gap: What do we know and where do we go from here?* (Adolescent Literacy Funders Meeting Report). New York: Carnegie Corporation.

Stahl, S.A. (1998). Four questions about vocabulary. In C.R. Hynd (Ed.), *Learning from text across conceptual domains* (pp. 73–94). Mahwah, NJ: Erlbaum.

Swanborn, M.S.L., & de Glopper, K. (1999). Incidental word learning while reading: A meta-analysis. *Review of Educational Research, 69*(3), 261–285.

Sweet, A.P. (1993). *State of the art: Transforming ideas for teaching and learning to read*. Washington, DC: U.S. Department of Education, Office of Educational Research and Improvement.

Trumbull, E., & Farr, B. (2005). *Language and learning: What teachers need to know*. Norwood, MA: Christopher-Gordon.

Walqui, A., & DeFazio, A. (2003). *The selection of written texts for English learners: Teaching reading to adolescent English learners*. San Francisco: WestEd.

Core Understanding 3

Applebee, A.N., & Langer, J.A. (1983). Instructional scaffolding: Reading and writing as natural language activities. *Language Arts, 60*(2), 168–175.

Applebee, A.N., Langer, J.A., Nystrand, M., & Gamoran, A. (2003). Discussion-based approaches to developing understanding: Classroom instruction and student performance in middle and high school English. *American Educational Research Journal, 40*(3), 685–730.

Bruner, J.S. (1975). The ontogenesis of speech acts. *Journal of Child Language, 2*(1), 1–19.

Cambourne, B. (2002). Holistic, integrated approaches to reading and language arts instruction: The constructivist framework of instructional theory. In A.E. Farstrup & S.J. Samuels (Eds.), *What research has to say about reading instruction* (3rd ed., pp. 25–47). Newark, DE: International Reading Association.

Eeds, M., & Wells, D. (1989). Grand conversations: An exploration of meaning construction in literature study groups.

Research in the Teaching of English, 23(1), 4–29.

Goldenberg, C. (1993). Instructional conversations: Promoting comprehension through discussion. *The Reading Teacher*, 46(4), 316–326.

Langer, J.A. (1993). Discussion as exploration: Literature and the horizon of possibilities. In G.E. Newell & R.K. Durst (Eds.), *Exploring texts: The role of discussion and writing in the teaching and learning of literature* (pp. 25–43). Norwood, MA: Christopher-Gordon.

Langer, J.A. (1999). *Beating the odds: Teaching middle and high school students to read and write well*. (CELA Research Report No. 12014). Albany: National Research Center on English Learning and Achievement, State University of New York.

Pressley, M. (2002). Metacognition and self-regulated comprehension. In A.E. Farstrup & S.J. Samuels (Eds.), *What research has to say about reading instruction* (3rd ed., pp. 291–309). Newark, DE: International Reading Association.

RAND Reading Study Group. (2002). *Reading for understanding: Toward an R&D program in reading comprehension*. Santa Monica, CA: RAND.

Sweet, A.P. (1993). *State of the art: Transforming ideas for teaching and learning to read*. Washington, DC: U.S. Department of Education, Office of Educational Research and Improvement.

Vygotsky, L.S. (1978). *Mind in society: The development of higher psychological processes* (M. Cole, V. John-Steiner, S. Scribner, & E. Souberman, Eds. & Trans.). Cambridge, MA: Harvard University Press. (Original work published 1934)

Walker, B. (1996). Discussions that focus on strategies and self-assessment. In L.B. Gambrell & J.F. Almasi (Eds.), *Lively discussions! Fostering engaged reading* (pp. 286–296). Newark, DE: International Reading Association.

Core Understanding 4

Burgess, K.A., Lundren, K.A., Lloyd, J.W., & Pianta, R.C. (2001). *Preschool teachers' self-reported beliefs and practices about literacy instruction* (CIERA Report No. 2-012). Ann Arbor: Center for the Improvement of Early Reading Achievement, University of Michigan.

Cambourne, B. (2002). Holistic, integrated approaches to reading and language arts instruction: The constructivist framework of an instructional theory. In A.E. Farstrup & S.J. Samuels (Eds.), *What research has to say about reading instruction* (3rd ed., pp. 25–47). Newark, DE: International Reading Association.

Clarke, L.K. (1988). Invented versus traditional spelling in first graders' writings: Effects on learning to spell and read. *Research in the Teaching of English*, 22(3), 281–309.

Clay, M.M. (1975). *What did I write?* Exeter, NH: Heinemann.

DeFord, D. (1981). Literacy: Reading, writing, and other essentials. *Language Arts*, 58(6), 652–658.

Duke, N.K., & Pearson, P.D. (2002). Effective practices for developing reading comprehension. In A.E. Farstrup & S.J. Samuels (Eds.), *What research has to say about reading instruction* (3rd ed., pp. 205–242). Newark, DE: International Reading Association.

International Reading Association (IRA) & National Association for the Education of Young Children (NAEYC). (1998). Learning to read and write: Developmentally appropriate practices for young children. *The Reading Teacher*, 52(2), 193–216.

Langer, J.A. (1986). Reading, writing, and understanding: An analysis of the construction of meaning. *Written Communication*, 3(2), 219–267.

Langer, J.A. (2001). Beating the odds: Teaching middle and high school students to read and write well. *American Educational Research Journal*, 38(4), 837–880.

Morris, D. (1981). Concept of word: A developmental phenomenon in the beginning reading and writing processes. *Language Arts*, 58(6), 659–668.

Ogle, D., & McMann, S. (2003). Curriculum integration to promote literate thinking: Dilemmas and possibilities. In J. Flood, D. Lapp, J.R. Squire, & J.M. Jensen (Eds.), *Handbook of research on teaching the English language arts* (2nd ed., pp. 1035–1051). Mahwah, NJ: Erlbaum.

Pearson, P.D., & Tierney, R.J. (1984). On becoming a thoughtful reader: Learning to read like a writer. In A.C. Purves & O. Niles (Eds.), *Becoming readers in a complex society* (83rd yearbook of the National Society of the Study of Education, pp. 144–173). Chicago: University of Chicago Press.

Smith, F. (1994). *Writing and the writer* (2nd ed.). Hillsdale, NJ: Erlbaum.

Squire, J.R. (1983). Composing and comprehending: Two sides of the same basic process. *Language Arts*, 60(5), 581–589.

Sulzby, E., & Teale, W. (1991). Emergent literacy. In R. Barr, M.L. Kamil, P.B. Mosenthal, & P.D. Pearson (Eds.), *Handbook of reading research* (Vol. 2, pp. 727–757). New York: Longman.

Sweet, A.P. (1993). *State of the art: Transforming ideas for teaching and learning to read*. Washington, DC: U.S. Department of Education, Office of Educational Research and Improvement.

Taylor, B.M., Peterson, D., Rodriguez, M.C., & Pearson, P.D. (2002). *The CIERA school-change project: Supporting schools as they implement home-grown reading reform* (CIERA Report No. 2-016). Ann Arbor: Center for the Improvement of Early Reading Achievement, University of Michigan.

Tierney, R.J., & Shanahan, T. (1991). Research on the reading–writing relationship: Interactions, transactions, and outcomes. In R. Barr, M.L. Kamil, P.B. Mosenthal, & P.D. Pearson (Eds.), *Handbook of reading research* (Vol. 2, pp. 246–280). New York: Longman.

Vernon, S.A., & Ferreiro, E. (1999).Writing development: A neglected variable in the consideration of phonological awareness. *Harvard Educational Review, 69*(4), 395–415.

Wilde, S. (1992). *You kan red this! Spelling and punctuation for whole language classrooms, K–6*. Portsmouth, NH: Heinemann.

Core Understanding 5

Alfassi, M. (1998). Reading for meaning: The efficacy of reciprocal teaching in fostering reading comprehension in high school students in remedial reading classes. *American Educational Research Journal, 35*(2), 309–332.

Applebee, A.N., Langer, J.A., Nystrand, M., & Gamoran, A. (2003). Discussion-based approaches to developing understanding: Classroom instruction and student performance in middle and high school English. *American Educational Research Journal, 40*(3), 685–730.

Caine, R.N., & Caine, G. (1991). *Making connections: Teaching and the human brain*. Alexandria, VA: Association for Supervision and Curriculum Development.

Caine, R.N., & Caine, G. (1997). *Education on the edge of possibility*. Alexandria, VA: Association for Supervision and Curriculum Development.

Duke, N.K., & Pearson, P.D. (2002). Effective practices for developing reading comprehension. In A.E. Farstrup & S.J. Samuels (Eds.), *What research has to say about reading instruction* (3rd ed., pp. 205–242). Newark, DE: International Reading Association.

Greenleaf, C.L., Schoenbach, R., Cziko, C., & Mueller, F.L. (2001). Apprenticing adolescent readers to academic literacy. *Harvard Educational Review, 71*(1), 79–129.

Grigg, W.S., Daane, M.C., Jin, Y., & Campbell, J.R. (2003). *The nation's report card: Reading 2002* (NCES Report No. 2003-521). Washington, DC: U.S. Department of Education, National Center for Education Statistics.

Guthrie, J.T., & Davis, M.H. (2003). Motivating struggling readers in middle school through an engagement model of classroom practice. *Reading & Writing Quarterly, 19*(1), 59–85.

Guthrie, J.T., Wigfield, A., & VonSecker, C. (2000). Effects of integrated instruction on motivation and strategy use in reading. *Journal of Educational Psychology, 92*(2), 331–341.

International Reading Association (IRA) & National Council of Teachers of English (NCTE). (1996). *Standards for the English language arts*. Newark, DE; Urbana, IL: Authors.

Langer, J.A. (1999). *Beating the odds: Teaching middle and high school students to read and write well* (CELA Research Report No. 12014). Albany: National Center on English Learning and Achievement, State University of New York.

Moje, E.B., Young, J.P., Readence, J.E., & Moore, D.W. (2000). Reinventing adolescent literacy for new times: Perennial and millennial issues. *Journal of Adolescent & Adult Literacy, 43*(5), 400–410.

No Child Left Behind Act of 2001, Pub. L. No. 107-110, 115 Stat. 1425 (2002).

Palincsar, A.S., & Brown, A.L. (1984). Reciprocal teaching of comprehension-fostering and comprehension-monitoring activities. *Cognition & Instruction, 1*(2), 117–175.

Pressley, M. (2002). Metacognition and self-regulated comprehension. In A.E. Farstrup & S.J. Samuels (Eds.), *What research has to say about reading instruction* (3rd ed., pp. 291–309. Newark, DE: International Reading Association.

RAND Reading Study Group. (2002). *Reading for understanding: Toward an R&D program in reading comprehension*. Santa Monica, CA: RAND.

Rosenblatt, L.M. (1978). *The reader, the text, the poem: The transactional theory of the literary work*. Carbondale: Southern Illinois University Press.

Rosenblatt, L.M. (1995). *Literature as exploration* (5th ed.). New York: Modern Language Association. (Original work published 1938)

Ruddell, R.B., Ruddell, M.R., & Singer, H. (Eds.). (1994). *Theoretical models and processes of reading* (4th ed.). Newark, DE: International Reading Association.

Scherer, M.M. (Ed.). (1997). How children learn [Special issue]. *Educational Leadership, 54*(6).

Sweet, A.P. (1993, November). *State of the art: Transforming ideas for teaching and learning to read*. Washington, DC: U.S. Department of Education, Office of Educational Research and Improvement.

Taylor, B.M., Peterson, D., Rodriguez, M.C., & Pearson, P.D. (2002). *The CIERA school-change project: Supporting schools as they implement home-grown reading reform* (CIERA Report No. 2-016). Ann Arbor: Center for the Improvement of Early Reading Achievement, University of Michigan.

Core Understanding 6

Allington, R.L., & Cunningham, P.M. (1996). *Schools that work: Where all children read and write*. New York: HarperCollins.

Allington, R.L., & Johnston, P.H. (2002). *Reading to learn: Lessons from exemplary fourth grade classrooms*. New York: Guilford.

Applebee, A.N, Langer, J.A., Nystrand, M., & Gamoran, A. (2003). Discussion-based approaches to developing understanding: Classroom instruction and student performance in middle and high school English. *American Educational Research Journal, 40*(3), 685–730.

Atwell, N. (1987). *In the middle: Writing, reading, and learning with adolescents*. Upper Montclair, NJ: Boynton/Cook.

Bisset, D. (1969). *The amount and effect of recreational reading in selected fifth grade classes*. Unpublished doctoral dissertation, Syracuse University, NY.

Bloome, D. (1991). Anthropology and research on teaching the English language arts. In J. Flood, J.M. Jensen, D. Lapp, & J.R. Squire (Eds.), *Handbook of research on teaching the English language arts* (pp. 46–56). New York: Macmillan.

Cazden, C.B. (1986). Classroom discourse. In M.C. Wittrock (Ed.), *The handbook of research on teaching* (3rd ed., pp. 432–463). New York: Macmillan.

Cazden, C.B. (1988). *Classroom discourse: The language of teaching and learning*. Portsmouth, NH: Heinemann.

Chomsky, C. (1972). Stages in language development and reading exposure. *Harvard Educational Review, 42*(1), 1–33.

Cox, B., & Sulzby, E. (1984). Children's use of reference in told, dictated, and handwritten stories. *Research in the Teaching of English, 18*(4), 345–365.

Cullinan, B.E. (1987). *Children's literature in the reading program*. Newark, DE: International Reading Association.

Cunningham, P.M., & Allington, R.L. (2003). *Classrooms that work: They can ALL read and write* (3rd ed.). Boston: Allyn & Bacon.

Duke, N.K. (2000). 3.6 minutes a day: The scarcity of informational text in first grade. *Reading Research Quarterly, 35*(2), 202–224.

Durkin, D. (1974). A six-year study of children who learned to read in school at the age of four. *Reading Research Quarterly, 10*, 9–61.

Dyson, A.H. (1987). The value of "time off task": Young children's spontaneous talk and deliberate text. *Harvard Educational Review, 57*(4), 396–420.

Field, T. (1980). Preschool play: Effects of teacher/child ratios and organization of classroom space. *Child Study Journal, 10*(3), 191–205.

Froebel, F. (1974). *The education of man* (W.N. Hailmann, Trans.). Clifton, NJ: Augustus M. Kelly.

Galda, L., Ash, G.E., & Cullinan, B.E. (2000). Children's literature. In M.L. Kamil, P.B. Mosenthal, P.D. Pearson, & R. Barr (Eds.), *Handbook of reading research* (Vol. 3, pp. 361–380). Mahwah, NJ: Erlbaum.

Galda, L., & Cullinan, B.E. (2003). Literature for literacy: What research says about the benefits of using trade books in the classroom. In J. Flood, D. Lapp, J.R. Squire, & J.M. Jensen (Eds.), *Handbook of research on teaching the English language arts* (2nd ed., pp. 640–648). Mahwah, NJ: Erlbaum.

Hoffman, J.V., Roser, N.L., & Farest, C. (1988). Literature sharing strategies in classrooms serving students from economically disadvantaged and language different home environments. In J.E. Readance & R.S. Baldwin (Eds.), *Dialogues in literacy research* (37th yearbook of the National Reading Conference, pp. 331–337). Chicago: National Reading Conference.

Ivey, G. (2003). "The teacher makes it more explainable" and other reasons to read aloud in the intermediate grades. *The Reading Teacher, 56*(8), 812–814.

Ivey, G., & Broaddus, K. (2001). "Just plain reading": A survey of what makes students want to read in middle school classrooms. *Reading Research Quarterly, 36*(4), 350–377.

Jett-Simpson, M. (1989). Reading comprehension through creative dramatics. In J.W. Stewig & S.L. Sebesta (Eds.), *Using literature in the elementary classroom* (pp. 63–71). Urbana, IL: National Council of Teachers of English.

Johnson, D.W., & Johnson, R.T. (1987). *Learning together and alone: Cooperative, competitive, and individualistic learning* (2nd ed.). Englewood Cliffs, NJ: Prentice Hall.

Kaufman, D. (2001). Organizing and managing the language arts workshop: A matter of motion. *Language Arts, 79*(2), 114–123.

Krashen, S.D. (1996). *Every person a reader: An alternative to the California Task Force report on reading*. Culver City, CA: Language Education Associates.

Langer, J.A. (2001). Beating the odds: Teaching middle and high school students to read and write well. *American Educational Research Journal, 38*(4), 837–880.

Langer, J.A. (2002). *Effective literacy instruction: Building successful reading and writing programs*. Urbana, IL: National Council of Teachers of English.

Loughlin, C.E., & Martin, M.D. (1987). *Supporting literacy: Developing effective learning environments*. New York: Teachers College Press.

Moore, G. (1986). Effects of spatial definition of behavior setting on children's behavior: A quasi-experimental field study. *Journal of Environmental Psychology, 6*, 205–231.

Morrow, L.M. (1988). Young children's responses to one-to-one story readings in school settings. *Reading Research Quarterly, 23*(1), 89–107.

Morrow, L.M. (1990). Preparing the classroom environment to promote literacy during play. *Early Childhood Research Quarterly, 5*(4), 537–554.

Morrow, L.M. (1996). *Motivating reading and writing in diverse classrooms: Social and physical contexts in a literature-based program* (Research Report No. 28). Urbana, IL: National Council of Teachers of English.

Morrow, L.M., O'Connor, E.M., & Smith, J. (1990). Effects of a story reading program on the literacy development of at-risk kindergarten children. *Journal of Reading Behavior, 22*(3), 255–275.

Neuman, S.B. (1995). Enhancing adolescent mothers' guided participation in literacy. In L.M. Morrow (Ed.), *Family literacy: Connections in schools and communities* (pp. 104–114). Newark, DE: International Reading Association.

Neuman, S.B., & Celano, D. (2001). Access to print in low-income and middle-income communities: An ecological study of four neighborhoods. *Reading Research Quarterly, 36*(1), 8–26.

Neuman, S.B., & Roskos, K. (1997). Literacy knowledge in practice: Contexts of participation for young writers and readers. *Reading Research Quarterly, 32*(1), 10–32.

Pappas, C.C., & Brown, E. (1987). Learning to read by reading: Learning how to extend the functional potential of language. *Research in the Teaching of English, 21*(2), 160–177.

Pearson, P.D. (1996). Foreword. In E. McIntyre & M. Pressley (Eds.), *Balanced instruction: Strategies and skills in whole language* (pp. xv–xviii). Norwood, MA: Christopher-Gordon.

Piaget, J., & Inhelder, B. (1969). *The psychology of the child* (H. Weaver, Trans.). New York: Basic Books.

Pressley, M., Allington, R.L., Wharton-McDonald, R., Block, C.C., & Morrow, L.M. (2001). *Learning to read: Lessons from exemplary first-grade classrooms*. New York: Guilford.

RAND Reading Study Group. (2002). *Reading for understanding: Toward an R&D program in reading comprehension*. Santa Monica, CA: RAND.

Richardson, J.S. (2000). *Read it aloud! Using literature in the secondary content classroom*. Newark, DE: International Reading Association.

Rivlin, L., & Weinstein, C.S. (1984). Educational issues, school settings, and environmental psychology. *Journal of Environmental Psychology, 4*, 347–364.

Rusk, R., & Scotland, J. (1979). *Doctrines of the great educators* (5th ed.). New York: St. Martin's.

Rosenblatt, L.M. (1978). *The reader, the text, the poem: The transactional theory of the literary work*. Carbondale: Southern Illinois University Press.

Schoenbach, R., Braunger, J., Greenleaf, C., & Litman, C. (2003). Apprenticing adolescents to reading in subject-area classrooms. *Phi Delta Kappan, 85*(2), 133–138.

Schoenbach, R., Greenleaf, C., Cziko, C., & Hurwitz, L. (1999). *Reading for understanding: A guide to improving reading in middle and high school classrooms*. San Francisco: Jossey-Bass.

Slavin, R.E. (1983). Non-cognitive outcomes. In J.M. Levine & M.C. Wang (Eds.), *Teacher and student perceptions: Implications for learning* (pp. 341–385). Hillsdale, NJ: Erlbaum.

Spivak, M. (1973). Archetypal place. *Architectural Forum, 40*, 40–44.

Sweet, A.P. (1993). *State of the art: Transforming ideas for teaching and learning to read*. Washington, DC: U.S. Department of Education, Office of Educational Research and Improvement.

Taylor, B.M., Pearson, P.D., Clark, K.F., & Walpole, S. (1999). *Beating the odds in teaching all children to read* (CIERA Report No. 2-006). Ann Arbor: Center for the Improvement of Early Reading Achievement, University of Michigan.

Taylor, D. (1983). *Family literacy: Young children learning to read and write*. Exeter, NH: Heinemann.

Teale, W.H. (1982). Toward a theory of how children learn to read and write naturally. *Language Arts, 59*(6), 555–570.

Teale, W.H. (1984). Reading to young children: Its significance for literacy development. In H. Goelman, A. Oberg, & F. Smith (Eds.), *Awakening to literacy* (pp. 110–121). Exeter, NH: Heinemann.

Teale, W.H., & Sulzby, E. (1987). Literacy acquisition in early childhood: The roles of access and mediation in storybook reading. In D.A. Wagner (Ed.), *The future of literacy in a changing world* (pp. 111–130). New York: Pergamon.

Vygotsky, L.S. (1978). *Mind in society: The development of higher psychological processes* (M. Cole, V. John-Steiner, S. Scribner, & E. Souberman, Eds. & Trans.). Cambridge, MA: Harvard University Press. (Original work published 1934)

Core Understanding 7

Allington, R.L., & McGill-Franzen, A. (2003). The impact of summer setback on the reading achievement gap. *Phi Delta Kappan, 85*(1), 68–75.

Brandt, D. (1990). *Literacy as involvement: The acts of writers, readers, and texts*. Carbondale: Southern Illinois University Press.

Cambourne, B. (1988). *The whole story: Natural learning and the acquisition of literacy in the classroom*. Auckland, New Zealand: Ashton Scholastic.

Cambourne, B. (1995). Toward an educationally relevant theory of literacy learning: Twenty years of inquiry. *The Reading Teacher, 49*(3), 182–190.

Cambourne, B. (2002). Holistic, integrated approaches to reading and language arts instruction: The constructivist framework of an instructional theory. In A.E. Farstrup & S.J. Samuels (Eds.), *What research has to say about reading instruction* (3rd ed., pp. 25–47). Newark, DE: International Reading Association.

Campbell, J.R., Voelkl, K.E., & Donahue, P.L. (1997). *NAEP 1996 trends in academic progress* (NCES Publication No. 97-985). Washington, DC: U.S. Department of Education, National Center for Education Statistics.

Ford, M.E. (1992). *Motivating humans: Goals, emotions, and personal agency beliefs*. Newbury Park, CA: Sage.

Gambrell, L.B., Almasi, J.F., Xie, Q., & Heland, V.J. (1995). Helping first graders get a running start in reading. In L.M. Morrow (Ed.), *Family literacy: Connections in schools and communities* (pp. 143–154). Newark, DE: International Reading Association.

Gambrell, L.B., Palmer, B., & Codling, R.M. (1993). *Motivation to read*. Washington, DC: U.S. Department of Education, Office of Educational Research and Improvement.

Greenleaf, C.L., Schoenbach, R., Cziko, C., & Mueller, F.L. (2001). Apprenticing adolescent readers to academic literacy. *Harvard Educational Review, 71*(1), 79–129.

Guthrie, J.T., & Anderson, R.E. (1999). Engagement in reading: Processes of motivated, strategic, knowledgeable, social readers. In J.T. Guthrie & D.E. Alvermann (Eds.), *Engaged reading: Processes, practices, and policy implications* (pp. 17–45). New York: Teachers College Press.

Guthrie, J.T., & Davis, M.H. (2003). Motivating struggling readers in middle school through an engagement model of classroom practice. *Reading & Writing Quarterly, 19*(1), 59–85.

Guthrie, J.T., Van Meter, P., Hancock G.R., McCann, A., Anderson, E., & Alao, S. (1998). Does Concept-Oriented Reading Instruction increase strategy use and conceptual learning from text? *Journal of Educational Psychology, 90*(2), 261–278.

Guthrie, J.T., & Wigfield, A. (2000). Engagement and motivation in reading. In M.L. Kamil, P.B. Mosenthal, P.D. Pearson, & R. Barr. (Eds.) *Handbook of reading research* (Vol. 3, pp. 403–422). Mahwah, NJ: Erlbaum.

Ivey, G. (1999a). A multicase study in the middle school: Complexities among young adolescent readers. *Reading Research Quarterly, 34*(2), 172–192.

Ivey, G. (1999b). Reflections on teaching struggling middle school readers. *Journal of Adolescent and Adult Literacy, 42*(5), 372–381.

Kamil, M.L. (2003). *Adolescents and literacy: Reading for the 21st century*. Washington, DC: Alliance for Excellent Education.

Langer, J.A. (1999). *Beating the odds: Teaching middle and high school students to read and write well* (CELA Research Report No. 12014). Albany: National Center on English Learning and Achievement, State University of New York.

Maehr, M.L. (1976). Continuing motivation: An analysis of a seldom considered educational outcome. *Review of Educational Research, 46*(3), 443–462.

McCombs, B.L. (1989). Self-regulated learning and academic achievement: A phenomenological view. In B.J. Zimmerman & D.H. Schunk (Eds.), *Self regulated learning and academic achievement: Theory, research, and practice* (pp. 67–123). New York: Springer-Verlag.

Moje, E.B., Young, J.P., Readence, J.E., & Moore, D.W. (2000). Reinventing adolescent literacy for new times: Perennial and millennial issues. *Journal of Adolescent & Adult Literacy, 43*(5), 400–410.

Morrow, L.M. (1992). The impact of a literature-based program on literacy achievement, use of literature, and attitudes of children from minority backgrounds. *Reading Research Quarterly, 27*(3), 250–275.

Morrow, L.M. (1996). *Motivating reading and writing in diverse classrooms: Social and physical contexts in a literature-based program* (Research Report No. 28). Urbana, IL: National Council of Teachers of English.

Morrow, L.M., & Weinstein, C.S. (1986). Encouraging voluntary reading: The impact of a literature program on children's use of library centers. *Reading Research Quarterly, 21*(3), 330–346.

National Academy of Education. (1991). *Research and the renewal of education*. Stanford, CA: Author.

Oldfather, P. (1993). What students say about motivating experiences in a whole language classroom. *The Reading Teacher, 46*(8), 672–681.

RAND Reading Study Group. (2002). *Reading for understanding: Toward an R&D program in reading comprehension*. Santa Monica, CA: RAND.

Ryan, R.M., & Deci, E.L. (2000). Intrinsic and extrinsic motivations: Classic definitions and new directions. *Contemporary Educational Psychology, 25*, 54–67.

Savery, J.R., & Duffy, T.M. (1995). Problem-based learning: An instructional model and its constructivist framework. *Educational Technology, 35*(5), 31–38.

Snow, C.E., & Biancarosa, G. (2003). *Adolescent literacy and the achievement gap: What do we know and where do we go from here?* (Adolescent Literacy Funders Meeting Report). New York: Carnegie Corporation.

Spaulding, C.L. (1992). The motivation to read and write. In J.W. Irwin & M.A. Doyle (Eds.), *Reading/writing connections: Learning from research* (pp. 177–201). Newark, DE: International Reading Association.

Stanovich, K.E. (1986). Matthew effects in reading: Some consequences of individual differences in the acquisition of literacy. *Reading Research Quarterly, 21*(4), 360–407.

Wang, M.C., Haertel, G.D., & Walberg, H.J. (1990). What influences learning? A content analysis of review literature. *Journal of Educational Research, 84*(1), 30–43.

Wood, E., Willoughby, T., & Woloshyn, V.E. (1995). An introduction to cognitive strategies in the secondary school. In E. Wood, V.E. Woloshyn, & T. Willoughby (Eds.), *Cognitive strategy instruction for middle and high schools* (pp. 1–4), Cambridge, MA: Brookline.

Core Understanding 8

Adams, M.J. (1990). *Beginning to read: Thinking and learning about print*. Cambridge, MA: MIT Press.

Berdiansky, B., Cronnell, B., & Koehler, J. (1969). *Spelling-sound relations and primary form-class descriptions for speech-comprehension vocabularies of 6–9 year olds* (Technical Report No. 15). Inglewood, CA: Southwest Regional Laboratory for Educational Research and Development.

Bruce, L.D. (1964). The analysis of word sounds by young children. *British Journal of Educational Psychology, 34*, 158–170.

Calfee, R. (1977). Assessment of individual reading skills: Basic research and practical applications. In A.S. Reber & D.L. Scarborough (Eds.), *Toward a psychology of reading* (pp. 289–323). New York: Erlbaum.

Carbo, M. (1987). Reading style research: "What works" isn't always phonics. *Phi Delta Kappan, 68*(6), 431–435.

Clay, M.M. (1979). *Reading: The patterning of complex behaviour*. Auckland, New Zealand: Heinemann.

Ehri, L.C., & Wilce, L.S. (1980). The influence of orthography on readers' conceptualization of the phonemic structure of words. *Applied Psycholinguistics, 1*(4), 371–385.

Goodman, Y.M. (1986). Children coming to know literacy. In W. Teale & E. Sulzby

(Eds.), *Emergent literacy: Reading and writing* (pp. 1–14). Norwood, NJ: Ablex.

Goswami, U. (1986). Children's use of analogy in learning to read: A developmental study. *Journal of Experimental Child Psychology, 42*(1), 73–83.

Goswami, U. (1988). Orthographic analogies and reading development. *Quarterly Journal of Experimental Psychology, 40A*, 239–268.

Goswami, U. (2000). Phonological and lexical processes. In M.L. Kamil, P.B. Mosenthal, P.D. Pearson, & R. Barr (Eds.), *Handbook of reading research* (Vol. 3, pp. 251–267). Mahwah, NJ: Erlbaum.

Goswami, U., & Bryant, P. (1990). *Phonological skills and learning to read*. Hillsdale, NJ: Erlbaum.

Hanna, P.R., Hanna, J.S., Hodges, R.E., & Rudorf, E. (1966). *Phoneme-grapheme correspondences as cues to spelling improvement* (USOE Publication No. 32008). Washington, DC: Government Printing Office.

Hansen, J., & Bowey, J.A. (1994). Phonological analysis skills, verbal working memory, and reading ability in second grade children. *Child Development, 65*, 938–950.

Liberman, I.Y., Shankweiler, D., Fisher, F., & Carter, B. (1974). Explicit syllable and phoneme segmentation in the young child. *Journal of Experimental Child Psychology, 18*(2), 201–212.

Lie, A. (1991). Effects of a training program for stimulating skills in word analysis in first-grade children. *Reading Research Quarterly, 26*(3), 234–250.

Mann, V.A. (1986). Phonological awareness: The role of reading experience. *Cognition, 24*, 65–92.

McClure, K.K., Ferreira, F., & Bisanz, G.L. (1996). Effects of grade, syllable segmentation, and speed of presentation on children's word blending ability. *Journal of Educational Psychology, 88*(4), 670–681.

Morais, J., Bertelson, P., Cary, L., & Alegria, J. (1986). Literacy training and speech segmentation. *Cognition, 24*(1–2), 45–64.

Moustafa, M. (1997). *Beyond traditional phonics: Research discoveries and reading instruction*. Portsmouth, NH: Heinemann.

Perfetti, C.A., Beck, I., Bell, L., & Hughes, C. (1987). Phonemic knowledge and learning to read are reciprocal: A longitudinal study of first grade children. *Merrill-Palmer Quarterly, 33*(3), 283–319.

Read, C., Zhang, Y.F., Nie, H.Y., & Ding, B.Q. (1986). The ability to manipulate speech sounds depends on knowing alphabetic writing. *Cognition, 24*(1–2), 31–44.

Rosner, J. (1974). Auditory analysis training with prereaders. *The Reading Teacher, 27*(4), 379–384.

Scholes, R.J. (1998). The case against phonemic awareness. *Journal of Research in Reading, 21*(3), 177–189.

Stahl, S.A., & Murray, B.A. (1994). Defining phonological awareness and its relationship to early reading. *Journal of Educational Psychology, 86*(2), 221–234.

Teale, W., & Sulzby, E. (1986). *Emergent literacy: Reading and writing*. Norwood, NJ: Ablex.

Treiman, R. (1983). The structure of spoken syllables: Evidence from novel word games. *Cognition, 15*(1–3), 49–74.

Treiman, R. (1985). Onsets and rimes as units of spoken syllables: Evidence from children. *Journal of Experimental Child Psychology, 39*(1), 161–181.

Treiman, R. (1986). The division between onsets and rimes in English syllables. *Journal of Memory & Language, 25*, 476–491.

Treiman, R., & Baron, J. (1981). Segmental analysis ability: Development and relation to reading ability. In G.E. MacKinnon & T.G. Waller (Eds.), *Reading research: Advances in theory and practice* (Vol. 3, pp. 159–197). New York: Academic.

Treiman, R., & Chafetz, J. (1987). Are there onset- and rime-like units in printed words? In M. Coltheart (Ed.), *The psychology of reading* (7th International Symposium on Attention and Performance, pp. 281–298). Hillsdale, NJ: Erlbaum.

Tunmer, W.E., & Nesdale, A.R. (1985). Phonemic segmentation and beginning reading. *Journal of Educational Psychology, 77*(4), 417–427.

Venezky, R.L. (1967). English orthography: Its graphical structure and its relation to sound. *Reading Research Quarterly, 2*(3), 75–106.

Venezky, R.L. (1970). Regularity in reading and spelling. In H. Levin & J.P. Williams (Eds.), *Basic studies on reading* (pp. 37–56). New York: Basic Books.

Winner, H., Landerl, K., Linortner, R., & Hummer, P. (1991). The relationship of phonemic awareness to reading acquisition: More consequence than precondition but still important. *Cognition, 40*, 219–249.

Wylie, R.E., & Durrell, D.D. (1970). Teaching vowels through phonograms. *Elementary English, 47*(6), 787–791.

Yaden, D.B., Jr., & Templeton, S. (Eds.). (1986). *Metalinguistic awareness and beginning literacy: Conceptualizing what it means to read and write*. Portsmouth, NH: Heinemann.

Core Understanding 9

Adams, M.J. (1990). *Beginning to read: Thinking and learning about print*. Cambridge, MA: MIT Press.

Adams, M.J., & Bruck, M. (1995). Resolving the "great debate." *American Educator, 19*(2), 10–20.

Allen, R.V. (1976). *Language experiences in communication*. Boston: Houghton Mifflin.

Allington, R.L. (1997, August/September). Overselling phonics. *Reading Today, 15*(1), pp. 15–16.

Allington, R.L. (2001). *What really matters for struggling readers: Designing research-based programs*. New York: Longman.

Allington, R.L. (2005). Ideology is still trumping evidence. *Phi Delta Kappan, 86*(6), 462–468.

Alvermann, D.E. (2002). Effective literacy instruction for adolescents. *Journal of Literacy Research, 34*(2), 189–208.

Anderson, R.C., Hiebert, E., Scott, J., & Wilkinson, I. (1985). *Becoming a nation of readers: The report of the Commission on Reading*. Champaign: University of Illinois, Center for the Study of Reading.

Au, K.H. (1993). *Literacy instuction in multicultural settings*. Fort Worth, TX: Harcourt College.

Ball, E.W., & Blachman, B.A. (1991). Does phoneme awareness training in kindergarten make a difference in early word recognition and developmental spelling? *Reading Research Quarterly, 26*(1), 49–66.

Beck, I., & Juel, C. (1995). The role of decoding in learning to read. *American Educator, 19*(2), 8, 21–25, 39–42.

Blachman, B.A. (2000). Phonological awareness. In M.L. Kamil, P.B. Mosenthal, P.D. Pearson, & R. Barr (Eds.), *Handbook of reading research* (Vol. 3, pp. 483–502). Mahwah, NJ: Erlbaum.

Bond, G.L., & Dykstra, R. (1997). The cooperative research program in first grade reading instruction. *Reading Research Quarterly, 32*(4), 348–427. (Original work published 1967)

Bus, A.G., & van IJzendoorn, M.H. (1999). Phonological awareness and early reading: A meta-analysis of experimental training studies. *Journal of Educational Psychology, 91*(3), 403–414.

Camilli, G., Vargas, S., & Yurecko, M. (2003). Teaching children to read: The fragile link between science and federal education policy. *Education Policy Analysis Archives, 11*(15). Retrieved May 10, 2003, from http://epaa.asu.edu/epaa/v11n15

Cantrell, S.C. (1999). Effective teaching and literacy learning: A look inside primary classrooms. *The Reading Teacher, 52*(4), 370–378.

Chall, J. (1983). *Learning to read: The great debate*. New York: McGraw-Hill. (Original work published 1967)

Chamot, A. (1993, May). Instructional practices enhance student achievement. *Forum, 16*(4), 1, 4.

Chaney, C. (1992). Language development, metalinguistic skills, and print awareness in 3-year-old children. *Applied Psycholinguistics, 13*(4), 485–514.

Clarke, L.K. (1988). Invented versus traditional spelling in first graders' writings: Effects on learning to spell and read. *Research in the Teaching of English, 22*(3), 281–309.

Clymer, T. (1996). The utility of phonic generalizations in the primary grades. *The Reading Teacher, 50*(3), 182–187. (Original work published 1963)

Crawford, L.W. (1993). *Language and literacy in multicultural classrooms*. Boston: Allyn & Bacon.

Cummins, J. (1986). Empowering minority students: A framework for intervention. *Harvard Educational Review, 56*(1), 18–36.

Cunningham, A.E. (1990). Explicit versus implicit instruction in phonemic awareness. *Journal of Experimental Child Psychology, 50*, 429–444.

Cunningham, P.M. (1992). What kind of phonics instruction will we have? In C.K. Kinzer & D.J. Leu (Eds.), *Literacy research, theory, and practice: Views from many perspectives* (41st yearbook of the National Reading Conference, pp. 17–31). Chicago: National Reading Conference.

Cunningham, P.M., & Allington, R.L. (2003). *Classrooms that work: They can ALL read and write* (3rd ed.). Boston: Allyn & Bacon.

Dahl, K.L., Scharer, P.L., Lawson, L.L., & Grogan, P.R. (1999). Phonics instruction and student achievement in whole language first-grade classrooms. *Reading Research Quarterly, 34*(3), 312–341.

Delpit, L.D. (1986). Skills and other dilemmas of a progressive black educator. *Harvard Educational Review, 56*(4), 379–385.

Delpit, L.D. (1988). The silenced dialogue: Power and pedagogy in educating other people's children. *Harvard Educational Review, 58*(3), 280–287.

Duffy, G.G., & Hoffman, J.V. (1999). In pursuit of an illusion: The flawed search for a perfect method. *The Reading Teacher, 53*(1), 10–16.

Ehri, L.C. (1991). The development of the ability to read words. In R. Barr, M.L. Kamil, P.B. Mosenthal, & P.D. Pearson (Eds.), *Handbook of reading research* (Vol. 2, pp. 383–417. New York: Longman.

Foorman, B.R. (1995). Research on "the great debate": Code-oriented versus whole language approaches to reading instruction. *School Psychology Review*, *24*, 376–392.

Foorman, B.R., Francis, D.J., Fletcher, J.M., Schatschneider, C., & Mehta, P. (1998). The role of instruction in learning to read: Preventing reading failure in at-risk children. *Journal of Educational Psychology*, *90*(1), 37–55.

Fountas, I.C., & Pinnell, G.S. (1996). *Guided reading: Good first teaching for all children*. Portsmouth, NH: Heinemann.

Freppon, P.A., & Dahl, K.L. (1991). Learning about phonics in a whole language classroom. *Language Arts*, *68*(3), 190–197.

Galda, L., Ash, G.E., & Cullinan, B.E. (2000). Children's literature. In M.L. Kamil, P.B. Mosenthal, P.D. Pearson, & R. Barr (Eds.), *Handbook of reading research* (Vol. 3, pp. 361–380). Mahwah, NJ: Erlbaum.

Galda, L., & Cullinan, B.E. (2003). Literature for literacy: What research says about the benefits of using trade books in the classroom. In J. Flood, D. Lapp, J.R. Squire, & J.M. Jensen (Eds.), *Handbook of research on teaching the English language arts* (2nd ed., pp. 640–648). Mahwah, NJ: Erlbaum.

Gay, G. (1988). Designing relevant curricula for diverse learners. *Education & Urban Society*, *20*(4), 327–340.

Harste, J.C., Woodward, V.A., & Burke, C.L. (1984). *Language stories and literacy lessons*. Exeter, NH: Heinemann.

Hatcher, P.J., Hulme, C., & Ellis, A.W. (1994). Ameliorating early reading failure by integrating the teaching of reading and phonological skills: The phonological linkage hypothesis. *Child Development*, *65*, 41–57.

Heath, S.B., Mangiola, L., Schecter, S.R., & Hull, G.A. (Eds.). (1991). *Children of promise: Literate activity in linguistically and culturally diverse classrooms*. Washington, DC: National Educational Association.

Henderson, E.H., & Beers, J.W. (Eds.). (1980). *Developmental and cognitive aspects of learning to spell: A reflection of word knowledge*. Newark, DE: International Reading Association.

House, E.R., Glass, G.V., McLean, L.F., & Walker, D.F. (1978). No simple answer: Critique of the follow through evaluation. *Harvard Educational Review*, *48*, 128–160.

International Reading Association (IRA). (1997). *The role of phonics in reading instruction* (Position statement). Newark, DE: Author. Retrieved June 7, 2005, from http://www.reading.org/resources/issues/positions_phonics.html

International Reading Association (IRA). (1998). *Phonemic awareness and the teaching of reading* (Position statement). Newark, DE: Author. Retrieved June 7, 2005, from http://www.reading.org/resources/issues/positions_phonemic.html

Invernizzi, M.A. (1992). The vowel and what follows: A phonological frame of orthographic analysis. In S. Templeton & D. Bear (Eds.), *Development of orthographic knowledge and the foundations of literacy: A memorial Festschrift for Edmund H. Henderson* (pp. 105–136). Hillsdale, NJ: Erlbaum.

IRA takes a stand on phonics. (1997, April/May). *Reading Today*, *14*(5), pp. 1, 4.

Ivey, G., & Baker, M.I. (2004). Phonics instruction for older students? Just say no. *Educational Leadership*, *61*(6), 35–39.

Juel, C. (1988). Learning to read and write: A longitudinal study of 54 children from first through fourth grades. *Journal of Educational Psychology*, *80*(4), 437–447.

Juel, C. (1991). Beginning reading. In R. Barr, M.L. Kamil, P.B. Mosenthal, & P.D. Pearson (Eds.), *Handbook of reading research* (Vol. 2, pp. 759–788). New York: Longman.

Juel, C. (1994). *Learning to read and write in one elementary school*. New York: Springer-Verlag.

Juel, C., & Minden-Cupp, C. (2000). Learning to read words: Linguistic units and instructional strategies. *Reading Research Quarterly*, *35*(4), 458–492.

Kasten, W.C., & Clarke, B.K. (1989). *Reading/writing readiness for preschool and kindergarten children: A whole language approach*. Sanibel: Florida Educational Research and Development Council. (ERIC Document Reproduction Service No. ED312041)

Knapp, M.S., & Shields, P.M. (1990). Reconceiving academic instruction for the children of poverty. *Phi Delta Kappan*, *71*(10), 753–758.

Knobel, M. (2001). "I'm not a pencil man": How one student challenges our notions of literacy "failure" in school. *Journal of Adolescent & Adult Literacy*, *44*(5), 404–414.

Krashen, S.D. (2001). More smoke and mirrors: A critique of the National Reading Panel report on fluency. *Phi Delta Kappan*, *83*(2), 119–123.

Krashen, S.D. (2002). Speculation and conjecture. *Phi Delta Kappan*, *84*(2), 157–158.

Levy, A.K., Wolfgang, C.H., & Koorland, M.A. (1992). Sociodramatic play as a method for enhancing the language performance of kindergarten-age students: Research on kindergarten [Special issue]. *Early Childhood Research Quarterly*, *7*(2), 245–262.

Lundberg, I., Frost, J., & Petersen, O. (1988). Effects of an extensive program for stimulating phonological awareness in preschool children. *Reading Research Quarterly*, *23*(3), 263–284.

Mann, V. (1986). Phonological awareness: The role of reading experience. *Cognition*, *24*, 65–92.

McCartney, K., & Rosenthal, R. (2000). Effect size, practical importance, and social policy for children. *Child Development*, *71*(1), 173–180.

Morais, J., Bertelson, P., Cary, L., & Alegria, J. (1986). Literacy training and speech segmentation. *Cognition*, *24*(1–2), 45–64.

Morris, D., & Perney, J. (1984). Developmental spelling as a predictor of first grade reading achievement. *The Elementary School Journal*, *84*(4), 441–457.

Moustafa, M. (1995). Children's productive phonological recoding. *Reading Research Quarterly*, *30*(3), 464–476.

Moustafa, M. (1997). *Beyond traditional phonics: Research discoveries and reading instruction*. Portsmouth, NH: Heinemann.

National Council of Teachers of English (NCTE). (2004). *On reading, learning to read, and effective reading instruction: An overview of what we know and how we know it* (NCTE guideline by the Commission on Reading). Urbana, IL: Author. Retrieved March 18, 2005, from http://www.ncte.org/about/over/positions/category/read/118620.htm

National Institute of Child Health and Human Development (NICHD). (2000). *Report of the National Reading Panel. Teaching children to read: An evidence-based assessment of the scientific research literature on reading and its implications for reading instruction* (NIH Publication No. 00-4769). Washington, DC: U.S. Government Printing Office.

Neuman, S.B. (1999). Books make a difference: A study of access to literacy. *Reading Research Quarterly*, *34*(3), 286–311.

O'Connell, M.P., & Wood, M. (1992). *Becoming a reader: A developmental approach to reading instruction*. Boston: Allyn & Bacon.

Ovando, C.J. (1993). Language diversity and education. In J.A. Banks & C.A. McGhee Banks (Eds.), *Multicultural education: Issues and perspectives* (2nd ed., pp. 215–235). Boston: Allyn & Bacon.

Pearson, P.D. (1993). Teaching and learning reading: A research perspective. *Language Arts*, *70*(6), 502–511.

Pearson, P.D. (1996). Foreword. In E. McIntyre & M. Pressley (Eds.), *Balanced instruction: Strategies and skills in whole language* (pp. xv–xviii). Norwood, MA: Christopher-Gordon.

Pearson, P.D. (2000). Reading in the 20th century. In T. Good (Ed.), *American education: Yesterday, today, and tomorrow* (yearbook of the National Society for the Study of Education, pp. 152–208). Chicago: University of Chicago Press.

Pogrow, S. (1992). What to do about Chapter 1: An alternative view from the street. *Phi Delta Kappan*, *73*(8), 624–630.

Pressley, M., Allington, R.L., Wharton-McDonald, R., Block, C.C., & Morrow, L.M. (2001). *Learning to read: Lessons from exemplary first-grade classrooms*. New York: Guilford.

Purcell-Gates, V., McIntyre, E., & Freppon, P. (1995). Learning written storybook language in school: A comparison of low-SES children in skills-based and whole language classrooms. *American Educational Research Journal*, *32*(3), 659–685.

Read, C. (1975). *Children's categorizations of speech sounds in English* (Research Report No. 17). Urbana, IL: National Council of Teachers of English.

Read, C. (1986). *Children's creative spelling*. Boston: Routledge & Kegan Paul.

Ribowsky, H. (1985). *The effects of a code emphasis approach and a whole language approach upon emergent literacy of kindergarten children* (Report No. CS-008-397). Alexandria, VA: ERIC Document Reproduction Service. (Report No. ED269720)

Schickedanz, J.A. (1986). *More than ABC's: The early stages of reading and writing*. Washington, DC: National Association for the Education of Young Children.

Schlagal, R.C. (1992). Patterns of orthographic development into the intermediate grades. In S. Templeton & D.R. Bear (Eds.), *Development of orthographic knowledge and the foundations of literacy: A memorial Festschrift for Edmund H. Henderson* (pp. 31–52). Hillsdale, NJ: Erlbaum.

Schoenbach, R., Greenleaf, C.L., Cziko, C. & Hurwitz, L. (1999). *Reading for understanding: A guide to improving reading in middle and high school classrooms*. San Francisco: Jossey-Bass.

Schweinhart, L.J., Weikart, D., & Larner, M. (1986). Consequences of three preschool curriculum models through age 15. *Early Childhood Research Quarterly, 1*(1), 15–45.

Shannon, P. (1996). Mad as Stanovich hell. *Language Arts, 73*(1), 14–19.

Snow, C.E., Burns, M.S., & Griffin, P. (Eds.). (1998). *Preventing reading difficulties in young children*. Washington, DC: National Academy Press.

Stahl, S.A. (1998). Teaching children with reading problems to decode: Phonics and "not-phonics" instruction. *Reading and Writing Quarterly, 14*(2), 165–188.

Stahl, S.A., McKenna, M.C., & Pagnucco, J.R. (1994). The effects of whole language instruction: An update and a reappraisal. *Educational Psychologist, 29*(4), 175–185.

Stanovich, K.E. (1991). Word recognition: Changing perspectives. In R. Barr, M.L. Kamil, P.B. Mosenthal, & P.D. Pearson (Eds.), *Handbook of reading research* (Vol. 2, pp. 418–452). New York: Longman.

Stebbins, L.B., St. Pierre, R.G., Proper, E.C., Anderson, R.B., & Cerva, T.R. (1977). *Education as experimentation: A planned variation model, an evaluation of follow through* (Vol. 4-A). Cambridge, MA: ABT.

Stice, C.F., & Bertrand, N.P. (1990). *Whole language and the emergent literacy of at-risk children: A two-year comparative study*. Nashville: Tennessee State University Center for Excellence.

Strickland, D.S. (1998). *Teaching phonics today: A primer for educators*. Newark, DE: International Reading Association.

Swanson, H.L., Trainin, G., Necoechea, D.M., & Hammill, D.D. (2003). Rapid naming, phonological awareness, and reading: A meta-analysis of the correlation evidence. *Review of Educational Research, 73*(4), 407–440.

Sweet, A.P. (1993). *State of the art: Transforming ideas for teaching and learning to read*. Washington, DC: U.S. Department of Education, Office of Educational Research and Improvement.

Taylor, B.M., Pearson, P.D., Clark, K.F., & Walpole, S. (1999). *Beating the odds in teaching all children to read* (CIERA Report No. 2-006). Ann Arbor: Center for the Improvement of Early Reading Achievement, University of Michigan.

Tharp, R.G. (1989). Psychocultural variables and constants: Effects on teaching and learning in schools. *American Psychologist, 44*(2), 349–359.

Thompson, R., Mixon, G., & Serpell, R. (1996). Engaging minority students in reading: Focus on the urban learner. In L. Baker, P. Afflerbach, & D. Reinking (Eds.), *Developing engaged readers in school and home communities* (pp. 43–63). Mahwah, NJ: Erlbaum.

Troia, G.A. (1999). Phonological awareness intervention research: A critical review of the experimental methodology. *Reading Research Quarterly, 34*(1), 28–52.

Tunmer, W.E., Herriman, M., & Nesdale, A. (1988). Metalinguistic abilities and beginning reading. *Reading Research Quarterly, 23*(2), 134–158.

Weaver, C. (1994). *Reading process and practice: From socio-psycholinguistics to whole language* (2nd ed.). Portsmouth, NH: Heinemann.

Weaver, C. (Ed.). (1998). *Reconsidering a balanced approach to reading*. Urbana, IL: National Council of Teachers of English.

Weaver, C., Gillmeister-Krause, L., & Vento-Zogby, G. (1996). *Creating support for effective literacy education: Workshop materials and handouts*. Portsmouth, NH: Heinemann.

Wharton-McDonald, R., Pressley, M., & Hampston, J.M. (1998). Outstanding literacy instruction in first grade: Teacher practices and student achievement. *The Elementary School Journal, 99*(2), 101–128.

Wilde, S. (1992). *You kan red this! Spelling and punctuation for whole language classrooms, K–6*. Portsmouth, NH: Hienemann.

Winner, H., Landerl, K., Linortner, R., & Hummer, P. (1991). The relationship of phonemic awareness to reading acquisition: More consequence than precondition but still important. *Cognition, 40*, 219–249.

Winsor, P.J., & Pearson, P.D. (1992). *Children at-risk: Their phonemic awareness development in holistic instruction* (Technical Report No. 556). Urbana: Center for the Study of Reading, University of Illinois.

Xue, Y., & Meisels, S.J. (2004). Early literacy instruction and learning in kindergarten: Evidence from the early childhood longitudinal study: Kindergarten class of 1998–1999. *American Educational Research Journal, 41*(1), 191–229.

Yatvin, J. (2002). Babes in the woods: The wanderings of the National Reading Panel. *Phi Delta Kappan, 83*(5), 364–369.

Yatvin, J., Weaver, C., & Garan, E. (2003). Reading First: Cautions and recommendations. *Language Arts, 81*(1), 28–33.

Zutell, J. (1979). Spelling strategies of primary school children and their relationship to

Piaget's concept of decentration. *Research in the Teaching of English*, *13*(1), 69–80.

Core Understanding 10

Alexander, P.A., & Murphy, P.K. (1999). Learner profiles: Valuing individual differences within classroom communities. In P.L. Ackerman, P.C. Kyllonen, & R.D. Roberts (Eds.), *Learning and individual differences: Process, trait, and content determinants* (pp. 413–436). Washington, DC: American Psychological Association.

Allington, R.L., & McGill-Franzen, A. (2003). The impact of summer setback on the reading achievement gap. *Phi Delta Kappan*, *85*(1), 68–75.

Applebee, A.N. (1996). *Curriculum as conversation: Transforming traditions of teaching and learning.* Chicago: University of Chicago Press.

Baumann, J.F. (1984). The effectiveness of a direct instruction paradigm for teaching main idea comprehension. *Reading Research Quarterly*, *20*(1), 93–115.

Beck, I.L., Omanson, R.C., & McKeown, M.G. (1982). An instructional redesign of reading lessons: Effects on comprehension. *Reading Research Quarterly*, *17*(4), 462–481.

Beers, K. (2003). *When kids can't read, what teachers can do: A guide for teachers 6–12.* Portsmouth, NH: Heinemann.

Braunger, J.B. (1996). Retelling: Reading assessment that's also good instruction. In R. Blum & J. Arter, (Eds.) *A handbook for student performance assessment in an era of restructuring* (pp. iv–12, 1–8). Alexandria, VA: Association for Supervision and Curriculum Development.

Brown, H., & Cambourne, B. (1990). *Read and retell: A strategy for the whole-language/natural learning classroom.* Portsmouth, NH: Heinemann.

Clay, M.M. (1985). *The early detection of reading difficulties: A diagnostic survey with recovery procedures* (3rd ed.). Auckland, New Zealand: Heinemann.

Clay, M.M. (1991). *Becoming literate: The construction of inner control.* Portsmouth, NH: Heinemann.

Cooper, J.D. (1993). *Literacy: Helping children construct meaning.* Boston: Houghton Mifflin.

Dole, J.A., Duffy, G.G., Roehler, L.R., & Pearson, P.D. (1991). Moving from the old to the new: Research on reading comprehension instruction. *Review of Educational Research*, *61*, 239–264.

Duke, N.K., & Pearson, P.D. (2002). Effective practices for developing reading comprehension. In A.E. Farstrup & S.J. Samuels (Eds.), *What research has to say about reading instruction* (3rd ed., pp. 205–242). Newark, DE: International Reading Association.

Englert, C.S., & Hiebert, E.H. (1984). Children's developing awareness of text structures in expository materials. *Journal of Educational Psychology*, *76*(1), 65–74.

Fournier, D.N.E., and Graves, M.F. (2002). Scaffolding adolescents' comprehension of short stories. *Journal of Adolescent & Adult Literacy*, *46*(1), 30–39.

Goodman, K.S. (1965). A linguistic study of cues and miscues in reading. *Elementary English*, *42*(6), 639–643.

Goodman, Y.M., & Marek, A.M. (1996). *Retrospective miscue analysis: Revaluing readers and reading.* Katonah, NY: Richard C. Owen.

Goodman, Y.M., Watson, D.J., & Burke, C.L. (1987). *Reading miscue inventory: Alternative procedures.* Katonah, NY: Richard C. Owen.

Graves, M.F., & Graves, B.B. (2003). *Scaffolding reading experiences: Designs for student success* (2nd ed.). Norwood, MA: Christopher-Gordon.

Greenleaf, C.L., Schoenbach, R., Cziko, C., & Mueller, F.L. (2001). Apprenticing adolescent readers to academic literacy. *Harvard Educational Review*, *71*(1), 79–129.

Guthrie, J.T., Van Meter, P., Hancock, G.R., McCann, A., Anderson, E., & Alao, S. (1998). Does concept-oriented reading instruction increase strategy use and conceptual learning from text? *Journal of Educational Psychology*, *90*(2), 261–278.

Guthrie, J.T., Van Meter, P., McCann, A.D., Wigfield, A., Bennett, L., Poundstone, C.C., et al. (1996). Growth of literacy engagement: Changes in motivations and strategies during concept-oriented reading instruction. *Reading Research Quarterly*, *31*(3), 306–332.

Guthrie, J.T., & Wigfield, A. (2000). Engagement and motivation in reading. In M.L. Kamil, P.B. Mosenthal, P.D. Pearson, & R. Barr (Eds.), *Handbook of reading research* (Vol. 3, pp. 403–422). Mahwah, NJ: Erlbaum.

Kamil, M.L. (2003). *Adolescents and literacy: Reading for the 21st century.* Washington, DC: Alliance for Excellent Education.

Langer, J.A. (2000). *Guidelines for teaching middle and high school students to read and write well: Six features of effective instruction.* Albany: National Research Center on

English Learning and Achievement, State University of New York.

Langer, J.A. (2001). Beating the odds: Teaching middle and high school students to read and write well. *American Educational Research Journal, 38*(4), 837–880.

McGee, L.M. (1982). Awareness of text structure: Effects on children's recall of expository text. *Reading Research Quarterly, 17*(4), 581–590.

Meyer, B.J.F., Brandt, D.M., & Bluth, G.J. (1980). Use of top-level structure in text: Key for reading comprehension of ninth-grade students. *Reading Research Quarterly, 16*(1), 73–103.

Moore, R.A., & Aspegren, C.M. (2001). Reflective conversations between two learners: Retrospective miscue analysis. *Journal of Adolescent & Adult Literacy, 44*(6), 492–503.

Morrow, L.M. (1990). Assessing children's understanding of story through their construction and reconstruction of narrative. In L.M. Morrow & J.K. Smith (Eds.), *Assessment for instruction in early literacy* (pp. 110–134). Englewood Cliffs, NJ: Prentice Hall.

National Council of Teachers of English (NCTE). (2004). *A call to action: What we know about adolescent literacy and ways to support teachers in meeting students' needs* (NCTE guideline by the Commission on Reading). Urbana, IL: Author. Retrieved May 21, 2005, from http://www.ncte.org/about/over/positions/category/read/118622.htm

Palincsar, A.S., & Brown, A.L. (1984). Reciprocal teaching of comprehension-fostering and comprehension-monitoring activities. *Cognition & Instruction, 1*(2), 117–175.

Paris, S.G., Lipson, M.Y., & Wixon, K.K. (1983). Becoming a strategic reader. *Contemporary Educational Psychology, 8*(3), 293–316.

Paris, S.G., Wasik, B.A., & Turner, J.C. (1991). The development of strategic readers. In R. Barr, M.L. Kamil, P.B. Mosenthal, & P.D. Pearson (Eds.), *Handbook of reading research* (Vol. 2, pp. 609–640). New York: Longman.

Pearson, P.D. (1993). Teaching and learning reading: A research perspective. *Language Arts, 70*(6), 502–511.

Pressley, M. (2002). Metacognition and self-regulated comprehension. In A.E. Farstrup & S.J. Samuels (Eds.), *What research has to say about reading instruction* (3rd ed., pp. 291–309). Newark, DE: International Reading Association.

Pressley, M., El-Dinary, P.B., Gaskins, I., Schuder, T., Bergman, J.L., Almasi, J., et al. (1992). Beyond direct explanation: Transactional instruction of reading comprehension strategies. *The Elementary School Journal, 92*(5), 513–555.

Pressley, M., Gaskins, I.W., Wile, D., Cunicelli, E.A., & Sheridan, J. (1991). Teaching strategy across the curriculum: A case study at Benchmark School. In J. Zutell & S. McCormick (Eds.), *Learner factors/teacher factors: Issues in literacy research and instruction* (40th yearbook of the National Reading Conference, pp. 219–228). Chicago: National Reading Conference.

Pressley, M., Schuder, T., & Bergman, J.L. (1992). A researcher-educator collaborative interview study of transactional comprehension strategies instruction. *Journal of Educational Psychology, 84*(2), 231–246.

RAND Reading Study Group. (2002). *Reading for understanding: Toward an R&D program in reading comprehension*. Santa Monica, CA: RAND.

Resnick, L.B. (1990). Literacy in school and out: Literacy in America [Special issue]. *Daedalus, 19*(2), 169–185.

Rinehart, S.D., Stahl, S.A., & Erickson, L.G. (1986). Some effects of summarization training on reading and studying. *Reading Research Quarterly, 21*(4), 422–438.

Rogoff, B. (1990). *Apprenticeship in thinking: Cognitive development in social context*. New York: Oxford University Press.

Schoenbach, R., Braunger, J., Greenleaf, C., & Litman, C. (2003). Apprenticing adolescents to reading in subject-area classrooms. *Phi Delta Kappan, 85*(2), 133–138.

Schoenbach, R., Greenleaf, C.L., Cziko, C., & Hurwitz, L. (1999). *Reading for understanding: A guide to improving reading in middle and high school classrooms*. San Francisco: Jossey-Bass.

Snow, C.E., Burns, M.S., & Griffin, P. (Eds.). (1998). *Preventing reading difficulties in young children*. Washington, DC: National Academy Press.

Sweet, A.P. (1993). *State of the art: Transforming ideas for teaching and learning to read*. Washington, DC: U.S. Department of Education, Office of Educational Research and Improvement.

Taylor, B.M. (1980). Children's memory for expository text after reading. *Reading Research Quarterly, 15*(3), 399–411.

Taylor, B.M., Pearson, P.D., Clark, K.F., & Walpole, S. (1999). *Beating the odds in teaching all children to read* (CIERA Report No. 2-006). Ann Arbor: Center for the

Improvement of Early Reading Achievement, University of Michigan.

Taylor, B.M., Peterson, D., Rodriguez, M.C., & Pearson, P.D. (2002). *The CIERA school-change project: Supporting schools as they implement home-grown reading reform* (CIERA Report No. 2-016). Ann Arbor: Center for the Improvement of Early Reading Achievement, University of Michigan.

Core Understanding 11

Adams, M.J. (1990). *Beginning to read: Thinking and learning about print*. Cambridge, MA: MIT Press.

Alexander, P.A., Graham, S., & Harris, K.R. (1998). A perspective on strategy research: Progress and prospects. *Educational Psychology Review, 10*(2), 129–154.

Alexander, P.A., & Jetton, T.L. (2000). Learning from text: A multidimensional and developmental perspective. In M.L. Kamil, P.B. Mosenthal, P.D. Pearson, & R. Barr (Eds.), *Handbook of Reading Research* (Vol. 3, pp. 285–310). Mahwah, NJ: Erlbaum.

Alexander, P.A., & Murphy, P.K. (1998). The research base for APA's learner-centered principles. In N.M. Lambert & B.L. Combs (Eds.), *Issues in school reform: A sampler of psychological perspectives on learner-centered schools* (pp. 25–60). Washington, DC: American Psychological Association.

Alidou, H. (2000). Preparing teachers for the education of new immigrant students from Africa. *Action in Teacher Education, 22*(2A), 101–108.

Allen, J. (2003). But they still can't (or won't) read! Helping children to overcome roadblocks to reading. *Language Arts, 80*(4), 268–274.

Allington, R.L. (1980). Poor readers don't get to read much in reading groups. *Language Arts, 57*(8), 873–875.

Allington, R.L. (1983). Fluency: The neglected reading goal. *The Reading Teacher, 36*(6), 556–561.

Allington, R.L. (2002). What I've learned about effective reading instruction from a decade of studying exemplary elementary classroom teachers. *Phi Delta Kappan, 83*(10), 740–747.

Allington, R.L., & Johnston, P.H. (2000). *What do we know about effective fourth-grade teachers and their classrooms?* (CELA Research Report No. 13010). Albany: National Research Center on English Learning and Achievement, State University of New York.

Allington, R.L., & Johnston, P.H. (2002). *Reading to learn: Lessons from exemplary fourth-grade classrooms*. New York: Guilford.

Allington, R.L., Johnston, P.H., & Day, J. (2002). Exemplary fourth-grade teachers. *Language Arts, 79*(6), 462–466.

Almasi, J.F. (1995). The nature of fourth graders' sociocognitive conflicts in peer-led and teacher-led discussion of literature. *Reading Research Quarterly, 30*(3), 314–351.

Al Otaiba, S., & Fuchs, D. (2002). Characteristics of children who are unresponsive to early literacy instruction: A review of the literature. *Remedial & Special Education, 23*(5), 300–316.

Anderson, R.C., & Freebody, P. (1981). Vocabulary knowledge. In J.T. Guthrie (Ed.), *Comprehension and teaching: Research reviews* (pp. 77–117). Newark, DE: International Reading Association.

Anderson, R.C., Hiebert, E., Scott, J., & Wilkinson, I. (1985). *Becoming a nation of readers: The report of the Commission on Reading*. Urbana, IL: Center for the Study of Reading; Washington, DC: National Academy of Education.

Anderson, R.C., Wilkinson, I.A.G., & Mason, J. (1991). A microanalysis of the small-group guided reading lesson: Effects of an emphasis on global story meaning. *Reading Research Quarterly, 26*, 417–441.

Anderson, R.C., Wilson, P.T., & Fielding, L.G. (1988). Growth in reading and how children spend their time outside of school. *Reading Research Quarterly, 23*(3), 285–303.

Applebee, A.N., Burroughs, R., & Stevens, A.S. (2000). Creating continuity and coherence in high school literature curricula. *Research in the Teaching of English, 34*(3), 396–429.

Applebee, A.N., & Langer, J.A. (1983). Instructional scaffolding: Reading and writing as natural activities. *Language Arts, 60*(2), 168–175.

Applebee, A.N., Langer, J.A., Nystrand, M., & Gamoran, A. (2003). Discussion-based approaches to developing understanding: Classroom instruction and student performance in middle and high school English. *American Educational Research Journal, 40*(3), 685–730.

Armbruster, B.B. (1984). The problem of "inconsiderate text." In G.G. Duffy, L.R. Roehler, & J.M. Mason (Eds.), *Comprehension instruction: Perspectives and suggestions* (pp. 202–217). New York: Longman.

Au, K.H. (1991, April). Organizing for instruction [Special issue]. *The Reading Teacher, 44*(8).

Au, K.H. (1993). *Literacy instruction in multicultural settings*. Fort Worth, TX: Harcourt College.

Au, K.H., & Raphael, T.E. (1998). Curriculum and teaching in literature based programs. In T.E. Raphael & K.H. Au (Eds.), *Literature based instruction: Reshaping the curriculum* (pp. 123–148). Norwood, MA: Christopher-Gordon.

Avery, C.W., & Avery, K.B. (2001). Kids teaching kids. *Journal of Adolescent & Adult Literacy*, *40*(5), 434–435.

Baker, K., & Allington, R.L. (2003). Strategies for literacy development for students with disabilities. In L.M. Morrow, L.B. Gambrell, & M. Pressley (Eds.), *Best practices in literacy instruction* (2nd ed., pp. 287–304). New York: Guilford.

Barr, R. (1989). The social organization of literacy instruction. In S. McCormick & J. Zutell (Eds.), *Cognitive and social perspectives for literacy research and instruction* (38th yearbook of the National Reading Conference, pp. 19–34). Chicago: National Reading Conference.

Baumann, J.F., Hoffman, J.V., Moon, J., & Duffy-Hester, A.M. (1998). Where are teachers' voices in the phonics/whole language debate? Results from a survey of U.S. elementary classroom teachers. *The Reading Teacher*, *51*(8), 636–650.

Beach, S.A. (1993). Oral reading instruction: Retiring the bird in the round. *Reading Psychology*, *14*(4), 333–338.

Beck, I.L. (1997, October/November). Response to "Overselling phonics." *Reading Today*, *15*(2), p. 17.

Beck, I.L., & McKeown, M.G. (2001). Text talk: Capturing the benefits of read-aloud experiences for young children. *The Reading Teacher*, *55*(1), 10–20.

Beck, I.L., McKeown, M.G., Hamilton, R.L., & Kucan, L. (1997). *Questioning the author: An approach for enhancing student engagement with text*. Newark, DE: International Reading Association.

Biddulph, J. (2002). *The guided reading approach: Theory and research*. Wellington, New Zealand: Learning Media.

Blachowicz, C.L.Z., & Fisher, P. (2000). Vocabulary instruction. In M.L. Kamil, P.B. Mosenthal, P.D. Pearson, & R. Barr (Eds.), *Handbook of reading research* (Vol. 3, pp. 503–524). Mahwah, NJ: Erlbaum.

Blachowicz, C.L.Z., & Fisher, P. (2003). Best practices in vocabulary instruction: What effective teachers do. In L.M. Morrow, L.B. Gambrell, & M. Pressley (Eds.), *Best practices in literacy instruction* (2nd ed., pp. 87–110). New York: Guilford.

Block, C.C., & Mangieri, J.N. (2002). Recreational reading: 20 years later. *The Reading Teacher*, *55*(6), 572–580.

Bond, G.L., & Dykstra, R. (1997). The cooperative research program on first-grade reading instruction. *Reading Research Quarterly*, *32*(4), 348–427. (Original work published 1967)

Bos, C.S., & Anders, P.L. (1989). *The effectiveness of interactive instructional practices on content area reading comprehension*. Washington, DC: Office of Special Education and Rehabilitative Services. (ERIC Document Reproduction Service No. ED329935)

Bos, C.S., & Anders, P.L. (1990). Effects of interactive vocabulary instruction on the vocabulary learning and reading comprehension of junior high learning disabled students. *Learning Disability Quarterly*, *13*(1), 31–42.

Bos, C.S., & Anders , P.L. (1992). Using interactive teaching and learning strategies to promote text comprehension and content learning for students with learning disabilities. *International Journal of Disability, Development, & Education*, *39*(3), 225–238.

Bransford, J.D., Brown, A.C., & Cocking, RR. (Eds.). (1999). *How people learn: Brain, mind, and school*. Washington, DC: National Academy Press.

Bridge, C., Winograd, P.N., & Haley, D. (1983). Using predictable materials vs. preprimers, to teach beginning sight words. *The Reading Teacher*, *36*(9), 884–891.

Brown, A., & Palincsar, A. (1989). Guided, cooperative learning and individual knowledge acquisition. In L.B. Resnick (Ed.), *Knowing, learning, and instruction: Essays in honor of Robert Glaser*. Hillsdale, NJ: Erlbaum.

Brown, R., & Coy-Ogan, L. (1993). The evolution of transactional strategies instruction in one teacher's classroom. *The Elementary School Journal*, *94*(2), 221–233.

Brown, R., Pressley, M., Van Meter, P., & Schuder, T. (1996). A quasi-experimental validation of transactional strategies instruction with low-achieving second-grade readers. *Journal of Educational Psychology*, *88*(1), 18–37.

Brozo, W.G., & Hargis, C.H. (2003). Taking seriously the idea of reform: One high school's efforts to make reading more responsive to all students. *Journal of Adolescent & Adult Literacy*, *47*(1), 14–23.

Bruner, J. (1975). The ontogenesis of speech acts. *Journal of Child Language, 2*(1), 1–19.

Caine, R.N., & Caine, G. (1997). *Education on the edge of possibility*. Alexandria, VA: Association for Supervision and Curriculum Development.

Cambourne, B. (2001). What do I do with the rest of the class? The nature of teaching-learning activities. *Language Arts, 79*(2), 124–135.

Cambourne, B., & Rousch, P. (1982). How do learning disabled children read? *Topics in Learning & Learning Disabilities, 1*, 59–68.

Cantrell, S.C. (1999). The effects of literacy instruction on primary students' reading and writing achievement. *Reading Research and Instruction, 39*(1), 3–26.

Chomsky, C. (1976). After decoding: What? *Language Arts, 53*(3), 288–296.

Clark, M.M. (1976). *Young fluent readers: What can they teach us?* London: Heinemann.

Clay, M.M. (1991a). *Becoming literate: The construction of inner control*. Portsmouth, NH: Heinemann.

Clay, M.M. (1991b). Introducing a new storybook to young readers. *The Reading Teacher, 45*(4), 264–273.

Cochran-Smith, M. (1984). *The making of a reader*. Norwood, NJ: Ablex.

Cohen, D.H. (1968). The effects of literature on vocabulary and reading achievement. *Elementary English, 45*(2), 209–213, 217.

Collins, C.C. (1991). Reading instruction that increases thinking abilities. *Journal of Reading, 34*, 510–516.

Cunningham, A.E., & Stanovich, K.E. (1998). What reading does for the mind. *American Educator, 22*(1–2), 8–15.

Cunningham, P.M. (2000). *Phonics they use: Words for reading and writing* (3rd ed.). New York: Longman.

Cunningham, P.M., & Allington, R.L. (2003). *Classrooms that work: They can ALL read and write* (3rd ed.). Boston: Allyn & Bacon.

Cunningham, P.M., Hall, D., & Defee, M. (1991). Non-ability grouped, multilevel instruction: A year in a first-grade classroom. *The Reading Teacher, 44*(8), 566–571.

Dahl, P.R. (1979). An experimental program for teaching high speed word recognition and comprehension skills. In J.E. Button, T. Lovitt, & T. Rowland (Eds.), *Communication research in learning disabilities and mental retardation* (pp. 33–65). Baltimore: University Park Press.

Darling-Hammond, L. (1999). *Reshaping teaching policy, preparation, and practice: Influences of the National Board for Professional Teaching Standards*. Washington, DC: American Association of Colleges of Teacher Education.

Davidson, J. (1985). What you think is going on, isn't: Eighth grade students' introspections of discussions in science and social studies lessons. In J.A. Niles & R. Lalik (Eds.), *Issues in literacy: A research perspective* (34th yearbook of the National Reading Conference). Rochester, NY: National Reading Conference.

Davis, F.B. (1944). Fundamental factors in reading comprehension. *Psychometrika, 9*, 185–197.

Dickinson, D.K., & Smith, M.W. (1994). Long-term effects of preschool teachers' book readings on low-income children's vocabulary and story comprehension. *Reading Research Quarterly, 29*(2), 104–122.

Doise, W., & Mugny, G. (1984). *The social development of the intellect* (A. St. James-Emler & N. Emler, Trans.). Oxford, England: Pergamon.

Dowhower, S.L. (1989). Repeated reading: Research into practice. *The Reading Teacher, 42*(7), 502–507.

Dowhower, S.L. (1991). Speaking of prosody: Fluency's unattended bedfellow. *Theory Into Practice, 30*(3), 165–175.

Dowhower, S.L. (1994). Repeated reading revisited. *Reading & Writing Quarterly, 10*(4), 343–358.

Dowhower, S.L. (1999). Supporting a strategic stance in the classroom: A comprehension framework for helping teachers help students to be strategic. *The Reading Teacher, 52*(7), 672–688.

Duchein, M.A., & Mealey, D.L. (1993). Remembrance of books past...long past: Glimpses into aliteracy. *Reading Research & Instruction, 33*(1), 13–28.

Duke, N.K. (2000). 3.6 minutes per day: The scarcity of informational texts in first grade. *Reading Research Quarterly, 35*(2), 202–224.

Durkin, D. (1966). *Children who read early: Two longitudinal studies*. New York: Teachers College Press.

Eeds, M., & Wells, D. (1989). Grand conversations: An exploration of meaning construction in literature study groups. *Research in the Teaching of English, 23*(1), 4–29.

Eldredge, J.L., Reutzel, D.R., & Hollingsworth, P.M. (1996). Comparing the effectiveness of two oral reading practices: Round-robin reading and the shared book experience. *Journal of Literacy Research, 28*(2), 201–225.

Elley, W.B. (1988). *New vocabulary: How do children learn new words?* Wellington: New

Zealand Council for Educational Research. (ERIC Document Reproduction Service No. ED298455)

Elley, W.B. (1992, July). *How in the world do students read? IEA study of reading literacy*. The Netherlands: International Association for the Evaluation of Educational Achievement. (ERIC Document Reproduction Service No. ED360613)

Finesilver, M. (1994). *An investigation of three methods to improve vocabulary learning at the middle school level*. Unpublished doctoral dissertation, National Louis University, Evanston, IL.

Fisher, C., & Adler, M.A. (1999). *Early reading programs in high poverty schools: Emerald Elementary beats the odds* (CIERA Report #3-009). Ann Arbor: Center for the Improvement of Early Reading Achievement, University of Michigan.

Fisher, D., Flood, J., & Lapp, D. (2003). Material matters: Using children's literature to charm readers (or why Harry Potter and the Princess Diaries matter). In L.M. Morrow, L.B. Gambrell, & M. Pressley (Eds.), *Best practices in literacy instruction* (2nd ed., pp. 167–186). New York: Guilford.

Fisher, D., Flood, J., Lapp, D., & Frey, N. (2004). Interactive read-alouds: Is there a common set of implementation practices? *The Reading Teacher, 58*(1), 8–17.

Flippo, R.F. (1998). Points of agreement: A display of professional unity in our field. *The Reading Teacher, 52*(1), 30–40.

Flippo, R.F. (2001). *Reading researchers in search of common ground*. Newark, DE: International Reading Association.

Flood, J., Lapp, D., Flood, S., & Nagel, G. (1992). Am I allowed to group? Using flexible patterns for effective instruction. *The Reading Teacher, 45*(8), 608–616.

Foorman, B.R., Fletcher, J.M., Francis, D.J., Beeler, T., & Winikates, D. (1997). Early interventions for children with reading problems: Study designs and preliminary findings. *Learning Disabilities: A Multidisciplinary Journal, 8*(1), 63–71.

Foorman, B.R., Francis, D.J., Fletcher, J.M., Schatschneider, C., & Mehta, P. (1998). The role of instruction in learning to read: Preventing reading failure in at-risk children. *Journal of Educational Psychology, 90*(1), 37–55.

Fountas, I.C., & Pinnell, G.S. (1996). *Guided reading: Good first teaching for all children*. Portsmouth, NH: Heinemann.

Fountas, I.C., & Pinnell, G.S. (1999). *Matching books to readers: Using leveled books in guided reading, K–3*. Portsmouth, NH: Heinemann.

Fountas, I.C., & Pinnell, G.S. (2001). *Guiding readers and writers, grades 3–6: Teaching comprehension, genre, and content literacy*. Portsmouth, NH: Heinemann.

Freeland, J.T., Skinner, C.H., Jackson, B., McDaniel, C.E., & Smith, S. (2000). Measuring and increasing silent reading comprehension rates: Empirically validating repeated readings intervention. *Psychology in the Schools, 37*(5), 415–429.

Galda, L., Ash, G.E., & Cullinan, B.E. (2000). Children's literature. In M.L. Kamil, P.B. Mosenthal, P.D. Pearson, & R. Barr (Eds.), *Handbook of reading research* (Vol. 3, pp. 361–380). Mahwah, NJ: Erlbaum.

Galda, L., & Cullinan, B.E. (2003). Literature for literacy: What research says about the benefits of using trade books in the classroom. In J. Flood, D. Lapp, J.R. Squire, & J.M. Jensen (Eds.), *Handbook of research on teaching the English language arts* (2nd ed., pp. 640–648). Mahwah, NJ: Erlbaum.

Gallik, J.D. (1999). Do they read for pleasure? Recreational reading habits of college students. *Journal of Adolescent & Adult Literacy, 42*(6), 480–488.

Gambrell, L.B. (1996). What research reveals about discussion. In J.F. Almasi & L.B. Gambrell (Eds.), *Lively discussions! Fostering engaged reading* (pp. 39–51). Newark, DE: International Reading Association.

Gersten, R., & Carnine, D. (1986). Direct instruction in reading comprehension. *Educational Leadership, 43*(7), 70–78.

Goatley, V.J., & Raphael, T.E. (1992). Non-traditional learners' written and dialogic response to literature. In C.K. Kinzer & D.J. Leu (Eds.), *Literacy research, theory, and practice: Views from many perspectives* (41st yearbook of the National Reading Conference, pp. 313–321). Chicago: National Reading Conference.

Goodman, Y.M. (1984). The development of initial literacy. In H. Goelman, A. Oberg, & F. Smith (Eds.), *Awakening to literacy* (pp. 102–109). Exeter, NH: Heinemann.

Goodman, Y.M., Watson, D.J., & Burke, C.L. (1987). *Reading miscue inventory: Alternative procedures*. Katonah, NY: Richard C. Owen.

Green, J.L., & Harker, J.O. (1982). Reading to children: A communicative process. In J.A. Langer & M.T. Smith-Burke (Eds.), *Reader meets author: Bridging the gap* (pp. 196–221). Newark, DE: International Reading Association.

Green, J.L., & Wallet, C. (1981). Mapping instructional conversations: A sociolinguistic ethnography. In J.L. Green & C. Wallet (Eds.), *Ethnography and language in educational settings* (pp. 161–205). Norwood, NJ: Ablex.

Greenleaf, C.L., Schoenbach, R., Cziko, C., & Mueller, F.L. (2001). Apprenticing adolescents to academic literacy. *Harvard Educational Review, 71*(1), 79–129.

Guthrie, J.T., & Davis, M.H. (2003). Motivating struggling readers in middle school through an engagement model of classroom practice. *Reading & Writing Quarterly, 19*(1), 59–85.

Guthrie, J.T., Schafer, W.D., Von Secker, C., & Alban, T. (2000). Contributions of instructional practices to reading achievement in a statewide improvement program. *Journal of Educational Research, 93*(4), 211–226.

Guthrie, J.T., Schafer, W.D., Wang, Y.Y., & Afflerbach, P. (1995). Relationships of instruction to amount of reading: An exploration of social, cognitive, and instructional connections. *Reading Research Quarterly, 30*(1), 8–25.

Harste, J., & Burke, C. (1980). Understanding the hypothesis: It's the teacher that makes the difference. In B. Farr & D. Strickler (Eds.), *Reading comprehension: A resource guide*. Bloomington: Indiana University Reading Programs.

Hart, B., & Risley, T.R. (1995). *Meaningful differences in the everyday experience of young American children*. Baltimore: Paul H. Brookes.

Heath, S.B. (1983). *Ways with words: Language, life, and work in communities*. Cambridge, England: Cambridge University Press.

Herman, P.A., Anderson, R.C., Pearson, P.D., & Nagy, W.E. (1987). Incidental acquisition of word meaning from expositions with varied text features. *Reading Research Quarterly, 22*(3), 263–284.

Hiebert, E.H. (1983). An examination of ability grouping for reading instruction. *Reading Research Quarterly, 18*(2), 231–255.

Hiebert, E.H. (1998). *Text matters in learning to read* (CIERA Report No. 1-001). Ann Arbor: Center for the Improvement of Early Reading Achievement, University of Michigan.

Hoffman, J.V. (1981). Is there a legitimate place for oral reading instruction in a developmental reading program? *The Elementary School Journal, 81*(5), 305–310.

Hoffman, J.V. (1987). Rethinking the role of oral reading in basal instruction. *The Elementary School Journal, 87*(3), 367–373.

Hoffman, J.V., McCarthey, S.J., Abbott, J., Christian, C., Corman, L., Curry, L., et al.

(1994). So what's new in the new basals? A focus in first grade. *Journal of Reading Behavior, 26*(1), 47–73.

Hoffman, J.V., McCarthey, S.J., Elliott, B., Bayles, D.L., Price, D.P., Ferree, A., et al. (1998). The literature-based basals in first-grade classrooms: Savior, Satan, or same-old, same-old? *Reading Research Quarterly, 33*, 168–197.

Hoffman, J.V., Roser, N.L., Salas, R., Patterson, E., & Pennington, J. (2000). *Text leveling and little books in first-grade reading* (CIERA Report No. 1-010). Ann Arbor: Center for the Improvement of Early Reading Instruction, University of Michigan.

Holdaway, D. (1979). *The foundations of literacy*. Sydney, Australia: Ashton Scholastic; Portsmouth, NH: Heinemann.

Horowitz, R., & Freeman, S. (1995). Robots versus spaceships: The role of discussion in kindergartners' and second graders' preferences for science texts. *The Reading Teacher, 49*(1), 30–40.

Hudgins, B.B., & Edelman, S. (1986). Teaching critical thinking skills to fourth and fifth graders through teacher-led small-group discussion. *Journal of Educational Research, 79*(6), 333–342.

Igoa, C. (1995). *The inner world of the immigrant child*. New York: St. Martin's.

Indrisano, R., & Paratore, J.R. (1991). Classroom contexts for literacy learning. In J. Flood, J.M. Jensen, D. Lapp, & J.R. Squire (Eds.), *Handbook of research on teaching the English language arts* (pp. 477–488). New York: Macmillan.

International Reading Association (IRA). (1999). *Using multiple methods of beginning reading instruction* (Position statement). Newark, DE: Author. Retrieved June 7, 2005, from http://www.reading.org/resources/issues/positions_multiple_methods.html

International Reading Association (IRA). (2000). *Excellent reading teachers* (Position statement). Newark, DE: Author. Retrieved June 7, 2005, from http://www.reading.org/resources/issues/positions_excellent.html

Ivey, G., & Baker, M.I. (2004). Phonics instruction for older students? Just say no. *Educational Leadership, 61*(6), 35–39.

Ivey, G., & Broaddus, K. (2001). "Just plain reading": A survey of what makes students want to read in middle school classrooms. *Reading Research Quarterly, 36*(4), 350–377.

Jenkins, J.R., Peyton, J.A., Sanders, E.A., & Vadasy, P.F. (2004). Effects of reading decodable texts in supplemental first-grade tutoring. *Scientific Studies of Reading, 8*(1), 53–85.

Johnson, C.J., & Anglin, J.M. (1995). Qualitative developments in the content and form of children's definitions. *Journal of Speech & Hearing Research, 38*(3), 12–29.

Johnson, D.W., & Johnson, R.T. (1979). Conflict in the classroom: Controversy and learning. *Review of Educational Research, 49*(1), 51–70.

Keene, E.O., & Zimmermann, S. (1997). *Mosaic of thought: Teaching comprehension in a reader's workshop*. Portsmouth, NH: Heinemann.

Klare, G. (1984). Readability. In P.D. Pearson, R. Barr, M.L. Kamil, & P.B. Mosenthal (Eds.), *Handbook of reading research* (Vol. 2, pp. 681–744). New York: Longman.

Klenk, L., & Kibby, M.W. (2000). Re-mediating reading difficulties: Appraising the past, reconciling the present, constructing the future. In M.L. Kamil, P.B. Mosenthal, P.D. Pearson, & R. Barr (Eds.), *Handbook of reading research* (Vol. 3, pp. 667–690). Mahwah, NJ: Erlbaum.

Knapp, N.F., & Winsor, A.P. (1998). A reading apprenticeship for delayed primary readers. *Reading Research & Instruction, 38*(1), 13–29.

Kuhn, M.R., & Stahl, S.A. (2000). *Fluency: A review of developmental and remedial practices* (CIERA Report No. 2-008). Ann Arbor: Center for the Improvement of Early Reading Achievement, University of Michigan.

Langer, J.A. (1993). Discussion as exploration: Literature and the horizon of possibilities. In G.E. Newell & R.K. Durst (Eds.), *Exploring texts: The role of discussion and writing in the teaching and learning of literature* (pp. 23–43). Norwood, MA: Christopher-Gordon.

Langer, J.A. (2001). Beating the odds: Teaching middle and high school students to read and write well. *American Educational Research Journal, 38*(4), 837–880.

Langer, J.A. (2002). *Effective literacy instruction: Building successful reading and writing programs*. Urbana, IL: National Council of Teachers of English.

Leal, D.J. (1992). The nature of talk about three types of text during peer group discussions. *Journal of Reading Behavior, 24*(3), 313–338.

Lou, Y., Abrami, P.C., Spence, J.C., Poulsen, C., Chambers, B., & d'Apollonia, S. (1996). Within-class grouping: A meta-analysis. *Review of Educational Research, 66*(4), 423–458.

Lyons, C.A., Pinnell, G.S., & DeFord, D.E. (1993). *Partners in learning: Teachers and children in reading recovery*. New York: Teachers College Press.

MacKinnon, J. (1993). *A comparison of three schema-based methods of vocabulary instruction*. Unpublished doctoral dissertation, Florida State University, Tallahassee, FL.

Martin, B., & Brogan, P. (1971). *Teacher's guide to the instant readers*. New York: Holt, Rinehart and Winston.

Martinez, M., & Roser, N. (1985). Read it again: The value of repeated readings during storytime. *The Reading Teacher, 38*(8), 782–786.

Martinez, M., Roser, N., & Strecker, S. (1999). "I never thought I could be a star": A Readers Theatre ticket to reading fluency. *The Reading Teacher, 52*(4), 326–334.

Mathewson, G.C. (1994). Model of attitude influence upon reading and learning to read. In R.B. Ruddell, M.R. Ruddell, & H. Singer (Eds.), *Theoretical models and processes of reading* (4th ed., pp. 1131–1161). Newark, DE: International Reading Association.

McGee, L. (1992). An exploration of meaning construction in first graders' grand conversations. In C.K. Kinzer & D.J. Leu (Eds.), *Literacy research, theory, and practice: Views from many perspectives* (41st yearbook of the National Reading Conference, pp. 177–187). Chicago: National Reading Conference.

McKenna, M.C. (1994). Toward a model of reading attitude acquisition. In E.H. Cramer & M. Castle (Eds.), *Fostering the love of reading: The affective domain in reading education* (pp. 18–40). Newark, DE: International Reading Association.

McKenzie, M. (1986). *Journeys into literacy*. Huddersfield, England: Schofield & Sims.

Meek, M. (1988). *How texts teach what readers learn*. Stroud, England: Thimble.

Miller, P.C., & Endo, H. (2004). Understanding and meeting the needs of ESL students. *Phi Delta Kappan, 85*(10), 786–791.

Milligan, J.L., & Berg, H. (1992). The effect of whole language on the comprehending ability of first grade children. *Reading Improvement, 29*(3), 146–154.

Morrow, L.M., & Asbury, E. (2003). Current practices in early literacy development. In L.M. Morrow, L.B. Gambrell, & M. Pressley (Eds.), *Best practice in literacy instruction* (2nd ed., pp. 43–64). New York: Guilford.

Morrow, L.M., Gambrell, L.B., & Pressley, M. (2003). *Best practices in literacy instruction* (2nd ed.). New York: Guilford.

Morrow, L.M., & Smith, J.K. (1990). The effects of group size on interactive storybook reading. *Reading Research Quarterly, 25*(3), 213–231.

Morrow, L.M., Tracey D.H., Woo, D.G., & Pressley, M. (1999). Characteristics of exemplary first grade literacy instruction. *The Reading Teacher, 52*(5), 462–476.

Morrow, L.M., & Weinstein, C.S. (1986). Encouraging voluntary reading: The impact of a literature program on children's use of library centers. *Reading Research Quarterly, 21*(3), 330–346.

Moss, B. (2003). *Exploring the literacy of fact: Children's nonfiction trade books in the elementary classroom: Solving problems in the teaching of literacy.* New York: Guilford. (ERIC Document Reproduction Service No. ED471790)

Moustafa, M., & Land, R.E. (2002). The reading achievement of economically disadvantaged children in urban schools using Open Court vs. comparably disadvantaged children in urban schools using nonscripted reading programs. In *Urban Learning, Teaching, and Research* (2002 yearbook, pp. 44–53). Washington, DC: American Educational Research Association. Retrieved May 21, 2005, from http://instructional1.calstatela.edu/mmousta/ The_Reading_Achievement_of_ Economically_Disadvantaged_Children_in_ Urban_Schools_Using_Open_Court.pdf

Mugny, G., & Doise, W. (1978). Socio-cognitive conflict and the structure of individual and collective performances. *European Journal of Social Psychology, 8*, 181–192.

Nagy, W.E., Herman, P.A., & Anderson, R.C. (1985). Learning words from context. *Reading Research Quarterly, 20*, 233–253.

Nagy, W.E., & Scott, J.A. (2000). Vocabulary processes. In M.L. Kamil, P.B. Mosenthal, P.D. Pearson, & R. Barr (Eds.), *Handbook of reading research* (Vol. 3, pp. 269–284). Mahwah, NJ: Erlbaum.

National Institute of Child Health and Human Development (NICHD). (2000). *Report of the National Reading Panel. Teaching children to read: An evidence-based assessment of the scientific research literature on reading and its implications for reading instruction* (NIH Publication No. 00-4769). Washington, DC: U.S. Government Printing Office.

Ninio, A. (1980). Picture-book reading in mother-infant dyads belonging to two subgroups in Israel. *Child Development, 51*(2), 587–590.

Nystrand, M. (1997). *Opening dialogue: Understanding the dynamics of language and learning in the English classroom.* New York: Teachers College Press.

O'Flavahan, J., Stein, S., Wiencek, J., & Marks, T. (1992). *Interpretive development in peer discussion about literature: An exploration of the teacher's role* (Final report to the trustees of the National Council of Teachers of English). Urbana, IL: National Council of Teachers of English.

Opitz, M. (1998). *Flexible grouping in reading.* New York: Scholastic.

Palincsar, A.S. (1987). Reciprocal teaching: Can student discussions boost comprehension? *Instructor, 96*(5), 56–60.

Palincsar, A.S., & Brown, A.L. (1984). Reciprocal teaching of comprehension-fostering and comprehension-monitoring activities. *Cognition & Instruction, 1*(2), 117–175.

Palincsar, A.S., Brown, A.L., & Martin, S. (1987). Peer interaction in reading comprehension instruction. *Educational Psychologist, 22*(3–4), 231–253.

Pappas, C.C., & Brown, E. (1987). Learning to read by reading: Learning how to extend the functional potential of language. *Research in the Teaching of English, 21*(2), 160–177.

Paris, S.G., & Jacobs, J.E. (1984). The benefits of informed instruction for children's reading awareness and comprehension. *Child Development, 55*(6), 2083–2093.

Paris, S.G., Wasik, B.A., & Turner, J.C. (1991). The development of strategic readers. In R. Barr, M.L. Kamil, P.B. Mosenthal, & P.D. Pearson (Eds.), *Handbook of reading research* (Vol. 2, pp. 609–640). New York: Longman.

Pflaum, S., & Bryan, T. (1982). Oral reading research and learning diabled children. *Topics in Learning & Learning Disabilities, 1*, 33–42.

Philips, S. (1973). Participant structures and communicative competence: Warm Springs children in community and classroom. In C. Cazden, V. John, & D. Hymes (Eds.), *Functions of language in the classroom* (pp. 370–394). New York: Teachers College Press.

Pinnell, G.S., Lyons, C.A., DeFord, D.E., Bryk, A.S., & Seltzer, M. (1994). Comparing instructional models for the literacy education of high-risk first graders. *Reading Research Quarterly, 29*(1), 9–38.

Pinnell, G.S., Pikulski, J.J., Wixon, K.K., Campbell, J.R., Gough, P.B., & Beatty, A.S. (1995). *Listening to children read aloud: Data from NAEP's integrated reading performance record at grade 4.* Washington, DC: U.S. Department of Education, National Center for Education Statistics.

Pittelman, S.D., Levin, J.R., & Johnson, D.D. (1985). *An investigation of two instructional settings in the use of semantic mapping with poor readers* (Program Report No. 85-4). Madison: Wisconsin Center for Education Research, University of Wisconsin.

Poplin, M.S. (1988). Holistic/constructivist principles of the teaching/learning process: Implications for the field of learning disabilities. *Journal of Learning Disabilities, 21*(7), 401–416.

Prawat, R.S. (1989). Promoting access to knowledge, strategy, and disposition in students: A research synthesis. *Review of Educational Research, 59*(1), 1–41.

Pressley, M. (1998). *Reading instruction that works: The case for balanced teaching*. New York: Guilford.

Pressley, M. (2000). What should comprehension instruction be the instruction of? In M.L. Kamil, P.B. Mosenthal, P.D. Pearson, & R. Barr (Eds.), *Handbook of reading research* (Vol. 3, pp. 546–561). Mahwah, NJ: Erlbaum.

Pressley, M., Allington, R.L., Wharton-McDonald, R., Block, C.C., & Morrow, L.M. (2001). *Learning to read: Lessons from exemplary first-grade classrooms*. New York: Guilford.

Pressley, M., Rankin, J.L., & Yokoi, L. (1996). A survey of instructional practices of primary teachers nominated as effective in promoting literacy. *The Elementary School Journal, 96*(4), 363–384.

RAND Reading Study Group. (2002). *Reading for understanding: Toward an R&D program in reading comprehension*. Santa Monica, CA: RAND.

Rankin-Erickson, J.L., & Pressley, M. (2000). A survey of instructional practices of special education teachers nominated as effective teachers of literacy. *Learning Disabilities, 15*(4), 206–225.

Raphael, T.E. (1986). Teaching question answer relationships, revisited. *The Reading Teacher, 39*(6), 516–522.

Raphael, T.E., Florio-Ruane, S., & George, M. (2001). *Book Club Plus: A conceptual framework to organize literacy instruction* (CIERA Report No. 3-015). Ann Arbor: Center for the Improvement of Early Reading Achievement, University of Michigan.

Raphael, T.E., & McMahon, S.I. (1994). Book Club: An alternative framework for reading instruction. *The Reading Teacher, 48*(2), 102–116.

Rasinski, T.V. (2004). Creating fluent readers. *Educational Leadership, 61*(6), 46–51.

Rasinski, T.V., & Hoffman, J.V. (2003). Oral reading in the school literacy curriculum. *Reading Research Quarterly, 38*(4), 510–522.

Rasinski, T.V., Padak, N., Linek, W., & Sturtevant, E. (1994). Effects of fluency development on urban second grade readers. *Journal of Educational Research, 87*(3), 158–165.

Resnick, L.B. (1990). Literacy in school and out: Literacy in America [Special issue]. *Daedalus, 19*(2), 169–185.

Rhodes, L.K. (1979). Comprehension and predictability: An analysis of beginning reading materials. In J.C. Harste & R.F. Carey (Eds.), *New perspectives on comprehension* (pp. 100–131). Bloomington: Indiana University School of Education.

Rhodes, L.K. (1981). I can read! Predictable books as resources for reading and writing instruction. *The Reading Teacher, 34*(5), 511–518.

Rhodes, L.K., & Dudley-Marling, C. (1996). *Readers and writers with a difference: A holistic approach to teaching struggling readers and writers* (2nd ed.). Portsmouth, NH: Heinemann.

Richardson, J.S. (2000). *Read it aloud! Using literature in the secondary content classroom*. Newark, DE: International Reading Association.

Rinehart, S.D. (1999). "Don't think for a minute that I'm getting up there": Opportunities for Readers Theater in a tutorial for children with reading problems. *Reading Psychology, 20*(1), 71–89.

Roehler, L., & Duffy, G. (1991). Teachers' instructional actions. In R. Barr, M.L. Kamil, P.B. Mosenthal, & P.D. Pearson (Eds.), *Handbook of reading research* (Vol. 2, pp. 861–883). New York: Longman.

Rogers, T. (1991). Students as literary critics: The interpretive experiences, beliefs, and processes of ninth-grade students. *Journal of Reading Behavior, 23*(4), 391–423.

Rogoff, B. (1990). *Apprenticeship in thinking: Cognitive development in social context*. New York: Oxford University Press.

Rong, X.L., & Preissle, J. (1997). *Educating immigrant children: What we need to know to meet the challenges*. Thousand Oaks, CA: Corwin Press.

Roser, N.L., & Keehn, S. (2002). Fostering thought, talk, and inquiry: Linking literature and social studies. *The Reading Teacher, 55*(5), 416–426.

Roser, N.L., & Martinez, M.G. (2000). What Alice saw through the keyhole: Visions of children's literature in the elementary classroom. *Journal of Children's Literature, 26*(2), 18–27.

Roth, F.P., Speece, D.L., Cooper, D.H., & De la Paz, S. (1996). Unresolved mysteries: How do metalinguistic and narrative skills connect with early reading? *Journal of Special Education, 30*(3), 257–277.

Routman, R. (1991). *Invitations: Changing as teachers and learners K–12*. Portsmouth, NH: Heinemann.

Rowe, D.W. (1987). Literacy learning as an intertextual process. In J.E. Readence & R.S. Baldwin (Eds.), *Research in literacy: Merging perspectives* (36th yearbook of the National Reading Conference, pp. 101–112). Chicago: National Reading Conference.

Ryder, R.J., Sekulski, J.L., & Silberg, A. (2003). *Results of direct instruction reading program evaluation: Longitudinal results: First through third grade, 2000–2003*. Milwaukee: University of Wisconsin.

Sacks, C.H., & Mergendoller, J.R. (1997). The relationship between teachers' theoretical orientation toward reading and student outcomes in kindergarten children with different initial reading abilities. *American Educational Research Journal, 34*(4), 721–739.

Samuels, S.J. (1979). The method of repeated reading. *The Reading Teacher, 32*, 403–408.

Samuels, S.J. (1994). Toward a theory of automatic information processing in reading, revisited. In R.B. Ruddell, M.R. Ruddell, & H. Singer (Eds.), *Theoretical models and processes of reading* (4th ed., pp. 359–380). Newark, DE: International Reading Association.

Schickedanz, J.A. (1978). "Please read that story again!" Exploring relationships between story reading and learning to read. *Young Children, 33*(5), 48–55.

Schoenbach, R., Braunger, J., Greenleaf, C., & Litman, C. (2003). Apprenticing adolescents to reading in subject-area classrooms. *Phi Delta Kappan, 85*(2), 133–138.

Schoenbach, R., Greenleaf, C.L., Cziko, C., & Hurwitz, L. (1999). *Reading for understanding: A guide to improving reading in middle and high school classrooms*. San Francisco: Jossey-Bass.

Schumm, J.S., Moody, S.W., & Vaughn, S. (2000). Grouping for reading instruction: Does one size fit all? *Journal of Reading Disabilities, 33*(5), 477–488.

Schwartz, R.M., & Raphael, T.E. (1985). Concept of definition: A key to improving students' vocabulary. *The Reading Teacher, 39*(2), 198–205.

Shannon, P. (1985). Reading instruction and social class. *Language Arts, 62*(6), 604–613.

Short, K.G., Harste, J.C., & Burke, C. (1996). *Creating classrooms for authors and inquirers* (2nd ed.). Portsmouth, NH: Heinemann.

Slavin, R. (1990). *Cooperative learning: Theory, research, and practice*. Englewood Cliffs, NJ: Prentice Hall.

Smith, L.L., & Joyner, C.R. (1990). Comparing recreational reading levels with reading levels from an informal reading inventory. *Reading Horizons, 30*(4), 293–299.

Snow, C.E. (1983). Literacy and language: Relationships during the preschool years. *Harvard Educational Review, 53*(2), 165–189.

Snow, C.E. (1991). The theoretical basis for relationships between language and literacy development. *Journal of Research in Childhood Education, 6*(1), 5–10.

Snow, C.E., Burns, M.S., & Griffin, P. (Eds.). (1998). *Preventing reading difficulties in young children*. Washington, DC: National Academy Press.

Stahl, S.A., Richek, M.A., & Vandevier, R.J. (1991). Learning meaning vocabulary through listening: A sixth-grade replication. In J. Zutell & S. McCormick (Eds.), *Learner factors/teacher factors: Issues in literacy research and instruction* (40th yearbook of the National Reading Conference, pp. 185–192). Chicago: National Reading Conference.

Stahl, S.A., & Vancil, S.J. (1986). Discussion is what makes semantic maps work in vocabulary instruction. *The Reading Teacher, 40*(1), 62–69.

Stallings, J. (1980). Allocated academic learning time revisited, or beyond time on task. *Educational Researcher, 9*, 11–16.

Stallings, J. (1995). Ensuring teaching and learning in the 21st century. *Educational Researcher, 24*(6), 4–8.

Strickland, D.S., & Ascher, C. (1992). Low-income African American children and public schooling. In P.W. Jackson (Ed.), *Handbook of research on curriculum* (pp. 609–625). New York: Macmillan.

Sulzby, E. (1985). Children's emergent reading of favorite storybooks: A developmental study. *Reading Research Quarterly, 20*(4), 458–481.

Sweigart, W. (1991). Classroom talk, knowledge development, and writing. *Research in the Teaching of English, 25*(4), 469–496.

Tatham, S.M. (1970). Reading comprehension of materials written with select oral language patterns: A study at grades two and four. *Reading Research Quarterly, 5*(3), 402–426.

Taubenheim, B., & Christensen, J. (1978). Let's shoot "Cock Robin"! Alternatives to "round robin" reading. *Language Arts*, *55*(8), 975–977.

Taylor, B.M., Pearson, P.D., Clark, K.F., & Walpole, S. (1999). *Beating the odds in teaching all children to read* (CIERA Report No. 2-006). Ann Arbor: Center for the Improvement of Early Reading Achievement, University of Michigan.

Taylor, D. (1983). *Family literacy: Young children learning to read and write*. Exeter, NH: Heinemann.

Taylor, N.E., & Connor, U. (1982). Silent vs. oral reading: The rational instructional use of both processes. *The Reading Teacher*, *35*(4), 440–443.

Teale, W.H., & Sulzby, E. (Eds.). (1986). *Emergent literacy: Writing and reading*. Norwood, NJ: Ablex.

Thompson, R., Mixon, G., & Serpell, R. (1996). Engaging minority students in reading: Focus on the urban learner. In L. Baker, P. Afflerbach, & D. Reinking (Eds.), *Developing engaged readers in school and home communities* (pp. 43–63). Mahwah, NJ: Erlbaum.

Topping, K. (1987). Paired reading: A powerful technique for parent use. *The Reading Teacher*, *40*(7), 608–614.

Topping, K. (1989). Peer tutoring and paired reading: Combining two powerful techniques. *The Reading Teacher*, *42*(7), 488–494.

Topping, K. (1995). *Paired reading, spelling, and writing: The handbook for teachers and parents*. New York: Cassell.

True, J. (1979). Round robin reading is for the birds. *Language Arts*, *56*(8), 918–921.

Tunmer, W.E., Herriman, M., & Nesdale, A. (1988). Metalinguistic abilities and beginning reading. *Reading Research Quarterly*, *23*(2), 134–158.

Vadasy, P.F., Jenkins, J.R., & Pool, K. (2000). Effects of a first grade tutoring program in phonological and early reading skills. *Journal of Learning Disabilities*, *33*, 579–590.

Villaume, S.K., & Hopkins, L. (1995). A transactional and sociocultural view of response in a fourth-grade literature discussion group. *Reading Research & Instruction*, *34*(3), 190–203.

Walqui, A. (2003). *Conceptual framework: Scaffolding instruction for English learners*. San Francisco: WestEd.

Wasik, B.A. (1998). Volunteer tutoring programs in reading: A review. *Reading Research Quarterly*, *33*(3), 266–291.

Watkins, M.W., & Edwards, V.A. (1992). Extracurricular reading and reading achievement: The rich stay rich and the poor don't read. *Reading Improvement*, *29*(4), 236–242.

Wells, C.G. (1986). *The meaning makers: Children learning language and using language to learn*. Portsmouth, NH: Heinemann.

Wharton-McDonald, R., Pressley, M., & Hampston, J.M. (1998). Literacy instruction in nine first-grade classrooms: Teacher characteristics and student achievement. *The Elementary School Journal*, *99*(2), 101–128.

Wharton-McDonald, R., Pressley, M., Rankin, J., Mistretta, J., Yokoi, L., & Ettenberger, S. (1997). Effective primary-grades instruction = balanced literacy instruction. *The Reading Teacher*, *50*(6), 518–521.

White, J. (1990). Involving different social and cultural groups in discussion. In W.W. Wilen (Ed.), *Teaching and learning through discussion: The theory, research, and practice of the discussion method* (pp. 147–174). Springfield, IL: Charles C. Thomas.

Wiencek, J., & O'Flavahan, J.F. (1994). From teacher-led to peer discussion about literature: Suggestions for making the shift. *Language Arts*, *71*(7), 488–498.

Wilhelm, J.D. (2001). *Improving comprehension with think-aloud strategies*. New York: Scholastic.

Wilhelm, J.D., Baker, T.N., & Dube, J. (2001). *Strategic reading: Guiding students to lifelong literacy 6–12*. Portsmouth, NH: Boynton/Cook.

Wilkerson, B.A. (1999). Awareness and anticipation: Utilizing LEA and DR-TA in the content classroom. In O.G. Nelson & W.M. Linek (Eds.), *Practical classroom applications of language experience: Looking back, looking forward* (pp. 148–155). Boston: Allyn & Bacon.

Wilkinson, I.A.G., & Townsend, M.A.R. (2000). From rata to rimu: Grouping instruction in best practice in New Zealand classrooms. *The Reading Teacher*, *53*(6), 460–471.

Winkeljohann, R., & Gallant, R. (1979). Queries: Why oral reading? *Language Arts*, *56*, 950–953.

Wong, S.D., Groth, L.A., & O'Flavahan, J. (1994). *Characterizing teacher-student interaction in Reading Recovery lessons* (Reading Research Report No. 17). Athens: National Reading Research Center, University of Georgia.

Wong Fillmore, L. (2000). Loss of family languages: Should educators be concerned? *Theory Into Practice*, *29*(40), 203–210.

Wong Fillmore, L., & Meyer, L. (1992). The curriculum and linguistic minorities. In P. Jackson (Ed.), *Handbook of research on curriculum: A project of the AERA* (pp. 626–658). New York: Macmillan.

Worthy, J., & Broaddus, K. (2002). Fluency beyond the primary grades: From group performance to silent, independent reading. *The Reading Teacher, 55*(4), 334–343.

Worthy, J., & Prater, K. (2002). "I thought about it all night": Readers Theatre for reading fluency and motivation. *The Reading Teacher, 56*(3), 294–297.

Yoon, J. (2002). Three decades of sustained silent reading: A meta-analytic review of the effects of SSR on attitude toward reading. *Reading Improvement, 39*(4), 186–195.

Core Understanding 12

Allington, R.L. (1977). If they don't read much, how they ever gonna get good? *Journal of Reading, 21*(1), 57–61.

Allington, R.L. (1980). Poor readers don't get to read much in reading groups. *Language Arts, 5*(8), 873–875.

Allington, R.L., & Cunningham, P.M. (1996). *Schools that work: Where all children read and write*. New York: HarperCollins.

Allington, R.L., & McGill-Franzen, A. (2003). The impact of summer setback on the reading achievement gap. *Phi Delta Kappan, 85*(1), 68–75.

Alvermann, D., Boyd, F., Brozo, W., Hinchman, K.A., Moore, D.W., & Sturtevant, E. (2002). *Principled practices for a literate America: A framework for literacy and learning in the upper grades*. New York: Carnegie Corporation.

Anderson, R.C., Wilson, P.T., & Fielding, L.G. (1988). Growth in reading and how children spend their time outside of school. *Reading Research Quarterly, 23*(3), 285–303.

Baumann, J.F., & Duffy, A.M. (1997). *Engaged reading for pleasure and learning* (Report from the National Reading Research Center). Athens, GA: National Reading Research Center. (ERIC Document Reproduction Service No. ED413579)

Beers, K. (1996). No time, no interest, no way! The three voices of aliteracy, Pt. 1. *School Library Journal, 42*(2), 30–33.

Beers, K. (2003). *When kids can't read: What teachers can do: A guide for teachers 6–12*. Portsmouth, NH: Heinemann.

Block, C.C. (2001). Case for exemplary instruction especially for students who begin school without the precursors for literacy success. In *49th yearbook of the National Reading Conference* (pp. 110–122). Chicago: National Reading Conference.

Block, C.C., & Mangieri, J.N. (2002). Recreational reading: 20 years later. *The Reading Teacher, 55*(6), 572–580.

Borman, G.D., & D'Agostino, J.V. (1996). Title I and student achievement: A meta-analysis of federal results. *Educational Evaluation & Policy Analysis, 18*(4), 309–326.

Brozo, W.G., & Hargis, C.H. (2003). Taking seriously the idea of reform: One high school's efforts to make reading more responsive to all students. *Journal of Adolescent & Adult Literacy, 47*(1), 14–23.

Collins, C.C. (1980). Sustained silent reading periods: Effect on teachers' behaviors and students' achievement. *The Elementary School Journal, 81*(2), 108–114.

Cunningham, P.M., & Allington, R.L. (2003). *Classrooms that work: They can ALL read and write* (3rd ed.). Boston: Allyn & Bacon.

Duke, N.K. (2000). For the rich, it's richer: Print experiences and environments offered to children in very low- and very high-socioeconomic status first-grade classrooms. *American Educational Research Journal, 37*(2), 441–478.

Elley, W.B. (1992, July). *How in the world do students read? IEA study of literacy*. The Netherlands: International Association for the Evaluation of Educational Achievement. (ERIC Document Reproduction Service No. ED360613)

Elley, W.B., & Mangubhai, F. (1983). The impact of reading on second language learning. *Reading Research Quarterly, 19*(1), 53–67.

Fractor, J.S., Woodruff, M., Martinez, M., & Teale, W. (1993). Let's not miss opportunities to promote voluntary reading: Classroom libraries in the elementary school. *The Reading Teacher, 46*(6), 476–484.

Gallik, J.D. (1999). Do they read for pleasure? Recreational reading habits of college students. *Journal of Adolescent & Adult Literacy, 42*(6), 480–488.

Glenn, N.D. (1994). Television watching, newspaper reading, and cohort differences in verbal ability. *Sociology of Education, 67*(3), 216–230.

Guice, S., & Allington, R.L. (1994). *It's more than reading real books! 10 ways to enhance the implications of literature-based instruction*. Albany: National Research Center on Literature Teaching and Learning, State University of New York.

Guthrie, J., & Greaney, V. (1991). Literacy acts. In R. Barr, M.L. Kamil, P.B. Mosenthal, & P.D. Pearson (Eds.), *Handbook of reading research* (Vol. 2, pp. 68–96). New York: Longman.

Hayes, D.P., & Grether, J. (1983). The school year and vacations: When do students learn? *Cornell Journal of Social Relations*, *17*(1), 56–71.

Herman, P.A., Anderson, R.C., Pearson, P.D., & Nagy, W.E. (1987). Incidental acquisition of word meaning from expositions with varied text features. *Reading Research Quarterly*, *22*(3), 263–284.

Holdaway, D. (1979). *The foundations of literacy*. Sydney, Australia: Ashton Scholastic; Portsmouth, NH: Heinemann.

Ingham, J. (1982). *Books and reading development: The Bradford book flood experiment* (2nd ed.). Exeter, NH: Heinemann.

International Reading Association (IRA). (1999). *Providing books and other print materials for classroom and school libraries* (Position statement). Newark, DE: Author. Retrieved June 7, 2005, from http://www. reading.org/resources/issues/positions_ libraries.html

Irving, A. (1980). *Promoting voluntary reading for children and young people*. Paris: UNESCO.

Ivey, G., & Broaddus, K. (2001). "Just plain reading": A survey of what makes students want to read in middle school classrooms. *Reading Research Quarterly*, *36*(4), 350–377.

Krashen, S.D. (1993). *The power of reading: Insights from the research*. Englewood, CO: Libraries Unlimited.

Krashen, S.D. (1996). *Every person a reader: An alternative to the California Task Force report on reading*. Culver City, CA: Language Education Associates.

Lamme, L.L. (1976). Are reading habits and abilities related? *The Reading Teacher*, *30*(1), 21–27.

Langer, J.A. (2001). Beating the odds: Teaching middle and high school students to read and write well. *American Educational Research Journal*, *38*(4), 837–880.

Libraries called key. (2004, February/March). *Reading Today*, *21*(4), pp. 1, 4.

Libsch, M.K., & Breslow, M. (1996). Trends in non-assigned reading by high school seniors. *NASSP Bulletin*, *80*(584), 111–116.

Mahiri, J., & Godley, A.J. (1998). Rewriting identity: social meanings of literacy and "re-visions" of self. *Reading Research Quarterly*, *33*(4), 416–433.

McQuillan, J., & Au, J. (2001). The effect of print access on reading frequency. *Reading Psychology*, *22*(3), 225–248.

Moore, D.W., Bean, T.W., Birdyshaw, D., & Rycik, J.A. (1999). *Adolescent literacy*. A position statement for the Commission on Adolescent Literacy of the International Reading Association. Newark, DE: International Reading Association. Retrieved June 7, 2005, from http://www. reading.org/downloads/positions/ps1036_ adolescent.pdf

Morrow, L.M. (1998). *Motivating lifelong voluntary readers*. Unpublished manuscript.

Neuman, S.B. (1999). Books make a difference: A study of access to literacy. *Reading Research Quarterly*, *34*(3), 286–311.

Neuman, S.B., & Celano, D. (2001). Access to print in low-income and middle-income communities: An ecological study of four neighborhoods. *Reading Research Quarterly*, *36*(1), 8–26.

Neuman, S.B., & Celano, D. (2002). *The importance of the library for vulnerable young children* (Final report to the William Penn Foundation). Philadelphia: William Penn Foundation.

Neuman, S.B., & Celano, D. (2004). Save the libraries! *Educational Leadership*, *61*(6), 82–85.

New study supports value of school libraries. (2004, April/May). *Reading Today*, *21*(5), p. 25.

Pearson, P.D. (1993). Teaching and learning reading: A research perspective. *Language Arts*, *70*(6), 502–511.

Pearson, P.D., & Fielding, L. (1991). Comprehension instruction. In R. Barr, M.L. Kamil, P.B. Mosenthal, & P.D. Pearson (Eds.), *Handbook of reading research* (Vol. 2, pp. 815–860). New York: Longman.

Pinnell, G.S. (1989). Success for at-risk children in a program that combines reading and writing. In J.M. Mason (Ed.), *Reading and writing connections* (pp. 237–260). Boston: Allyn & Bacon.

Schumm, J.S., Vaughn, S., & Saumill, L. (1994). Assisting students with difficult textbooks: Teacher perceptions and practices. *Reading Research & Instruction*, *34*(1), 39–56.

Smith, C., Constantino, R., & Krashen, S.D. (1997). Difference in print environment for children in Beverly Hills, Compton, and Watts. *Emergency Librarian*, *24*(4), 8–9.

Smith, L.L., & Joyner, C.R. (1990). Comparing recreational reading levels with reading levels from an informal reading inventory. *Reading Horizons*, *30*(4), 293–299.

Spiegel, D.L. (1981). *Reading for pleasure: Guidelines*. Newark, DE: International Reading Association.

Stanovich, K.E. (1986). Matthew effects in reading: Some consequences of individual differences in the acquisition of literacy. *Reading Research Quarterly*, *21*(4), 360–407.

Taylor, B.M., Frye, B.J., & Maruyama, G.M.. (1990). Time spent reading and reading growth. *American Educational Research Journal*, *27*(2), 351–362.

Taylor, B.M., Pearson, P.D., Clark, K.F., & Walpole, S. (1999). *Beating the odds in teaching all children to read* (CIERA Report No. 2-006). Ann Arbor: Center for the Improvement of Early Reading Achievement, University of Michigan.

Wiesendanger, K.D., & Bader, L. (1989). SSR: Its effects on students reading habits after they complete the program. *Reading Horizons*, *29*(3), 162–166.

Core Understanding 13

Allington, R.L. (1977). If they don't read much, how they ever gonna get good? *Journal of Reading*, *21*(1), 57–61.

Allington, R.L., & McGill-Franzen, A. (2003). The impact of summer setback on the reading achievement gap. *Phi Delta Kappan*, *85*(1), 68–75.

Allington, R.L., & Walmsley, S.A. (Eds.). (1995). *No quick fix: Rethinking literacy programs in America's elementary schools*. Newark, DE: International Reading Association.

American Educational Research Association (AERA). (2000). *High-stakes testing in preK–12 education* (Position statement). Washington, DC: Author. Retrieved May 20, 2005, from http://www.aera.net/policyand programs/?id=378

Atwell, N. (1998). *In the middle: New understandings about reading, writing and learning* (2nd ed.). Portsmouth, NH: Heinemann.

Barr, M.A., & Syverson, M.A. (1999). *Assessing literacy with the Learning Record: A handbook for teachers, grades 6–12*. Portsmouth, NH: Heinemann.

Bennett, M.B. (2003). From practice to preaching: Helping content area teachers teach comprehension. *Voices From the Middle*, *11*(1), 31–34.

Black, P., & Wiliam, D. (1998). Inside the black box: Raising standards through classroom assessment. *Phi Delta Kappan*, *80*(2), 139–144.

Braunger, J.B. (1996). Retelling: Reading assessment that's also good instruction. In R. Blum & J. Arter, (Eds.) *A handbook for student performance assessment in an era of restructuring* (pp. iv–12, 1–8). Alexandria, VA: Association for Supervision and Curriculum Development.

Brown, C.S., & Lytle, S.L. (1988). Merging assessment and instruction: Protocols in the classroom. In S.M. Glazer, L.W. Searfoss, & L.M. Gentile (Eds.), *Reexamining reading diagnosis: New trends and procedures* (pp. 94–102). Newark, DE: International Reading Association.

Brown, H., & Cambourne, B. (1990). *Read and retell: A strategy for the whole-language/ natural learning classroom*. Portsmouth, NH: Heinemann.

Chall, J.S. (1996). *Stages of reading development* (2nd ed.). Fort Worth, TX: Harcourt College.

Clay, M.M. (1985). *The early detection of reading difficulties: A diagnostic survey with recovery procedures* (3rd ed.). Auckland, New Zealand: Heinemann.

Clay, M.M. (1991). *Becoming literate: The construction of inner control*. Portsmouth, NH: Heinemann.

Clay, M.M. (2002). *An observation survey: Of early literacy achievement* (2nd ed.). Portsmouth, NH: Heinemann.

Cooper, J.D., & Kiger, N.D. (2005). *Literacy assessment: Helping teachers plan instruction* (2nd ed.). Boston: Houghton Mifflin.

Daniels, H. (2002). *Literature circles: Voice and choice in book clubs and reading groups* (2nd ed.). Portland, ME: Stenhouse.

Darling-Hammond, L. (1991). The implications of testing policy for quality and equality. *Phi Delta Kappan*, *73*(3), 220–225.

Darling-Hammond, L. (1997). *The right to learn: A blueprint for creating schools that work*. San Francisco: Jossey-Bass.

Gallagher, C.W. (2004). Turning the accountability tables: Ten progressive lessons from one "backward" state. *Phi Delta Kappan*, *85*(5), 352–360.

Goldberg, M.F. (2004). The test mess. *Phi Delta Kappan*, *85*(5), 361–366.

Goodman, Y.M., & Marek, A.M. (1996). *Retrospective miscue analysis: Revaluing readers and reading*. Katonah, NY: Richard C. Owen.

Goodman, Y.M., Watson, D.J., Burke, C.L. (1987). *Reading miscue inventory: Alternative procedures*. Katonah, NY: Richard C. Owen.

Grigg, W.S., Daane, M.C., Jin, Y., & Campbell, J.R. (2003). *The nation's report card: Reading 2002* (NCES Report No. 2003-521). Washington, DC: U.S. Department of Education, National Center for Education Statistics.

International Reading Association (IRA). (1999). *High-stakes assessments in reading* (Position statement). Newark, DE: Author. Retrieved June 7, 2005, from http://www.reading.org/resources/issues/positions_high_stakes.html

International Reading Association (IRA) & National Council of Teachers of English (NCTE). (1996). *Standards for the English language arts*. Newark, DE; Urbana, IL: Authors.

Krashen, S.D. (2001). More smoke and mirrors: A critique of the National Reading Panel report on fluency. *Phi Delta Kappan*, *83*(2), 119–123.

Kuhn, M.R., & Stahl, S.A. (2000). *Fluency: A review of developmental and remedial practices* (CIERA Report No. 2-008). Ann Arbor: Center for the Improvement of Early Reading Achievement, University of Michigan.

LaBerge, D., & Samuels, S.J. (1974). Toward a theory of automatic information processing in reading. *Cognitive Psychology*, *6*, 293–323.

Leslie, L., & Caldwell, J. (2001). *Qualitative reading inventory–3*. New York: Longman.

McDonald, J.P. (2001). Students' work and teachers' learning. In A. Lieberman & L. Miller (Eds.), *Teachers caught in the action: Professional development that matters* (pp. 209–235). New York: Teachers College Press.

Meier, D. (2003). So what does it take to build a school for democracy? *Phi Delta Kappan*, *85*(1), 15–21.

Meisels, S.J., & Piker, R.A. (2001). *An analysis of early literacy assessments used for instruction* (CIERA Report No. 2-013). Ann Arbor: Center for the Improvement of Early Reading Achievement, University of Michigan.

Mokharti, K., & Reichard, C. (2002). Assessing students' metacognitive awareness. *Journal of Educational Psychology*, *94*(2), 249–260.

Moore, R.A., & Aspegren, C.M. (2001). Reflective conversations between two learners: Retrospective miscue analysis. *Journal of Adolescent & Adult Literacy*, *44*(6), 492–503.

National Institute of Child Health and Human Development (NICHD). (2000). *Report of the National Reading Panel. Teaching children to read: An evidence-based assessment of the scientific research literature on reading and its implications for reading instruction* (NIH Publication No. 00-4769). Washington, DC: U.S. Government Printing Office.

Neuman, S.B., & Celano, D. (2001). Access to print in low-income and middle-income communities: An ecological study of four neighborhoods. *Reading Research Quarterly*, *36*, 8–26.

No Child Left Behind Act of 2001, Pub. L. No. 107-110, 115 Stat. 1425 (2002).

Perfetti, C.A. (1985). *Reading ability*. New York: Oxford University Press.

Pinnell, G.S., Pikulski, J.J., Wixon, K.K., Campbell, J.R., Gough, P.B., & Beatty, A.S. (1995). *Listening to children read aloud: Data from NAEP's integrated reading performance record at grade 4*. Washington, DC: U.S. Department of Education, National Center for Education Statistics.

Pressley, M. (2002). Metacognition and self-regulated comprehension. In A.E. Farstrup & S.J. Samuels (Eds.), *What research has to say about reading instruction* (3rd ed., pp. 291–309). Newark, DE: International Reading Association.

RAND Reading Study Group. (2002). *Reading for understanding: Toward an R&D program in reading comprehension*. Santa Monica, CA: RAND.

Rhodes, L.K. (1993). *Literacy assessment: A handbook of instruments*. Portsmouth, NH: Heinemann.

Rhodes, L.K., & Dudley-Marling, C. (1996). *Readers and writers with a difference: A holistic approach to teaching struggling readers and writers* (2nd ed.). Portsmouth, NH: Heinemann.

Ruddell, R.B., & Ruddell, M.R. (1994). Language acquisition and literacy processes. In R.B. Ruddell, M.R. Ruddell, & H. Singer (Eds.), *Theoretical models and processes of reading* (4th ed., pp. 83–104). Newark, DE: International Reading Association.

Samuels, S.J. (2002). Reading fluency: Its development and assessment. In A.E. Farstrup & S.J. Samuels (Eds.), *What research has to say about reading instruction* (3rd ed., pp. 166–183). Newark, DE: International Reading Association.

Schoenbach, R., Braunger, J., Greenleaf, C., & Litman, C. (2003). Apprenticing adolescents to reading in subject-area classrooms. *Phi Delta Kappan*, *85*(2), 133–138.

Schoenbach, R., Greenleaf, C.L., Cziko, C., & Hurwitz, L. (1999). *Reading for understanding: A guide to improving reading in middle and high school classrooms*. San Francisco: Jossey-Bass.

Stallman, A.C., & Pearson, P.D. (1990). Formal measures of early literacy. In L.M. Morrow & J.K. Smith (Eds.), *Assessment for instruction in early literacy* (pp. 7–44). Englewood Cliffs, NJ: Prentice Hall.

Stanovich, K.E. (1980). Toward an interactive-compensatory model of individual differences in the development of reading fluency. *Reading Research Quarterly*, *16*(1), 32–71.

Taylor, B.M., Pearson, P.D., Clark, K.F., & Walpole, S. (1999). *Beating the odds in teaching all children to read* (CIERA Report No. 2-006). Ann Arbor: Center for the Improvement of Early Reading Achievement, University of Michigan.

Wixon, K.K., Fisk, M.C., Dutro, E., & McDaniel, J. (2002). *The alignment of state standards and assessment in elementary reading* (CIERA Report No. 3-024). Ann Arbor: Center for the Improvement of Early Reading Achievement, University of Michigan.

Conclusion

Allington, R.L. (2002). What I've learned about effective reading instruction from a decade of studying exemplary elementary classroom teachers. *Phi Delta Kappan*, *83*(10), 740–747.

Allington, R.L., & Cunningham, P.M. (1996). *Schools that work: Where all children read and write*. New York: HarperCollins.

Allington, R.L., & McGill-Franzen, A. (1997, May). *Improving schools' responses to children on the edge*. Paper presented at the International Reading Association Annual Convention, Atlanta, GA.

Applebee, A.N., Langer, J.A., Nystrand, M., & Gamoran, A. (2003). Discussion-based approaches to developing understanding: Classroom instruction and student performance in middle and high school English. *American Educational Research Journal*, *40*(3), 685–730.

Baumann, J.F. (1997, May). *Reflections on teaching struggling readers across grade levels*. Paper presented at the International Reading Association Annual Convention, Atlanta, GA.

Brown, H., & Cambourne, B. (1990). *Read and retell: A strategy for the whole-language/natural learning classroom*. Portsmouth, NH: Heinemann.

Carnegie Task Force. (1996, September). *Years of promise: A comprehensive learning strategy for America's children* (Report of the Carnegie Task Force on Learning in the Primary Grades). New York: Carnegie Corporation.

Clay, M.M. (1991). *Becoming literate: The construction of inner control*. Portsmouth, NH: Heinemann.

Dreher, M.J., & Slater, W.H. (1992). Elementary school literacy: Critical issues. In M.J. Dreher & W.H. Slater (Eds.), *Elementary school literacy: Critical issues* (pp. 3–25). Norwood, MA: Christopher-Gordon.

Flippo, R.F. (1998). Points of agreement: A display of professional unity in our field. *The Reading Teacher*, *52*(1), 30–40.

Flippo, R.F. (2001). *Reading researchers in search of common ground*. Newark, DE: International Reading Association.

Guthrie, J.T., Schafer, W.D., Wang, Y.Y., & Afflerbach, P. (1995). Relationships of instruction to amount of reading: An exploration of social, cognitive, and instructional connections. *Reading Research Quarterly*, *30*(1), 8–25.

Harste, J.C., Burke, C.L., & Woodward, V.A. (1982). Children's language and world: Initial encounters with print. In J.A. Langer & M.T. Smith-Burke (Eds.), *Reader meets author: Bridging the gap* (pp. 105–131). Newark, DE: International Reading Association.

Juel, C. (1992). Longitudinal research on learning to read and write with at-risk students. In M.J. Dreher & W.H. Slater (Eds.), *Elementary school literacy: Critical issues* (pp. 73–99). Norwood, MA: Christopher-Gordon.

Krashen, S.D. (2004). *The power of reading: Insights from the research* (2nd ed.). Westport, CT: Libraries Unlimited.

Langer, J.A. (2001). Beating the odds: Teaching middle and high school students to read and write well. *American Educational Research Journal*, *38*(4), 837–880.

McQuillan, J. (2001). If you build it, they will come: A book flood program for struggling readers in an urban high school. In B. Ericson (Ed.), *Teaching reading in high school English classes* (pp. 69–83). Urbana, IL: National Council of Teachers of English.

Meier, D. (1995). *The power of their ideas: Lessons for America from a small school in Harlem*. Boston: Beacon.

Morrow, L.M., Tracey D.M., Woo, D.G., & Pressley, M. (1999). Characteristics of exemplary first grade literacy instruction. *The Reading Teacher*, *52*(5), 462–476.

Myers, M. (1996). *Changing our minds: Negotiating English and literacy*. Urbana, IL: National Council of Teachers of English.

Putnam, L.R. (1994). Reading instruction: What do we know now that we didn't know thirty years ago? *Language Arts*, *71*(5), 362–366.

Rosenholtz, S.J. (1989). *Teachers' workplace: The social organization of schools*. New York: Longman.

Routman, R. (1996). *Literacy at the crossroads: Crucial talk about reading, writing, and other teaching dilemmas*. Portsmouth, NH: Heinemann.

Schoenbach, R., Braunger, J., Greenleaf, C., & Litman, C. (2003). Apprenticing adolescents to reading in subject-area classrooms. *Phi Delta Kappan*, *85*(2), 133–138.

Schoenbach, R., Greenleaf, C., Cziko, C., & Hurwitz, L. (1999). *Reading for understanding: A guide to improving reading in middle and high school classrooms*. San Francisco: Jossey-Bass.

Sharp, D.L.M., Bransford, N.V., Goldman, S.R., Kinzer, C., & Soraci, S., Jr. (1992). Literacy in an age of integrated-media. In M.J. Dreher & W.H. Slater (Eds.), *Elementary school literacy: Critical issues* (pp. 183–210). Norwood, MA: Christopher-Gordon.

Smith, F. (1983). Twelve easy ways to make learning to read difficult. In F. Smith (Ed.), *Essays into literacy: Selected papers and some afterthoughts* (pp. 12–25). Portsmouth, NH: Heinemann.

Smith, F. (2003). *Unspeakable acts, unnatural practices: Flaws and fallacies in "scientific" reading instruction*. Portsmouth, NH: Heinemann.

Taylor, B.M., Pearson, P.D., Clark, K.F., & Walpole, S. (1999). *Beating the odds in teaching all children to read* (CIERA Report No. 2-006). Ann Arbor: Center for the Improvement of Early Reading Achievement, University of Michigan.

Yatvin, J. (1992, November). *Beginning a school literacy improvement project: Some words of advice* (Literacy Improvement Series for Elementary Educators). Portland, OR: Northwest Regional Educational Laboratory.

Index